Spencer Maurice's
Family Provision on Death

Spencer Maurice's Family Provision on Death

Seventh Edition

Alexandra Mason
of Gray's Inn, Barrister

Marian Conroy
of the Inner Temple, Barrister

LONGMAN

ISBN 0752 00087 X

Published by
Longman Group Ltd
21–27 Lamb's Conduit Street
London WC1N 3NJ

Associated offices
Australia, Hong Kong, Malaysia, Singapore and USA

First Published 1953
Second edition 1961
Third edition 1970
Fourth edition 1979
Fifth edition 1983
Sixth edition 1987
Seventh edition 1994

A CIP catalogue record for this book is available from the British Library.

Printed and bound in Great Britain by Biddles Ltd, Guildford

Contents

Preface

Since 1953 six editions of this Book have appeared, all of them written by Spencer G Maurice. Unfortunately Spencer Maurice died in 1991 and in preparing this edition we greatly regret we have not had the benefit of his advice or experience. This Book has proved of considerable practical use to the legal profession over many years and we hope that the same will be the case with this edition and that Spencer Maurice would not have been disappointed by our efforts to follow in his footsteps.

It is now 18 years since the Inheritance (Provision for Family and Dependants) Act 1975 came into force and there is no longer a lack of reported cases, although there remain areas on which there is little or no authority and the mental gymnastics required by some of the sections continue to plague judges and practitioners alike. Because of the time which has passed since the commencement of the Act and because it is seven years since the last edition we have reviewed the entire Book. We have made amendments to the order in which the Book is set out and have made major additions to Chapter 9 on the practice on applications, taking into account the recent changes to the jurisdiction of the county court and including a separate section on the practice on compromise. We have elected to reduce the references to cases on the Inheritance (Family Provision) Act 1938 and to the Law Commission report on which the present Act was based, reference should be had to earlier editions for fuller references to such cases and to the Law Commission report. However, we have not completely excluded such references as some of the cases remain of assistance and it remains useful to understand the reasoning behind the provisions included in the Act, particularly with respect to some of the more obscure sections.

We have endeavoured to state the law as at 31st August 1994.

17, Old Buildings
Lincoln's Inn
28 October 1994

Alexandra Mason
Marian Conroy

Table of Cases

Table of Statutes

Table of Statutory Instruments

Chapter 1

Introduction

The preamble to the Inheritance (Provision for Family and Dependants) Act 1975 (c 63) describes it as 'An Act to make fresh provision for empowering the court to make orders for the making out of the estate of a deceased person of provision for the spouse, former spouse, child, child of the family or dependant of that person; and for matters connected therewith.'. The Act (as it will be called in this Book) received the Royal Assent on 12 November 1975. It came into force on 1 April 1976 (s 27(3)) and may be cited by its short title (s 27(1)). As the preamble indicates, the Act permits the court to make an order varying the disposition of a deceased person's estate effected by his will or the law relating to intestacy, or the combination of his will and that law. It replaces the legislation first brought onto the Statute Book by the Inheritance (Family Provision) Act 1938 ('the Act of 1938') and subsequently amended and extended by the Intestates' Estate Act 1952 ('the Act of 1952'), the Matrimonial Causes (Property and Maintenance) Act 1958, the Matrimonial Causes Act 1965, the Family Provision Act 1966 and the Family Law Reform Act 1969. The whole of the Act of 1938 and such parts of the subsequent Acts as were made obsolete by the Act were repealed thereby (s 26(2) and Sched). It is, however, provided by s 26(3) that the repeal of the earlier enactments shall not affect their operation in relation to any application made thereunder, whether before or after the commencement of the Act, with reference to the death of any person who died before its commencement. Section 26(4) preserves in force orders and directions made under the former law, whether before or after the commencement of the Act, and applies to such orders the powers of variation and discharge contained in s 6 of the Act. The Act has itself been amended by the Administration of Justice Act 1982 and the Matrimonial and Family Proceedings Act 1984. The Finance Act 1986, s 100(1) provides that on and after the passing of that Act (25 July 1986), the tax charged under the Capital Transfer Tax Act 1984 shall be known as inheritance tax and the Capital Transfer Tax Act 1984 may be cited as the Inheritance Tax Act 1984. The references in this book to that tax and the last-mentioned Act have accordingly been amended. The text of the Act, however, remains unamended in that references to capital transfer tax will still be found there.

The Act gave statutory effect to recommendations contained in the Law Commission's Second Report on Family Property: Family Provision on Death (Law Com No 61: (1974) HC 324; hereinafter cited as Law Com No 61), in particular to the recommendation that, so far as should be practicable in the differing circumstances, the claim of a surviving spouse upon the family assets should at least be equal to that of a divorced spouse, and the court's power to order financial provision for a surviving spouse should be as wide as its powers to order financial provision on a divorce. In the result maintenance is no longer retained as the objective in determining family provision for a surviving spouse who is not judicially separated, but still provides the basis upon which provision may be made for other persons eligible to make an application under the Act. The class of persons so eligible has, however, been enlarged It seems clear that the enlargement did not have retrospective effect (cf *Hogan v Hogan* [1983] 1 WLR 1232, a decision of the Judicial Committee of the Privy Council under the Testator's Family and Guardianship of Infants Act 1916 (New South Wales) and the Children (Equality of Status) Act 1976 (New South Wales)): but the point must by now be academic. Other important changes in the law effected by the Act were the extension of the powers of the court to make whatever orders may in the circumstances of the particular case be appropriate for provision out of the property available for that purpose and the prevention of evasion of the Act by dispositions and contracts made *inter vivos*.

Because of the special position of surviving spouses under the Act, cases under the Act of 1938 are only of very limited guidance. In the case of claims by other applicants, where the criterion of provision remains maintenance and the Act has not effected any major changes of principle, such cases may retain some value but having regard to the increase in the number of reported cases under the Act the citation of such cases on other than minor points is inpractice very unlikely. Although reference is made in this book to cases under the Act of 1938 care should be taken when referring to them to bear in mind the changes made by the Act and also the present acceptance of the principle that the test to be applied on considering an application under the Act is an objective one. Many of the cases under the Act of 1938 were decided without reference to that principle and on a more subjective basis.

See page 76 for a possible amendment to s 1(1) of the Act (categories of applicant) proposed by the Law Commission (Law Com 187/1990).

Chapter 2

Territorial Jurisdiction And Who May Apply

1 Domicile of deceased

The Act only applies where the deceased died domiciled in England and Wales after 1 April 1976 (ss 1(1) and 27(3)) but there is no condition attached to the domicile of the applicant. The Act has no application to Scotland or Northern Ireland (s 27(2)). The latter has its own statutory regime: the Inheritance (Family Provision) Act (Northern Ireland) 1960, amended by the Family Provision (Northern Ireland) Act 1969 and repealed and replaced by the Inheritance (Provision for Family and Dependants) Act (Northern Ireland) Order 1979 (SI 1979 No 924). In Scotland the law of succession protects the position of widows and children.

When making an application under the Act it is incumbent upon the applicant to show that the deceased died domiciled in England and Wales: *Mastaka v Midland Bank Executor and Trustee Co Ltd* [1941] Ch 192. A statement of where the deceased died domiciled should routinely be included in any application under the Act. In *Mastaka v Midland Bank and Trustee Co Ltd* the testatrix married a Russian in England from whom she shortly afterwards separated and about whose subsequent life and domicile nothing was known. At this time, a wife took her husband's domicile on marriage. The testatrix died in 1939. By her will she made no provision for her daughter, who applied for maintenance. Refusing to make an order, Farwell J held that the daughter had failed to discharge the onus which lay upon her of proving that the testatrix died domiciled in England and Wales.

A deceased is domiciled at the date of their death in the jurisdiction in which they, at that date, had their permanent home (see *Dicey and Morris, The Conflict of Laws*, 12th edn at 115).

A summary of the main principles of domicile follows. However, if a question as to domicile arises reference should be made to the leading texts (such as *Dicey and Morris*) for a more detailed exposition.

English law determines where a person is domiciled for the purposes of the Act. There are three categories of domicile: domicile of origin, domicile of choice and domicile of dependency. Together the three types ensure that no person can be without a domicile. The latter is relevant only where the deceased was (at death) an unmarried child under 16 years of age or a person suffering from a mental disorder. Until 1 January 1974 married women were taken to have their husband's domicile, a rule referred to as 'the last barbarous relic of a wife's servitude': *Gray v Formosa* [1963] P 259 per Denning MR at 267. Since 1 January 1974 a married woman is an independent person (see the Domicile and Matrimonial and Proceedings Act 1973, s 1(1)). The age of independence in this context is 16 years of age, not the same as that of majority. The age of majority was reduced from 21 to 18 years of age as of 1 January 1970 by virtue of s 1(1) of the Family Law Reform Act 1969.

At birth every person acquires a domicile of origin which is presumed to continue until displaced by a domicile of choice after the attainment of independence. Rules exist to determine every person's domicile of origin and they depend upon the legal status of the relationship between a child and its parents at birth. Every independent person can acquire a domicile of choice by residing in a jurisdiction of their choosing with the intention to reside there permanently or at least indefinitely.

Apart from the statutory requirement as to domicile, it also appears that the deceased must die possessed of property which is either situated in England and Wales at the time of their death or otherwise within the jurisdiction of the courts of England and Wales. In the absence of special circumstances, a grant of representation will not be made in England and Wales unless there is property within England and Wales to be administered (see the Probate Registrar's Direction, 30 November 1932). A grant of representation must exist before an application under the Act can be made (see pp 110–111). However, if an application under the Act was envisaged, a grant would (it is anticipated) be made in appropriate circumstances limited to the prosecution of, or the defence of, such an application even if there was no property in

England and Wales to be administered (Probate Registrar's Direction, 30 November 1932). If the deceased died domiciled in England and Wales leaving movables (as defined by English rules of conflict of laws) wherever situate, the court, on an application under the Act, could make provision out of those movables. However, if the deceased died domiciled in England and Wales possessed of immovables (similarly defined) situate outside England and Wales, the court, on an application under the Act would be very unlikely to order provision for the applicant out of those immovables as English rules of conflict of laws state that succession to and capacity to dispose of immovables is determined by the law of the place where the immovables are situated, the *lex situs*. This view is supported by Commonwealth authority and persuasive academic comment (see *Re Donnelly* [1927] 28 SRNSW 34, *Re Roper* [1927] NZLR 731, *Re Paulin* [1950] VLR 462, *Re Perkins* [1958] SRNSW 1, *Re Bailey* [1985] 2 NZLR 656, *Heuston v Barber* [1990] 19 NSWLR 354, *Miller* (1990) 39 ICLQ 261).

Had it not been for the inclusion of a choice of law clause, the Act would, on the general principles of conflicts of law, have applied to the movables wherever situated of a deceased person domiciled in England and Wales and to the immovables in England and Wales of deceased persons wherever domiciled. As it is, where a person dies domiciled in a country (eg New Zealand) having legislation comparable to the Act, no order can be made in the courts of that country in respect of immovables in England, because the *lex situs* applies to those immovables. Further complications can arise where applications for maintenance are made in two (or more) territorial jurisdictions: *Re Paulin* [1950] VLR 462.

Where there is doubt as to the proper law, and the relevant foreign law is one which protects the position of widows and children, it may be a finely balanced question which system of law would be more advantageous to a potential applicant under the Act.

Where necessary, determination of the deceased's domicile at death can be treated as a preliminary issue: *Re Harmsworth* [1982] CLY 3388. Contesting the deceased's domicile as a preliminary issue will not give rise to a jurisdiction in the court enabling it to order that the defendant give the plaintiff security for their costs: *Visco v Minter* [1969] P 82 and RSC Ord 23. As to the evidence of domicile that can be adduced, it is commonly said that there is no circumstance in a person's life, however trivial, which ought to be left out of account: *Drevon v Drevon* (1864) 34 LJ Ch 129. A statement of the deceased's domicile in a grant of representation is not conclusive but has been described as prima facie evidence of the domicile stated: *Eames v Hacon* (1881) 18 Ch D 347 per Jessel MR at 352.

2 Categories of applicants

Section 1(1) of the Act divides into the following categories the persons who may apply to the court under s 2 (see Chapter 4) on the ground that the disposition of the deceased's estate effected by his will (which includes codicil (s 25(1))) or the law relating to intestacy, or the combination of his will and that law, is not such as to make reasonable financial provision for the applicant:

(a) the wife or husband of the deceased;
(b) a former wife or former husband of the deceased who has not remarried;
(c) a child of the deceased;
(d) any person (not being a child of the deceased) who, in the case of any marriage to which the deceased was at any time a party, was treated by the deceased as a child of the family in relation to that marriage;
(e) any person (not being a person included in (a) to (d) above) who immediately before the death of the deceased was being maintained, either wholly or partly, by the deceased, and it is provided by s 1(3) that a person shall be treated as being maintained by the deceased, either wholly or partly, as the case may be, if the deceased, otherwise than for full valuable consideration, was making a substantial contribution in money or money's worth towards the reasonable needs of that person.

Section 24 of the Act provides that s 46(1)(vi) of the Administration of Estates Act 1925, in so far as it provides for the devolution of property on the Crown, the Duchy of Lancaster or the Duke of Cornwall as *bona vacantia* shall have effect subject to the provisions of the Act. This enables a person to apply under the Act for provision where the deceased has died wholly or partly intestate without statutory next of kin.

3 Evidence of relationship to deceased

It is essential for an applicant to prove that he or she is an applicant within one of the categories in s 1(1) of the Act by producing the appropriate certificates of birth, marriage or death, or other relevant evidence, such as evidence of dependency for applicants under s 1(1) (e). In *Re Peete, Peete v Crompton* [1952] 2 All ER 599 a widow making application for maintenance produced a certificate of her marriage, in 1919, to the testator, in which she was described as a widow, but she was unable to produce a certificate of the death of her first husband. Roxburgh J held that while, prima facie, a marriage certificate was evidence of the capacity of the parties to marry, that presumption could be displaced if some evidence were given which caused the court to doubt the validity of the marriage. In the present case there was evidence which put the matter in issue, since the statement in the certificate that the plaintiff was a widow depended on her uncorroborated statement made to the registrar at the time of the ceremony, which statement was founded on hearsay. Accordingly, the plaintiff had not proved that she was the testator's widow and she had no claim against his estate.

Re Peete was considered by Harman J in *Re Watkins, Watkins v Watkins* [1953] 1 WLR 1323. In the latter case the plaintiff married her first husband in 1913. He deserted her in 1921, but returned in 1922 and asked her to take him back; she, however, refused, and since then had neither seen nor heard from or of him. She remained in touch with the husband's father until the father's death in 1927, and with the husband's sister until the sister's death in 1937, but the husband was never mentioned between them. From information which subsequently proved incorrect the plaintiff believed the husband to have died in 1942. In 1948 she went through a form of marriage with the testator, and was described on the marriage certificate as a widow. The testator died in 1951 and Harman J held that on the evidence before him he was entitled to presume that the first husband was dead at the time when the plaintiff went through a form of marriage with the testator, so that she was legally married to him and thus entitled to make an application for provision under the Act of 1938. (See s 25(4) of the Act for a possible approach in similar circumstances today). *Re Peete* was doubted in *Re Hussain, Hussain v Rahaman* (CAT (Civil) No 921 of 1980).

4 Spouses and former spouses

Applications by the wife or husband of the deceased are permitted by s 1(1)(a) and a former wife or former husband of the deceased who has not remarried are permitted by (s 1(1)(b)). The remarriage of a widow or widower after the deceased's death does not prevent such a person applying for provision under s 1(1)(a). Clearly, however, remarriage would be a highly relevant consideration for the court to take into account in the case of an application under s 1(1)(a), or under s 6 for variation or discharge or suspension of an order for periodical payments (see pp 87–90). In the case of (a) an applicant who was a former husband or former wife of the deceased or (b) an applicant who was the husband or wife of the deceased in a case where the marriage with the deceased was the subject of a decree of judicial separation and at the date of death the decree was in force and the separation was continuing, it is expressly provided by s 19(2) that any order for the making of periodical payments made under s 2 or under s 5 (an interim order) in favour of such an applicant shall cease to have effect on the applicant's remarriage except in relation to any arrears due under the order on the date of the remarriage (see also pp 83–87 and Chapter 6).

The position of a person who had in good faith entered into a void marriage was formerly protected by s 6(1) of the Law Reform (Miscellaneous Provisions) Act 1970; but by s 6(3) of that Act such a person was debarred from relief not only if the marriage had been dissolved or annulled during the deceased's lifetime and the dissolution or annulment was recognised by the law of England and Wales, but also if the survivor had remarried either before or since the death of the deceased. Now, by virtue of s 25(4) of the Act, the survivor is debarred from relief only if there has been such a dissolution or annulment or she or he remarried during the lifetime of the deceased.

Formerly, a person whose marriage was terminated in another jurisdiction was not eligible to apply under para (*b*) of s 1(1) (though such a person might be able to qualify under para (*e*)) and the definition in s 25(1) of 'former wife' or 'former husband' was confined to a person whose marriage with the deceased had, during the deceased's lifetime, been dissolved or annulled by a decree of divorce or of nullity of marriage made under the Matrimonial Causes Act 1973. Section 25 of the Matrimonial and Family Proceedings Act 1984 amends the Act so as to give persons whose marriages have been terminated outside England and Wales the same rights to apply for provision under the Act as persons whose marriages are terminated under the Matrimonial Causes Act 1973. Section 25 (1) of the Act is amended (by s 25(2) of the Act of 1984) so as to define 'former wife' and 'former husband' as meaning a person whose marriage with the deceased was during the lifetime of the deceased either:

(a) dissolved or annulled by a decree of divorce or a decree of nullity of marriage granted under the law of any part of the British Islands, or

(b) dissolved or annulled in any country or territory outside the British Islands by a divorce or annulment which is entitled to be recognised as valid by the law of England and Wales.

An application under the Act can be made in a case in which the marriage was terminated in England and Wales, Scotland, Northern Ireland, the Channel Islands or the Isle of Man ('the British Islands' as defined by s 5 and Sched 1 of the Interpretation Act 1978), and in countries outside the British Islands. The requirement that the deceased be domiciled in England and Wales (see s 1(1) of the Act) is not, however, affected. Where a marriage is terminated by a decree of nullity, the grounds on which the decree was made are immaterial (see *Lamerton v Personal Representatives of Lamerton* (1966) 110 SJ 288 (where the marriage had been annulled by a decree made under s 21 of the Supreme Court of Judicature (Consolidation) Act 1925 (see now the Supreme Court Act 1981, s 26) on the ground that the marriage had never been consummated owing to the applicant's incapacity)). Section 25(6) of the Act provides that any reference to an order or decree made under the Matrimonial Causes Act 1973 or under any section of that Act shall be construed as including a reference to an order or decree which is deemed to have been made under that Act or under that section thereof, as the case may be; and s 25(7) provides that any reference in the Act to an enactment is a reference to that enactment as amended by or under any subsequent enactment. In considering whether or not a former wife or former husband has remarried it is necessary to have regard to s 25(5) which provides that any reference in the Act to remarriage or to a person who has remarried includes a reference to a marriage which is by law void or voidable or to a person who has entered into such a marriage, as the case may be, and that a marriage shall be treated for the purposes of the Act as a remarriage, in relation to any party thereto, notwithstanding that the previous marriage of that party was void or voidable.

Section 18(2) of the Administration of Justice Act 1982 inserts in the Wills Act 1837 a new section, s 18A (applicable where the testator died on or after 1 January 1983). Subsection (1) of s 18A, as amended by s 53 of the Family Law Act 1986, provides that where, after a testator has made a will, a decree of a court of civil jurisdiction in England and Wales dissolves or annuls his marriage or his marriage is dissolved or annulled and the divorce or annulment is entitled to recognition in England and Wales by virtue of Pt II of the Family Law Act 1986 (which is concerned with recognition of divorces, annulments and legal separations), (a) the will shall take effect as if any appointment of the former spouse as an executor or as the executor and trustee of the will were omitted; and (b) any devise or bequest to the former spouse shall lapse, except in so far as a contrary intention appears from the will. It is, however, provided by subs (2) of s 18A that s 18A(1)(b) is without prejudice to any right of the former spouse to apply for financial provision under the Act.

A wife of a polygamous marriage is entitled to claim under s 1(1)(a) of the Act. Foster J so held on a preliminary point of law in *Re Sehota, Kaur v Kaur* [1978] 1 WLR 1506, where the applicant was a party to a Hindu marriage formally valid under Indian law at the time when it was contracted. The testator (who had acquired an English domicile) had left the whole of his residuary estate to another wife. In deciding that the applicant was entitled to apply for provision, Foster J having pointed out that there is no definition of 'the wife' in the Act, held that the Act was not merely a consolidating Act so as to constrain him to construe the words as he might have done in construing similar words in the Act of 1938. He had regard to the fact that s 47(1) of the Matrimonial Causes Act 1973 provides that a court in England and Wales shall not be precluded from granting matrimonial relief or making a declaration concerning the validity of a marriage by reason only that the marriage in question was entered into under a law which permits polygamy; though his Lordship did not in fact think that the applicant was seeking matrimonial relief in asking for reasonable provision from her deceased husband's estate.

5 Children

Section 1(1)(c) of the Act permits any child of the deceased to make an application. 'Child' includes an illegitimate child and a child *en ventre sa mère* at the death of the deceased (s 25(1)) and an adult child is not precluded from making an application. In a case in which a child is illegitimate and claims that the deceased was his father, the question of paternity may be tried as a preliminary issue and evidence directed to this issue alone may be ordered to be lodged. 'Child' also includes an adopted child of the deceased by virtue of the status conferred by adoption (see the Adoption Act 1976, s 39 and s 73(3) and Sched 4).

The effect of adoption was considered in *Re Collins* [1990] Fam 56. A minor son and adult daughter applied under s 1(1)(c) for provision to be made for them from the estate of their deceased mother. The deceased had died intestate in 1980 and her estate amounting to £35,000 passed to her surviving spouse. A decree nisi had been granted prior to the deceased's death. The minor son was adopted on 19 March 1987 and made an application under the Act on 3 June 1987. Hollings J dismissed his application. At the date the application was made the minor was not the deceased's child but was for all purposes the child of his adoptive parents (see the Adoption Act 1976, s 39(2)). Further (and by analogy with *Whytte v Ticehurst* [1986] Fam 64 stating that an application under the Act was not a 'cause of action' within s 1(1) of the Law Reform (Miscellaneous Provisions) Act 1934) the minor son had not prior to the date of his adoption obtained an interest which would survive his adoption (Adoption Act 1976, s 42(4)). A right to apply under the Act was no more than a hope. The adult daughter's application succeeded and the learned judge approved the view that the receipt of state assistance by an applicant was not relevant when considering whether reasonable financial provision had been made for them: *Re E*, E *v* E [1966] 1 WLR 709 applied.

Where by virtue of s 27 or s 28 of the Human Fertilisation and Embryology Act 1990 (effective 1 1991) a person is to be treated as the mother or father of a child, they are to be treated as the parent of that child for all purposes (s 29(1)) save where the child is treated by virtue of adoption as being the child of any other person (ss 27(2) and 28(5)). References to any two people in any enactment, deed or other instrument or document are to be read accordingly (s 29(3)) and so references to a 'child' in the Act are to be read subject to the provisions of the Act of 1990.

A person is treated as the mother of a child if she is carrying or has carried that child as a result of the placing in her of an embryo or of sperm and eggs (s 27(1)). Where a woman is carrying a child or has carried a child as a result of the placing in her of an embryo or of sperm and eggs or her artificial insemination and:

(a) at the time of such placing or insemination she was married and the embryo was not created with the sperm of her spouse then that spouse is treated as the father of the child unless it is shown that he did not consent to the placing in the woman of an embryo or sperm and eggs or her insemination (s 28(2)); or

(b) s 28(2) is inapplicable but the said placing or insemination took place in the course of treatment provided for the woman and a man together but the embryo was not created with the sperm of that man, that man is treated as the father of the child (s 28(3)).

Where s 28(2) or (3) of the Act of 1990 applies no other person is to be treated as the father of the child (s 28(4)) but neither subs (2) nor (3) of s 28 applies to any child who by common law rules is treated as the legitimate child of the parties to a marriage (s 28(5)(a)).

It is sometimes the case that a surviving child who is mentally or physically retarded will be entirely dependent upon state assistance and can expect to remain so dependent for the remainder of their lives. Applications under the Act can, of course, be made on their behalf (see *Re Wood* [1982] LSG 774 and *Ashton* (1990) LSG (13) 87, 19 for an illustration of and discussion of some of the problems that arise).

In extending the right to make an application to any child, Parliament, accepting the recommendation of the Law Commission (Law Com No 61, para 79), departed from the former law, under which only a daughter who had not been married, or who was, by reason of some mental or physical disability, incapable of maintaining herself, and a son who had not attained the age of 21 years, or who was, by reason of some mental or physical disability, incapable of maintaining himself, could apply (s 1(1)(b), (c), (d) of the Act of 1938, as amended).

6 Child of the family

Power to make an application is conferred by para (d) of s 1(1) of the Act on any person (not being a child of the deceased) who, in the case of any marriage to which the deceased was at any time a party, was treated by the deceased as a child of the family in relation to that marriage. The inclusion of this class was in accordance with the recommendation of the Law Commission (Law Com No 61, para 70). Under the Matrimonial Causes Act 1973, on the grant of a decree of divorce, nullity or judicial separation either spouse could be ordered to make provision for a 'child of the family' (ss 23, 52(1)). Such a child included a child of the marriage and a child treated by both parties to the marriage as a child of the family. The Law Commission had this power in mind when it recommended that a child of the family be able to apply under the Act. However, under the Act it is only necessary that the deceased treat the applicant as a child of the family. Section 1(1)(d) of the Act enables stepchildren of a deceased to apply for provision to be made for them.

It is to be observed that, where a man and a woman have lived together without ever marrying a child of one of them cannot be an applicant on the death of the other under s 1(1)(d), because there has been no marriage; but such a child may be eligible to claim under s 1(1)(e) as a person who immediately before the death of the deceased was being maintained by the deceased.

In *Re Callaghan* [1985] Fam 1 (see p 69) Booth J held that 'child' in s 1(1)(d) was not restricted to a minor or dependent child. It had been argued that the terms of s 3(3) of the Act concerned with the education and training of the applicant and the extent to which the deceased had assumed and discharged responsibility for the applicant's maintenance, indicated that only a minor or dependent child could qualify. This argument was rejected; s 3(3) only contains additional matters to which the court is to have regard in considering an application under the Act by a child of the family. Booth J further held that 'child of the family' referred to the relationship between the deceased and the applicant and did not suggest that only a minor could make an application. In *Re Leach* [1986] Ch 226 the appellate court (O'Connor, Slade and Robert Goff LJJ) approved *Re Callaghan*. The applicant's mother had died in 1959. In the following year her father remarried, the applicant was 32 years of age at the time. On the father's death virtually the whole of his estate passed to the applicant's stepmother. The stepmother died intestate in 1981. The court said that the mere display of affection, kindness or hospitality by a stepparent to a stepchild was not sufficient under s 1(1)(d). Rather, the stepparent must be shown to have assumed the position of a parent towards the applicant with all the attendant responsibilities and privileges of that relationship. In considering whether the applicant has been treated as a 'child of the family' evidence of the status of the relationship between the deceased and the applicant after the death of the first spouse was relevant as such treatment stemmed from the marriage. In *Re Leach* the applicant was a 'child of the family'.

It is open to question whether treatment of a person prior to marriage by the deceased can be relied upon by that applicant to establish that they fall within s 1(1)(d) of the Act. This was not an issue that required to be resolved in *Re Callaghan* or *Re Leach* although Mr Michael Wheeler QC at first instance in *Re Leach* ((1983) *The Times*, 8 December) appears to have considered that such conduct was relevant.

7 Persons maintained by the deceased

Para (e) of s 1(1) of the Act permits an application by any person (not being a person included in paras (a)–(d)) who immediately before the death of the deceased was being maintained, either wholly or partly, by the deceased. A person is treated as being maintained by the deceased either wholly or partly only if the deceased, otherwise than for full valuable consideration, was making a substantial contribution in money or money's worth towards that person's reasonable needs (s 1(3)) and had assumed responsibility to do so (s 3(4)). The inclusion of persons within this category was recommended by the Law Commission (Law Com No 61, para 94).

It is incumbent upon an applicant under s 1(1)(e) of the Act to show that they are a person who was being maintained by the deceased (within the terms of the Act) before the court can consider whether reasonable financial provision has been made for them: *Re Wilkinson* [1978] Fam 22 per Arnold J at 23. If they do so then it has been said that the object of the legislation is to remedy the injustice of one who has been put by a deceased person in a position of dependency and then deprived of financial support whether by accident or design: *Jelley v Iliffe* [1981] Fam 128 per Stephenson LJ at 137–138 approved in *Bishop v Plumley* [1991] 1 WLR 582 per Butler-Sloss LJ at 584.

In considering whether a person was being maintained immediately before the death of the deceased, it is not the de facto state of maintenance at the moment of the deceased's death that must be considered but something more substantial and enduring: the settled basis or general arrangement between the parties as regards maintenance during the deceased's lifetime. In *Re Dymott, Spooner v Carroll* (CAT (Civil) No 942 of 1980) the court found that the 'norm' of the relationship between the deceased and the applicant had been of two financially independent people sharing their lives together. The applicant's claim to have been maintained by the deceased immediately prior to his death was therefore rejected, although it was accepted that she was maintained by the deceased for a period of 8 months some 12 months prior to his death. However, a relationship of dependence which has existed for years will not be defeated by its termination during a few weeks of mortal sickness, (see *Re Beaumont, Martin v Midland Bank Trust Co Ltd* [1980] Ch 444, per Sir Robert Megarry V-C at 452, 456 and *Jelley v Iliffe* [1981] Fam 128 per Stephenson LJ at 136 and Griffiths LJ at 141). In *Kourkgy v Lusher* (1982) 12 Fam Law 86 Wood J held that the deceased had divested himself of financial responsibility for his partner and had left her shortly before his death, so that her claim against his estate failed (see also *Layton v Martin* (1986) 16 Fam Law 212, where the plaintiff seems to have accepted that she could not succeed in a claim under the Act (because her association with the deceased had ended nearly two years before his death) and tried, unsuccessfully, to found a claim for provision out of his estate on the grounds that before she went to live with him he had represented to her that he would provide for her by his will, and that she was entitled to rely either on proprietary estoppel or on an offer made to her and accepted by her conduct).

Section 1(1)(e) and (3) are qualified by s 3(4) of the Act. It is necessary for an applicant pursuant to s 1(1)(e) additionally to fulfil the criteria set down at s 3(4) and show that the deceased had assumed responsibility for their maintenance: *Re Beaumont* per Sir Robert Megarry V-C at 457 and *Jelley v Iliffe* per Stephenson LJ at 137. Where it is shown that the applicant was maintained by the deceased, assumption of responsibility by the deceased for such maintenance can usually be presumed: *Jelley v Iliffe* per Stephenson LJ at 137 disapproving dicta to the contrary in *Re Beaumont* per Sir Robert Megarry V-C at 458.

A person is to be treated as being maintained by the deceased, either wholly or partly, as the case may be, 'only' if the deceased, otherwise than for full valuable consideration, was making a substantial contribution in money or money's worth towards the reasonable needs of that person (s 1(3) and *Re Beaumont* per Sir Robert Megarry V-C at 450, 451; *Jelley v Iliffe* per Stephenson LJ at 136 and per Griffiths LJ at 141). Section 1(1)(e) and s (3) of the Act were introduced for the first time by the 1975 legislation. It is clear that they do not operate as alternatives but that s 1(3) exhaustively defines what is meant by 'being maintained' in s 1(1)(e) of the Act.

The exception 'otherwise than for full valuable consideration' applies whenever full valuable consideration is given, whether under contract or otherwise. See *Re McC* (1978) 9 Fam Law 26 for the suggestion that full valuable consideration was provided pursuant to contract. In *Re Wilkinson, Neale v Newell* [1978] Fam 22 the deceased paid for all food and household expenses. The deceased and the applicant suffered from arthritis but they shared light household duties and cooking with the applicant helping the deceased (as far as she was able) to dress. Arnold J held that such assistance and division of duties were not full valuable consideration for the substantial contribution made by the deceased to the applicant's reasonable needs. In *Re Beaumont* Sir Robert Megarry V-C supported the approach taken in *Re Wilkinson* but added that the proviso in s 1(3) was not reserved for situations where the supposed full valuable consideration was provided pursuant to contract. 'Full valuable consideration' is found wherever the flow of benefits from the applicant to the deceased is broadly commensurate with the contribution made by the deceased to the applicant: *Bishop v Plumley* [1991] 1 WLR 582 per Butler-Sloss LJ at 587.

In *Bishop v Plumley* the applicant and the deceased had lived together as man and wife. During a short separation the deceased made a will which made no provision for the applicant. The deceased provided the applicant (in later years) with rent-free accommodation but otherwise they pooled their resources. The applicant was extremely devoted to the deceased and provided him with great care and attention during a terminal illness. It was argued (unsuccessfully) that the applicant's exceptional care amounted to full valuable consideration for the substantial contribution made by the deceased to the applicant's reasonable needs. Butler-Sloss LJ (with whom Sir Patrick O'Connor and Purchas LJ concurred) said that the applicant's devotion could not be viewed in isolation from the relationship between the applicant and the deceased and that it could not have been the legislature's intention to put an uncaring partner in a stronger position than one who had provided devoted care.

For an application to succeed it must be shown that the deceased was making a 'substantial' contribution to the reasonable needs of the applicant. In *Re Wilkinson* the deceased had provided the applicant with full board and lodging at the deceased's expense. This was held to be a substantial contribution as was the provision of rent-free accommodation in *Jelley v Iliffe* and *Bishop v Plumley*. In *Jelley v Iliffe* Stephenson LJ spoke of the need for the court to balance what the applicant and the deceased contributed to see which way the scales of dependency tipped. It is, of course, necessary for the court to undertake a balancing exercise but

Stephenson LJ's comments have since been misinterpreted. Stephenson LJ did not say that it was sufficient simply for an applicant to show (on the hearing of the substantive application) that the balance of dependency was in their favour. If this was the case the provision within s 1(3) that the deceased's contribution has to be 'substantial' would be meaningless. Instead, Stephenson LJ, in dealing with an application to strike out the applicant's claim, said that there should be no striking out where the applicant could show that the balance of contributions suggested that the deceased's was the greater and had therefore shown a prima facie case, (see *Re Kirby* [1982] 3 FLR 249 for approval of this approach).

In *Harrington v Gill* (1983) 4 FLR 265 'reasonable needs' was held to mean 'reasonable requirements'. (See p 76 for a recent Law Commission proposal in respect of the treatment of cohabitees).

8 An objective test

In providing that an application may be made on the ground that the disposition of the deceased's estate 'is not such as to make reasonable financial provision for the applicant' s 1(1) of the Act adopts an objective test.

For some thirty years the courts applied a subjective test in considering whether or not reasonable provision had been made (see *Re Brownbridge, Brownbridge v Brownbridge* (1942) 193 LT Jo 185, *Re Styler, Styler v Griffith* [1942] Ch 387, *Re Howell, Howell v Lloyds Bank Ltd* [1953] 1 WLR 1034, *Re E, E v E* [1966] 1 WLR 709, *Re Harker-Thomas's Application, Harker-Thomas v Harker-Thomas* [1969] P 28). In *Re Goodwin, Goodwin v Goodwin* [1969] 1 Ch 283, however, Megarry J said that in his judgment the question was not subjective but objective, not whether the testator stood convicted of unreasonableness, but whether the provision in fact made was reasonable. The testator in that case left his widow £1,000, personal chattels worth about £150, and his residuary estate. He expected the residue to amount to between £8,000 and £9,000 but it amounted to only £1,550, and of this £1,100 consisted of the balance of an interest-free loan to the widow's son, who was sick and unable to make repayments. The net estate was nearly £19,000. The testator and the widow had been married in 1939, when he was 51 years of age and she was 48. At the time of the application she was 77. The defendants to the widow's application were the children of the testator's first marriage and their spouses. In those circumstances Megarry J said that he had to consider whether he was of the opinion that reasonable provision for the maintenance of the widow had been made and he had no hesitation in answering that question in the negative. His lordship said that what the testator intended his widow to have was a factor of great importance. In the circumstances she should have £8 a week, determinable on re-marriage, the payments to run from the testator's death, as that was the date from which any provision made by the will would normally have taken effect.

The Court of Appeal adopted the objective test and followed *Re Goodwin* in *Millward v Shenton* [1972] 1 WLR 711. The applicant in that case was a son of the testatrix. He was 54 years of age, married, and entirely incapacitated from earning a living. He and his wife lived entirely on state assistance amounting to about £12 a week, and he had chattels amounting to about £70 in value. The testatrix had had seven children, one of whom had recently died of cancer, and she left the whole of her estate of £3,144 to cancer research. The Court of Appeal held that the disposition of the estate did not make reasonable provision for the applicant and that reasonable provision would be eleven-twelfths of the estate. Any question as to whether the test to be applied is objective or subjective has now been laid to rest; for further confirmation see *Re Coventry, Coventry v Coventry* [1980] Ch 461 per Goff LJ at 488.

As the test is an objective one, any view expressed by a deceased person that he wishes a particular person to benefit will generally be of little significance: per Goff LJ at 488–489. An express reason for rejecting the applicant is a different matter and may be very relevant to the problem: *ibid* and see pp 37–41.

9 Meaning of maintenance

'Reasonable financial provision' has a different meaning depending upon whether the applicant is the surviving spouse or not. In the case of all applicants save for the surviving spouse (s 1(1)(a)) 'reasonable financial provision' is limited to maintenance (s 1(2)(b)). However, if the applicant is the deceased's surviving spouse, 'reasonable financial provision' is not limited to maintenance but means 'such financial provision as it would be reasonable in all the circumstances of the case for [the applicant] to receive, whether or not that provision is required for his or her maintenance' (s 1(2)(a)).

In *Re Borthwick, Borthwick v Beauvais* [1949] Ch 395 Harman J held that maintenance could not mean only mere subsistence. In *Re*

Coventry, Coventry v Coventry [1980] Ch 481, Goff LJ said (at 484–485) that maintenance was a word of somewhat limited meaning in its application to any person qualified to apply, other than a husband or wife. His Lordship went on to say that what was proper maintenance must in all cases depend upon all the facts and circumstances of the particular case being considered at the time, but that too limited a meaning was not to be put on it; it did not mean just enough to enable a person to get by; on the other hand it did not mean anything which might be regarded as reasonably desirable for the applicant's personal benefit or welfare. His Lordship said (at 490) that Mr Vivian Price QC (sitting as a deputy judge of the Chancery Division) might in *Re Christie, Christie v Keeble* [1979] Ch 168 have gone too far in putting a very wide interpretation on maintenance when he treated it (at 174) as referring to 'the applicant's way of life and well-being, his health, financial security and allied matters such as the well-being, health and financial security of his immediate family for whom he is responsible'. See *Re Duranceau* [1952] 3 DLR 714 per Roach J at 720 where 'maintenance' is described as 'sufficient to enable the dependant to live neither luxuriously nor miserably, but decently and comfortably according to his or her station in life'.

The applicant in *Re Dennis, Dennis v Lloyds Bank Ltd* [1981] 2 All ER 140, a son of the deceased applying under s 1(1)(c), sought leave to apply out of time (see s 4 and Chapter 5). He asked for a capital sum sufficient to pay the capital transfer tax, some £45,000 to £50,000, which he was liable to pay in respect of a gift of £90,000 received from the testator during the latter's lifetime and now expended. The applicant claimed that he had no assets with which to pay the tax and would be made bankrupt if he did not pay it. Browne-Wilkinson J held (at 145–146) that maintenance connoted only payments which, directly or indirectly, enabled the applicant in the future to discharge the cost of his daily living at whatever standard of living was appropriate to him. The provision that was to be made was to meet recurring expenses, being expenses of living of an income nature. That did not mean that the provision need be by way of income payments. The provision could be by way of a lump sum, for example, to buy a house in which the applicant could be housed, thereby relieving him *pro tanto* of income expenditure. His Lordship added that he was not suggesting that there might not be cases in which payment of existing debts might not be appropriate as a maintenance payment; for example, to pay the debts of an applicant in order to enable him to carry on a profit-making business or profession might well be for his maintenance. In the present case, however, there was no suggestion that payment of the capital transfer tax would do anything to help the applicant's future maintenance. It might save him from bankruptcy, but there was no evidence that being made bankrupt was going to prevent the applicant from earning his living. In the circumstances he had not shown that he had an arguable case. His application to bring proceedings out of time accordingly failed.

More recently, in *Riggs v Lloyds Bank plc* (CAT (Civil) No 1151 of 1992) the Court of Appeal held that payments ordered to be made to an applicant in order to assist her whilst her children were dependent did not, in the circumstances of that case, constitute 'maintenance'. The applicant was the deceased's adult daughter. The whole of the deceased's estate passed by will to his adult son. The applicant and her husband had two minor children aged 14 and 10 years respectively. They lived within their means (which were small). Although the applicant's case was not put to the judge at first instance on this basis, the judge decided to award the applicant a lump sum of £14,000 payable in two tranches to assist the applicant while her children remained dependent upon her. This order at first instance was overturned on two bases. First, the learned judge had relied on matters that were not fully explored in the evidence, namely, the minor children's needs. Secondly, the learned judge had treated as 'maintenance' payments which could not have been maintenance as there was no evidence to show that the applicant was in need.

Finally, the court in deciding what financial provision to order (if any) is entitled to consider the applicant's standard of living. In *Re Besterman, Besterman v Grusin* [1984] Ch 458 (see p 41) large provision was ordered for a widow out of the estate of a very wealthy testator and account was taken of the affluent lifestyle to which the applicant was accustomed. *Re Besterman* was an unusual case being an application by a widow where there were no competing claims cases to an estate valued at £1.37 million. However, reference has been made to an applicant's standard of living in claims by applicants other than surviving spouses. In *Re Dennis* the court was content to regard 'maintenance' as payments which (directly or indirectly) enabled the applicant to discharge the cost of daily living at 'whatever standard of living was appropriate': per Browne-Wilkinson J at 145. This approach was expressly adopted in *Re Jennings, Harlow v National Westminster Bank plc* [1994] 3 WLR 67 where the evidence indicated that the applicant (again an adult son) required no assistance to maintain his standard of living. (See also *Re Debenham* [1986] 1 FLR 404 and pp 68–69).

10 Intestacy

Section 1(1) of the Act legislates not only for the numerous cases where a will fails to make reasonable financial provision but also for the cases in which the intestacy rules work unfairly. *Re Coventry, Coventry v Coventry* [1980] Ch 461 was a case of intestacy, and Goff LJ said (at 488) that the problem of maintenance must be exactly the same whether one is dealing with a will or with an intestacy, or with a combination of both. The question is whether the operative dispositions make, or fail to make, reasonable provision in all the circumstances.

The Administration of Estates Act 1925 sets out the scheme of distribution where a deceased dies wholly or partially intestate. Where there is an issue as to that scheme reference should be made to texts dealing with intestacy in greater detail than is possible here. In general terms where an intestate is survived by:

(1) A spouse and issue: the spouse receives a fixed net sum, the 'statutory legacy', plus a life interest in half of the residue. The issue receive the remaining half of the residue plus the interest in remainder upon statutory trusts.
(2) A spouse and parents or siblings: the spouse receives the statutory legacy at a higher level and one half of the residue absolutely. The remaining half goes to the parents absolutely or siblings upon statutory trusts.
(3) Spouse or issue only: the spouse would take the whole of the estate of which the deceased died intestate absolutely, the issue would take the entirety on statutory trusts.
(4) No spouse or issue: the intestate's estate passes to the deceased's relatives in a set order of priority, failing which it goes to the Crown *bona vacantia*.

The statutory legacy is periodically increased. Where the deceased died after 1 March 1981 but on or before 1 June 1987 the statutory legacy is fixed at £40,000 and £85,000 (in situations (1) and (2) respectively above) (SI 1981 No 255). Where the deceased died after 1 June 1987 but on or before 1 December 1993 the statutory legacy is respectively £75,000 and £125,000 (SI 1987 No 799). Where the deceased died after 1 December 1993 the statutory legacy is respectively £125,000 and £200,000 (SI 1993 No 2906).

Applicants ought to note that if the deceased's estate or any part of it is to be distributed to the Crown as *bona vacantia*, the proposed applicant can make an application to the Treasury Solicitor or Duchy Solicitor for an ex gratia payment to be made to them. This course of action will rarely replace the making of an application under the Act but is one that merits consideration. For a full discussion of this option see Chatterton, 'In *bona vacantia*: ex gratia payments' (1987) LSG 3315.

11 Forfeiture Act 1982

The rule of public policy, the forfeiture rule, that a person should not be allowed to benefit from their own crime is now enshrined (in amended form) in s 1(1) of the Forfeiture Act 1982. In relation to the Act it is now clear that a person who has unlawfully killed another (within the meaning of that term in s 1(2) of the Forfeiture Act 1982) can, save where convicted of murder, apply under the Act for provision to be made for them from the estate of the deceased (s 3(1), (2)(a) of the Forfeiture Act 1982) regardless of when the unlawful killing took place (*ibid*, s 7(4)) if the application under the Act is made after the effective date under the 1982 legislation, 13 October 1982 (*ibid*, s 7(2)). However, an order may not be made so as to affect any interest in property which, in consequence of the rule, has been acquired before that date by a person other than the offender or a person claiming through him (*ibid*, ss 2(7), 7(4)).

In any claim under the Act the court is required to have regard (amongst other matters) to the applicant's conduct and any other matter which it considers relevant (s 3(1)(g)). In a case of unlawful killing the justice of the case and the degree of moral blame attaching to the applicant must be relevant considerations.

In *Re Royse, Royse v Royse* [1985] Ch 22, the applicant, convicted of her husband's manslaughter in July 1979 applied under the Act (in April 1982) for provision to be made for her from his estate. By his will the deceased had left his entire estate to the applicant who could not benefit due to the forfeiture rule. The appellate court found that s 3 of the Forfeiture Act 1982 was not available to assist the applicant as her application under the Act was made prior to the effective date for s 3 of the Act of 1982, namely 13 October 1982. Further, that even if s 3 of the Forfeiture Act 1982 had been available it would have been of no assistance to the applicant as her claim under the Act was bound to fail. The reason that the applicant lacked provision was not the disposition of the deceased's estate effected by his will but instead the operation of the forfeiture rule. This was not a valid precursor to an application under the Act.

12 Death of the applicant

The right of an applicant to apply for provision under the Act is personal and not a 'cause of action' which is vested in the applicant within s 1(1) of the Law Reform (Miscellaneous Provisions) Act 1934. Therefore, if the applicant dies before the court grants relief under the Act, their personal representatives are not able to continue the application for the benefit of the applicant's estate.

In *Whytte v Ticehurst* [1986] Fam 64, Booth J refused leave to continue proceedings to the personal representatives of a widow, who had claimed against her deceased husband's estate, but died before the hearing. It had been argued on the personal representatives' behalf that as provision for a surviving spouse under the Act was not limited to maintenance, death of that spouse would not extinguish their claim under the Act although it was conceded that the claim of any other category of applicant (necessarily limited to maintenance) must be extinguished by the death of the applicant. This argument was discounted, the Act is designed to make provision for the present and foreseeable needs of an applicant. This is no longer relevant where the applicant has died (see also *Re R, R v O* [1986] Fam Law 58).

In *Re Bramwell, Campbell v Tobin* [1988] 2 FLR 263, *Whytte v Ticehurst* was expressly followed and the court approved the use of RSC Ord 18, r 19 (corresponding to CCR Ord 13, r 5 in the county court) to strike out the application of a deceased applicant at an early stage.

Chapter 3

What the Court Must Take into Consideration

Under the former law there were various matters to which the court was required to have regard when considering an application for maintenance (see s 1(5), (6), (7) of the Act of 1938 and s 26(4), (5) of the Matrimonial Causes Act 1965). However, the court is now given much more specific guidelines by s 3 of the Act. Oliver J said in *Re Coventry, Coventry v Coventry* [1980] Ch 461 (at 474–475), that in regarding the circumstances and applying those guidelines it always had to be borne in mind that the Act, so far as it related to applicants other than spouses, was an Act the purpose of which was limited to the provision of reasonable maintenance. It was not the purpose of the Act to provide legacies or rewards for meritorious conduct. Subject to the court's powers under the Act and to fiscal demands, an Englishman still remained at liberty at his death to dispose of his own property in whatever way he pleased or, if he chose to do so, to leave that disposition to be regulated by the laws of intestate succession. In order to enable the court to interfere with and reform those dispositions it must be shown, not that the deceased acted unreasonably, but that, looked at objectively, his disposition or lack of disposition produced an unreasonable result in that it did not make any or any greater provision for the applicant—and that meant, in the case of an applicant other than a spouse, for that applicant's maintenance. His Lordships's words met with approval in the Court of Appeal (per Goff LJ at 488 and per Buckley LJ at 495).

Section 3(1) provides that, where an application is made for an order under s 2, the court shall, in determining whether the disposition of the deceased's estate effected by his will or the law relating to intestacy, or the combination of his will and that law, is such as to make reasonable financial provision for the applicant and, if the court considers that reasonable financial provision has not been made, in determining whether and in what manner it shall exercise its powers under that section, have regard to various matters (set out in paras (a) to (g)) which are relevant to every category of applicant: but they will not necessarily be applied in the same way for all categories of applicant. In the Court of Appeal in *Re Rowlands* [1984] FLR 813, Cumming-Bruce LJ (with whom Dunn LJ and Wood J agreed) said at 822):

> As a matter of construction, the first point to note on the provisions of s 3(1) is this. The court has to answer three questions. The first is the question whether reasonable financial provision for the applicant should be ordered out of the estate. In relation to that exercise, the court is enjoined to have regard to all the matters thereafter specified in the section. If the court answers the first question in the affirmative it then has to decide whether to exercise its power at all, and at that stage has again to have regard to all the matters thereafter set out by the draftsman in the subsection. If the court decides to exercise its powers, it then has to determine in what manner to exercise them, and again for that purpose to have regard to all the matters set out in the rest of the section. That is important because it is perfectly plain from the language that those factors set out in subs (1) fall for mandatory consideration by the court when answering each of the three questions which the legislation requires the court to answer.

See also *Re Coventry*, per Oliver J at 469 and per Goff LJ at 486–487, and *Moody v Stevenson* [1992] Ch 486 per Waite J at 497–8.

1 Regard must be had to existing facts

In considering the matters to which it is now required to have regard the court must take into account the facts as known to it at the date of the hearing (see s 3(5)). This means the hearing at first instance. The facts must be properly proved. If the matter goes to the Court of Appeal, that court is not concerned with events which may have happened since the judge delivered his judgment: *Re Coventry, Coventry v Coventry* [1980] Ch 461 per Goff LJ at 491 and per Geoffrey Lane LJ at 493. It is therefore of the utmost importance that the court is provided with up to date evidence at the date of the hearing at first instance. (See p 149 on appeals).

2 Resources, needs, obligations and responsibilities

Under s 3(1) of the Act the court must have regard to (para (a)) the financial resources and financial needs which the applicant has or is likely to have in the foreseeable future; (para (b)) the financial resources and financial needs which any other applicant for an order under s 2 has or is likely to have in the foreseeable future; (para (c)) the financial resources and financial needs which any beneficiary of the estate of the deceased has or is likely to have in the foreseeable future; and (para (d)) any obligations and responsibilities which the deceased had towards any applicant for an order under s 2 or towards any beneficiary of the estate of the deceased.

'Needs' means 'reasonable requirements': *Harrington v Gill* (1983) 4 FLR 265, per Dunn LJ at 271. Subsection (6) provides that in considering the financial resources of any person for the purposes of the section the court shall take into account his earning capacity and in considering the financial needs of any person for the purposes of the section the court shall take into account his financial obligations and responsibilities. 'Beneficiary' is defined by s 25(1) as (a) a person who under the will of the deceased or under the law relating to intestacy is beneficially interested in the estate or would be so interested if an order had not been made under the Act and (b) a person in whose favour the deceased has nominated money or property or in whose favour the deceased has made a *donatio mortis causa* of money or other property (which money or other property is by virtue of s 8(1) or s 8(2) (see pp 79–81) treated for the purposes of the Act as part of the net estate of the deceased). The requirement in s 1(6) of the Act of 1938 and s 26(4)(a) of the Matrimonial Causes Act 1965 that the court shall have regard to any past capital and income of the applicant has no counterpart in the Act: but it is clear from the decision of the Court of Appeal in *Re Besterman, Besterman v Grusin* [1984] Ch 458 that, at least in the case of a surviving spouse, a relevant consideration is the standard of living to which the applicant has been accustomed. 'Obligations and responsibilities' in s 1(1)(d) means obligations and responsibilities which the deceased had immediately before his death and do not include defunct obligations, see *Re Jennings, Harlow v National Westminster Bank plc* [1994] 3 WLR 67 and p 71.

Paragraphs (a), (b), (c) and (d) of s 3(1) recognise that the applicant may not be the most needy person interested in the estate by requiring the court to have regard to the financial resources and financial needs not only of the applicant but also of any other applicant and any beneficiary. It is not uncommon for there to be more than one applicant seeking relief: for example, a widow and a child of the deceased. Obviously, in all such cases the court must balance the respective claims. In *Kusminov v Barclays Bank Trust Co Ltd* [1989] Fam Law 66 Sir Stephen Brown P had to balance the claim under the Act of the deceased's widow to whom he had been married for 27 years against the claims of the beneficiaries, a niece and nephew of the deceased living in some poverty in the Soviet Union and also in need of a substantial capital sum. In *Malone v Harrison* [1979] 1 WLR 1353, Hollings J (at 1363) said that the financial resources and needs of the beneficiaries were relevant to the extent that any order contemplated by the court might affect those resources and needs, and to the extent that they might be used by way of comparison and to achieve fairness when assessing how much, if anything, should be awarded under the Act. In *Re Debenham* [1986] 1 FLR 404, Ewbank J (at 408) observed that in the context of paragraph (a) of s 3(1) in particular he must remember that he was dealing with the plaintiff, and not with her husband, who was not an applicant under the Act, and must beware of making provision which would be diverted to his benefit rather than to the plaintiff's. On the other hand it is clear from the judgment of Oliver LJ in *Re Besterman, Besterman v Grusin* [1984] Ch 458 (at 466), that when a lump sum is awarded to a surviving spouse it is immaterial that they may thereby be enabled to make provision for somebody else who is not an applicant (see p 41).

Moreover, the court has always paid regard to moral as well as legal claims on testators, so that the rights of dependants may be cut down, even though those dependants have, on their own merits, a good claim for maintenance. Thus, in *Re Joslin, Joslin v Murch* [1941] Ch 200 (see p 32 and *Worthington v Ongley and Kelly* [1910] 29 NZLR 1167), the court refused to interfere with the dispositions of a testator who had left the whole of his very small estate—approximately £370—to his mistress and his illegitimate children, who were penniless and in receipt of poor relief, and dismissed the application of his wife, to whom the testator had, during their joint lives, been bound to pay £1 a week under a deed of separation, and whose income was approximately £23 a year from property which she owned, together with £3 4s a week from taking in boarders. Farwell J said that in cases of this kind the court must consider moral as well as legal obligations, and that the testator was not only entitled, but bound to consider how far a duty—perhaps a moral duty—lay on him to provide for his mistress and their children.

Now that not only illegitimate children (see p 12) but also, in certain circumstances, mistresses and unmarried partners, for example (see p 15) are eligible to make an application, they and a widow and legitimate children may find themselves in direct conflict with one another. See also *Jessop v Jessop* [1992] 1 FLR 591 where the deceased clearly had moral obligations to both the applicant widow and the lady with whom he resided.

Equally the court may take into account the fact that a beneficiary had no moral or legal claim on the deceased. Thus, Ewbank J in *Re Debenham* [1986] 1 FLR 404 took into account the fact that the deceased owed no obligation to the charities who took the residuary estate under the will and in *Re Callaghan* [1985] Fam 1 Booth J contrasted the obligations which the deceased owed his stepson, which her Ladyship said were very considerable indeed, with those he owed his sisters (who took on his intestacy) which were those brought about by their blood relationship and by remembrance of that part of their lives which they had shared and therefore considerably less.

The reference in s 3(1) to resources which the applicant or any other beneficiary 'is likely to have in the foreseeable future' appears to refer to estates or interests indefeasibly vested in possession or reversion at the date of the application; the falling into possession of an estate or interest might well affect the duration of payments by way of maintenance to an applicant. However, in *Browne v Browne* [1989] 1 FLR 291, a case on a similar matter to be taken into account under s 25 of the Matrimonial Causes Act 1973 the Court of Appeal held that assets held in a discretionary trust out of the jurisdiction were capable of being 'financial resources' for the purposes of that Act, where the wife had 'effective control' or 'immediate access' to them, the trustees having never refused an application for funds. In view of this provision, the applicant should in every case file evidence making full disclosure as to his financial position, past and present, with a reference to any interest indefeasibly vested in possession or reversion. The applicant should state whether he has received any advances from the deceased in the past, and, if so, particulars of these should be given in this connection. The applicant should also state his age, his capacity to earn his living and the state of his health. Other interested persons are entitled but not bound (see p 142) to file evidence if they desire to do so.

The applicant's earning capacity has, of course, always been an important factor when the court is determining whether an award should be made. It appears from *Re Ducksbury, Ducksbury v Ducksbury* [1966] 1 WLR 1226 that the court will have regard to potential as well as actual earnings. The applicant, a daughter of the testator, was able to earn her living as a secretary, but preferred to work part-time and to pursue part-time studies of art, with the consequence that her earnings were small. Having found that the testator had a moral obligation to make some provision for her and, having made no such provision by his will, had failed to make reasonable provision for her maintenance, Buckley J ordered that she be paid £2 weekly out of the testator's estate until she married. His Lordship held that her choice of way of living did not increase her moral claim on the testator. In *Re Pearson-Gregory* ((1957) *The Times*, 11 October), Roxburgh J refused to make an order in favour of a daughter of a testator whose estate was £43,000 but under whose will the applicant received only chattels worth £400. She had an income of £800 a year from a trust fund provided by the testator in 1947, and Roxburgh J said that if she wanted to maintain the high standard of life into which she had been introduced, she must work. In *Re Bunning, Bunning v Salmon* [1984] Ch 480 Vinelott J, in awarding £60,000 to the widow of the deceased who had been separated from him for some four years before his death, took into account the expectation that the applicant would undertake some part-time employment.

Possession of a pension or receipt of insurance monies or lump sum benefits payable on death under the deceased's pension fund by an applicant or any beneficiary will also be material. Thus in *Jessop v Jessop* [1992] 1 FLR 591 the pension to which the applicant, the deceased's widow, was entitled from the deceased's employers was taken into account and the Court of Appeal in making an award to the widow, including an order under s 9 of the Act (jointly owned property), held that the judge had erred in apparently failing to take fully into account the sum of £40,000 which the defendant, who had lived with the deceased as his wife for many years, had also received from the pension scheme. In *Re Charman, Charman v Williams* [1951] 2 TLR 1095 Harman J, in refusing to make provision for the applicant who was the widow of the deceased, took into account a voluntary pension being paid by the employers. While account would no doubt still be taken of such provision it is possible that such payment would not be considered decisive having regard to the Court of Appeal's decision in *Rajabally v Rajabally* [1987] 2 FLR 390. In that case Nicholls J at first instance dismissed a claim by the widow in reliance upon assurances by two of the deceased's sons that they would not insist on their rights under the will. The Court of Appeal stated that it was not permissible to reach a conclusion on the question whether the will failed to make reasonable financial provision for the applicant on legally unenforceable assurances given at the hearing by various parties. See also *Browne v Browne* [1989] 1 FLR 291 (a case on s 25 of the Matrimonial Causes Act 1973).

The right to benefit under the social security legislation is also relevant. In the case of a small estate it may be reasonable for an applicant who is entitled to such benefit not to have further provision made for him, and in such a case the court may be reluctant to make an order, the effect of which will be to relieve public funds: *Re E, E v E* [1966] 1 WLR 709. An application will not, however, necessarily fail because social security benefits will be reduced by reason of an order under the Act: *Re Collins* [1990] Fam 56. Where an applicant or a beneficiary is in receipt of means tested benefit, careful consideration should be given, both on a contested application and in the event of a compromise, to the effect on such benefits of any proposed award and it may be possible to make such provision as will not greatly reduce them.

3 Size and nature of the estate

The court is directed by s 3(1)(e) of the Act to have regard to the size and nature of the deceased's net estate. There is no longer any prohibition against making an order necessitating a realisation which would be improvident having regard to the interests of the deceased's dependants and of the persons who, apart from the order, would be entitled to that property (cf s 1(5) of the Act of 1938). However, the requirement of para (e) of s 3(1) that the court shall have regard to the nature of the net estate appears to put upon the court an obligation to consider what the effect of realising any particular asset would be. In a proper case the whole estate might well have to be realised if that were the only means whereby proper provision for dependants might be secured (see *Re Farrow* [1987] 1 FLR 205 for a case where the nature of the estate had a limiting effect: the principal asset was a farm which passed to the deceased's sons and from which they made their livelihoods).

It may be that 'nature' has a wide enough connotation to include 'source'. Be that as it may, the court does in fact take account of the origin of the deceased's estate, though it could equally well do so when considering 'any other matter . . . which in the circumstances of the case the court may consider relevant' (s 3(1)(g)). Thus the court took account in *Re Styler, Styler v Griffith* [1942] Ch 387 of the fact that the greater part of the estate of the testatrix was derived from her husband; in *Re Brownbridge, Brownbridge v Brownbridge* (1942) 193 LT Jo 185 of the fact that the sole beneficiary under the will had in the last years of the testator's life considerably assisted him in his business and had become his business partner; in *Re Sivyer, Sivyer v Sivyer* [1967] 1 WLR 1482 of the fact that the principal asset of the deceased's estate was derived from the applicant's mother; in *Re Thornley, Thornley v Palmer* [1969] 1 WLR 1037 of the fact that the applicant had originally put up part of the money which started the joint life of the deceased and herself together; in *Re Callaghan* [1985] Fam 1 that the greater part of the deceased's estate derived from the applicant's mother and grandfather; and in *Re Wood, Wood v Wood* [1982] LS Gaz 774 that the deceased's estate derived from her family but as a result of her intestacy and the subsequent death of her second husband would pass to her stepson and away from the plaintiff, her own daughter. In view of the special position of a surviving spouse (see pp 41–54), the source of the deceased's assets (eg, the matrimonial home) is clearly of particular relevance. Thus in *Re Bunning, Bunning v Salmon* [1984] Ch 480 Vinelott J took into account the fact that the deceased husband's assets were built up by his own efforts largely before he married. On the other hand the fact that the applicant made a large contribution to the acquisition of the deceased's assets will not necessarily increase the amount of provision to be made. In *Stead v Stead* [1985] FLR 16 the Court of Appeal accepted that the applicant widow had made a substantial contribution to the value of the estate, having helped a great deal with family finances and helped the deceased on the farm which was owned by him and taken in paying guests, but went on to hold that as she was elderly and her need for capital was limited the judge's order as to periodical payments without payment of a lump sum would be upheld (see p 84).

Paragraph (e) of s 3(1) also requires the court to have regard to the size of the deceased's net estate. In *Re Coventry, Coventry v Coventry* [1980] Ch 461 Goff LJ (at 486) said that applications in small estates should be discouraged, because the costs tend to become wholly disproportionate to the end in view, while Geoffrey Lane LJ (at 492) with whom Buckley LJ (at 496) agreed, said that appeals to the Court of Appeal were to be strongly discouraged in small estates. See also *Re Joslin, Joslin v Murch* [1941] Ch 200, where Farwell J dismissed the application with costs, saying that he thought it right to prevent the very small provision made for the testator's mistress and their children from being reduced as a result of the proceedings *Re Trowell* ((1957) *The Times*, 29 November), where Roxburgh J made a 'derisory order' to discourage applications in the case of very small estates; *Re E, E v E* [1966] 1 WLR 709, a case in which the plaintiff was legally aided and Stamp J said that he would think it right if he had the power to do so to echo the words of Farwell J in *Re Joslin* and to prevent the very small provision made for the defendant from being reduced by the proceedings and dismissed the summons with costs; *Re Gregory, Gregory v Goodenough* [1970] 1 WLR 1455; and *Allcorn v Harvey* (1981) 131 NLJ 242.

In *Brill v Proud* (1984) 14 Fam Law 59 (see p 56) where a claim by a former wife was dismissed and an order for costs in the sum of £476, the amount of her legal aid contribution, was made against her, the Court of Appeal was critical of the fact that a small estate had been heavily depleted by costs and that the appellant had been granted legal aid to conduct her appeal. Sir John Arnold P said that the effect of costs should have been taken into account by the area legal aid committee. Latey J referred to the fact that the defendant's solicitors had very properly written to the committee with an estimate of the costs, but the plaintiff's legal aid certificate had not subsequently been discharged. His Lordship emphasised the duty of practitioners, when the estate was small, to inform the Legal Aid Board of the likely effect of costs.

Whether an estate is sufficiently large to justify an application must depend upon the facts, and whereas generally (as under the previous law), the smallness of the estate will be relevant, account must be taken of the special position of a surviving spouse: no matter how small the estate, the fact that a surviving spouse has contributed to it will give them a strong claim to provision out of it, and possibly to the whole of it. Ungoed-Thomas J in *Re Clayton, Clayton v Howell* [1966] 1 WLR 969, pointed out that the Act of 1938 placed no bottom limit to the value of the estate in respect of which an application could be made. Small sums mattered to very many people, and an order for payment of £1 a week or less might, in certain circumstances, make all the difference to a claimant. However small the estate, all the relevant circumstances had to be considered before the court's decision was made. The smallness of the estate excluded neither jurisdiction nor full consideration. Stamp J in *Re E* (at 716) said that it was no doubt true that often when proceedings were launched the plaintiff was unaware of the size of the estate, but where that fact had been ascertained the application ought in his judgment to be reconsidered. Where the plaintiff was, as in that case, legally aided he doubted not that this ought to be done. It is the knowledge that a trial will further deplete an already small fund which leads to so many claims being settled out of court. On the other hand, the cost of litigating claims has been lightened by the giving of jurisdiction not only to the county courts but also to masters and district judges (see Chapter 9).

Where the estate is a large one it will generally be easier to make suitable provision for an applicant, and a surviving spouse may expect to receive a substantial sum (see *Re Besterman, Besterman v Grusin* [1984] Ch 458 and p 41. In the case of other applicants, however, who are only entitled to awards by way of maintenance, an award will not be proportionately larger just because the estate is a large one (see *Re Inns, Inns v Wallace* [1947] Ch 576).

It will not necessarily be certain when an application comes before the court whether or not anything will exist out of which provision may be made. In such a case the application has to be determined on the position as presented to the court at the time of the hearing, when future prospects will be taken into account, if there is evidence justifying a conclusion that the estate is likely to appreciate or depreciate in the future. If there is no evidence to that effect, then the matter must be dealt with on the evidence as it stands, and if on that evidence an order would be, in effect, a nullity and would confer no benefit, the court will not make an order on the chance that it may, in some unforeseen circumstances, provide some benefit for the applicant. It is for the trial judge to use their judicial discretion whether to dismiss the application on the ground that there are no assets on which an order for provision could operate, or to make an order which would take effect in the event of assets existing. Where that discretion is properly exercised a higher court will not interfere with the decision of the trial judge (see *Leeder v Ellis* [1953] AC 52, a decision under the New South Wales Testator's Family Maintenance and Guardianship of Infants Act 1916–1938, where the Privy Council approved the observations of Street CJ in the Full Court of the Supreme Court of New South Wales).

4 Disability of applicants and beneficiaries

Paragraph (f) of s 3(1) of the Act requires the court to have regard to any physical or mental disability of any applicant for an order under s 2 and any beneficiary of the estate of the deceased. The health of the applicant was considered to be of importance in both *Re Debenham* [1986] 1 FLR 404 and *Re Wood, Wood v Wood* [1982] LS Gaz 774 giving rise in both cases to a moral obligation (in *Re Wood* said to be compelling) on the deceased, the applicant's mother in both cases, to assist the applicant.

It has been said in a number of cases concerning the Act of 1938 that it may be reasonable for a testator to intend a dependant suffering from disability, whether physical or mental, to take advantage of facilities for treatment offered by the state and to leave his estate, or the greater part of it, elsewhere. Conversely, it may be unreasonable to provide, at the expense of other dependants, for one who is in the state's care and who may possibly be in no position to enjoy the testator's bounty. The applicant in *Re Watkins, Hayward v Chatterton* [1949] 1 All ER 695 was the daughter of the testator. She had been a patient in a private mental hospital since 1945, and she was incapable of maintaining herself. Her private means amounted to approximately £140 a year. During his lifetime the testator had provided £250 a year for her upkeep in the hospital, but the provision made for her by his will would produce only £72 a year, while the cost of her maintenance in the private hospital was about £360 a year. Evidence was given that, in view of the provisions of the National Health Service Act 1946, the testator intended to leave the state to take care of his invalid daughter, and that he would only be responsible for her until the day to be appointed under the said Act for its commencement. Roxburgh J held that the testator was entitled to distribute his estate on the footing that his daughter should take advantage of the provisions of the said Act, and, therefore, the provision made for her by his will was reasonable having regard to her existing needs. The learned judge added that if he had come to the conclusion that the will did not make reasonable provision for the applicant's maintenance he would have made some additional provision for her in respect of the period between the testator's death and the period, say, of three months after the date of the order; that being a reasonable period for the removal of the applicant to some state institution, the Hospital where she was a patient not having been taken over by the state. Reference should be made to *Re E, E v E*

[1966] 1 WLR 530 for Stamp J's comments on the extent of this decision.

In *Re Pringle* ((1956) *The Times*, 2 February), on the other hand, Vaisey J made an order in favour of the applicant, who was the son of the testatrix and who was a mentally defective patient, resident in a mental hospital. Vaisey J found that the testatrix did not intend to leave anything to the applicant, not from lack of affection, but because she thought that, as he was being maintained by the state, she was entitled to leave her money elsewhere. His lordship referred to *Re Watkins* as 'a very different case from the present,' and ordered that the applicant be paid 10s a week, for the purchase of 'comforts' not provided by the hospital, out of the estate of the testatrix as from the date of her death for his life, or until cesser of his disability, or further order (see also *Re Williams* [1933] St R, S Aus 107, where an order was made in favour of the testator's widow although the allowance would go in relief of the cost of her support in a mental hospital; and *Re Brousseau* [1952] 4 DLR 664, a case under the Testator's Family Maintenance Act of British Columbia (Revised Statutes of British Columbia 1948), where Clyne J in the Supreme Court of British Columbia made an order in favour of the testator's widow, who had been in a public mental hospital for several years before the testator's death, and in so doing did not follow *Re Watkins* where, he observed, there were grounds for invoking state assistance).

In *Re Wood, Wood v Wood* [1982] LS Gaz 774 Mervyn Davies J recognised that the life of the severely handicapped applicant could be improved by the provision of capital even though she was permanently resident in hospital and this will be the case even if the applicant may lose state benefits as a result of provision being made. Under the present system of benefits applicants who are being cared for under the National Health system will not usually be in receipt of means tested benefits. However, those being cared for in private nursing homes may be receiving income support or the cost of their accommodation may be being subsidised by the local authority. In these cases benefits may be lost in whole or in part by a substantial payment. However, where an applicant is severely mentally handicapped it is probable that the court would insist on some sort of discretionary trust which may not be taken into account in assessing entitlement to benefit. Even if the applicant's entitlement to state benefit will be effected it may still be in the interests of the applicant to be awarded a lump sum which can be used to purchase items such as wheel chairs and pay for outings and holidays as well as being used to defray accommodation costs: *Millward v Shenton* [1972] 1 WLR 711.

The case of an applicant who is being maintained in an old people's home is similar to that of one in a mental hospital. In *Re Perry* ((1956) The Times, 19 April), Vaisey J made an order in favour of such an applicant, who was entirely dependent on public assistance and had been left nothing by his wife, the testatrix.

5 Conduct and other matters

Paragraph (g) of s 3(1) of the Act requires that the court shall have regard to 'any other matter, including the conduct of the applicant or any other person, which in the circumstances of the case the court may consider relevant'. In the case of an application by a former spouse the fact that the applicant and the deceased have been divorced and the result of that divorce in financial terms is highly relevant (see *Re Fullard, Fullard v King* [1982] Fam 42).

It is thought that the unmeritorious conduct of an applicant who is a surviving spouse will not usually be very relevant in view of the special position accorded to such an applicant by the Act (see pp 41–54). Nevertheless, it is desirable that the applicant should file evidence as to whether he or she was on friendly terms with the deceased. If the applicant is a surviving spouse, the court should be informed whether the applicant and the deceased were living together at the time of the deceased's death, and, if they have parted, the grounds of the separation and the financial arrangements then made. Having regard to the relevance of judicial separation to reasonable financial provision (see s 1(2) and pp 54–63), it is essential that such information should be before the court. The fact that the testator had exercised a special testamentary power of appointment in favour of the applicant would be relevant in deciding whether provision should be made out the testator's free estate.

In *Williams v Johns* [1988] 2 FLR 475 His Honour Judge Micklem took into account the conduct of the applicant, the adopted daughter of the deceased, who it was said had caused shame and distress to the deceased.

Section 1(7) of the Act of 1938 directed the court to have regard to the deceased's reasons for his dispositions. No such direction is contained in the Act. However, if the court considers them to be relevant the deceased's reasons may still be taken into account under s 3(1)(g). Having regard to the fact that the test to be applied is an objective one the deceased's reasons will be of less relevance in many cases under the Act than formerly: the court has to consider the objective reasonableness of the effect of the dispositions of the deceased's estate and not whether the deceased acted reasonably or unreasonably. Thus a clause in the will in general terms to the effect that nothing has been left to the surviving spouse because they have already been provided for will have no bearing on the matter where looked at objectively that is not the case, see for example *Moody v Stevenson* [1992] Ch 486. On the other hand a signed statement to the effect that nothing has been left to X because of X's conduct or referring to some other specific circumstance may be of greater importance.

Many of the cases under the Act of 1938 were concerned with the nature of the evidence which might be admissible under s 1(7) of that Act. These problems have largely been solved by s 21 of the Act which is concerned with the evidentiary aspect of statements made by the deceased, providing that in any proceedings under the Act a statement made by the deceased, whether orally or in a document or otherwise, shall be admissible under s 2 of the Civil Evidence Act 1968 as evidence of any fact stated therein in like manner as if the statement were a statement falling within subs (1) of that section. Any reference in that Act to a statement admissible, or given or proposed to be given, in evidence under s 2 thereof or to the admissibility or the giving in evidence of a statement by virtue of that section or to any statement falling within subs (1) thereof is to be construed accordingly. That subsection enables oral or written statements by a person to be admitted as evidence of any fact of which direct oral evidence by him would be admissible. Section 21 of the Act removes a doubt which existed as to whether s 2 (1) of the Civil Evidence Act covers statements by a deceased person who could never have given direct oral evidence since the proceedings in question are proceedings against his estate. Having regard to the changes referred to above, cases under the Act of 1938 no longer have much relevance and have been omitted from this edition, the majority of them being concerned with the very specific terms of s 1(7) of that Act. Section 3(1)(g) of the Act on the other hand when coupled with s 21 gives the court a wide discretion as to what it considers relevant to take into account.

In any case where a will does not provide for a possible applicant, the reasons for the provisions of the will should be made clear, either by means of a statement in the will itself, or by a separate document. There are two main groups of reasons: first, the person in question being well provided for in some other way; and, secondly, the person by his conduct having forfeited his natural claims on the testator, so as to be superseded by the superior claims of other persons. (As to the relevance of means, see pp 26–31, and as to the relevance of his conduct, see p 37).

If the grounds for the testator's disposition are financial, they should be set out. For example, a testator may have provided for his family by a settlement; or provision for a member of his family may have been made by a third person; or there may have been an order for secured periodical payments made under the Matrimonial Causes Act 1973 (see as to variation and discharge s 16 and pp 60–61,); or there may be a maintenance agreement providing for continuation of payments under the agreement after the death of the deceased (see as to variation and revocation s 17 and pp 61–62). Grounds for discrimination between children, if proper, should be stated; for example, where one child is provided for to the exclusion of others. A case where this might happen is where money is spent on the training or advancement in life of a child during the testator's lifetime so that they become self-supporting. It would not, in the case of a small estate, be unreasonable for another child, who had devoted their life to looking after their parents, to take the estate to the exclusion of the other child. Where there are reasonable grounds it is most important that the draftsman should make them clear so that it is at once obvious on the face of the will that an application made under the Act would be unlikely to succeed.

Where the ground for discrimination is based on a person's misconduct, or on what the testator considers to be misconduct, the ground on which the testator has acted should not be incorporated in the will, but in a signed statement referred to in the will and kept therewith. It has already been pointed out (see p 37) that matrimonial misconduct, unless very grave, will not normally disentitle the surviving spouse to provision. A bare statement, as in *Re Lidington, Lidington v Thomas* (*No* 2) [1940] Ch 927 that the testator left 'nothing whatsoever' to his wife will not carry any weight. In *Re Borthwick, Borthwick v Beauvais* [1949] Ch 395 the testator left a document in which he sought to justify his treatment of his wife, but Harman J allowed her maintenance. An infant child is unlikely to have forfeited all right to maintenance, but an adult child might —for example, by deliberately cutting themselves off from their family. It seems that a statement, even if it does not result in the dependant being deprived of all maintenance, may yet cut down the amount which the court will order to be paid. (See *Re Clarke*,

Clarke v Roberts [1986] 1 WLR 415, for a case where an inaccurate statement of reasons was ignored).

It is clearly undesirable that scandalous matter should be incorporated in the will itself; hence the desirability of a separate document when the testator's reasons are based on a person's misconduct. Such a document would be privileged, so far as its publication by the executors was necessary for the purpose of supporting the will, but, unlike a will, it would not be available for the general public to read. The court will not order to be struck out of a will words which might have an effect upon proceedings under the Act (see *In the Estate of C* ((1960) *The Times*, 28 July)).

In a *Practice Note* [1945] WN 210, Vaisey J said that, in applications under the Act of 1938, any suggestion of the testator's weakness of mind ought to be excluded. His Lordship could not see the relevance of it. He was confident that it was not an issue in such cases. He had consulted his brother judges and he thought he could say, without any impropriety, that, in such cases, any suggestion of unsoundness of mind, or even want of lucidity of mind, could not possibly be raised. It might be the reason why the will was in a rather queer form and it might be the reason why it was unintelligible, but it could not be one of the testator's reasons for making the bequest. It was a lack of reason, and the point ought not to be raised. In *Re Blanch, Blanch v Honhold* [1967] 1 WLR 987, an application by a widow, the applicant stated that (as was admitted) the testator had been obsessively, irrationally jealous of her relationships with other persons. Buckley J considered the Practice Note in question and said that, as Vaisey J apparently had consulted his brethren before he made the statement which was recorded in the Note, he had thought that perhaps it was desirable that he should consult some of his present brethren before delivering his judgment, and he had done so. His Lordship believed that Vaisey J in making the observations which he made, was speaking a little unguardedly and in wider terms than those in which he really meant to be understood. The Note as it stood should not be taken to be of general application. The Act of 1938 enjoined the court to have regard to any matter or thing which in the circumstances of the case it might consider relevant or material. There were likely in certain cases to be respects in which the state of the deceased's mind might properly be regarded as relevant and material. For instance, the state of the deceased's mind might be very material to the weight to be attributed to any reason he might have given in his lifetime for failing to make provision for a dependant or the making of any such provision as he did make for a dependant. Moreover, although the test of what must be regarded as reasonable provision should be an objective test, it might have to be made in the light of the competing claims on the deceased's bounty. If, as his Lordship thought, it might be relevant in one case to take into consideration that a dependant had devoted himself or herself to caring for the deceased during a long physical illness, it might be equally relevant in another case to take into account care during a long period of mental illness, and evidence would be admissible in that respect. In either case, the fact that a dependant had devoted time and trouble to caring for the deceased might be something to which some weight should be given in assessing the moral obligations of the deceased to the dependant in question. If the will had been admitted to probate, testamentary incapacity could not be alleged, and feebleness of mind, whether amounting to or falling short of testamentary capacity, could never be a 'reason' for the purposes of subs (7) of s 1 of the Act of 1938. The Practice Note should be read as indicating only that testamentary capacity, or the lack of it, was not a matter which should be investigated on an application under the Act, and that feebleness of mind or understanding could not constitute a reason for the deceased's conduct which was relevant for the purposes of that subsection. In the present case Buckley J felt no doubts that the deceased's irrational jealousy accounted for his complete failure to make any provision for the plaintiff, but it was not a reason which had any bearing on either whether it was reasonable for him to fail to provide for her, or what provision the court should order to be made for her, except in so far as the plaintiff's having apparently endured the state of affairs for about a year with a generous understanding might be said to enhance her moral claim upon the deceased's bounty. That decision seems to have undiminished force in the context of the law as it is today.

6 Special position of surviving spouse

When considering an application by a surviving spouse the court not only has to take into consideration the matters referred to in s 3(1) but also those set out in s 3(2) of the Act.

While Oliver LJ delivering the leading judgment in the Court of Appeal in *Re Besterman, Besterman v Grusin* [1984] Ch 458 was at pains (at 479–480) to emphasise that the case was a very unusual one, turning largely on its own facts, one of which was the very large size of the estate and another the absence of conflicting obligations, it is, nevertheless, a valuable decision on the position of a surviving spouse. The essential facts can be stated quite briefly. The plaintiff and the testator were married in 1958, when they were aged respectively 42 and 54, and lived together until he died in 1976. They enjoyed a high standard of living. The estate was valued at £1.37m. The testator bequeathed to the plaintiff only his domestic and personal chattels, £100,000 nominal War Stock for life, and the use for life of certain works of art. The main beneficiary was Oxford University. It was not in dispute that the bequests to the plaintiff did not constitute reasonable provision: the question in issue was the size of the provision which should be made. By an interim order the plaintiff was given a capital sum of £75,000, income of £11,500 per annum, and a further income of £3,500 per annum for the upkeep of the matrimonial home until sale. In addition, she had a widow's pension of £400 per annum. Judge Mervyn Davies QC (sitting as a judge of the Chancery Division) ordered that the plaintiff should have the War Stock absolutely, together with a lump sum of £125,000, and that she should be reimbursed any income tax which she was liable to pay. The Court of Appeal increased the lump sum to £275,000.

Oliver LJ referred to the particular importance of subs (2) of s 1 of the Act. As has already been observed (see pp 9, 20), a surviving spouse (unless judicially separated from the deceased at the time of his death) is placed in a special position because in his or her case 'reasonable financial provision' is defined by s 1(2)(a) as meaning 'such financial provision as it would be reasonable in all the circumstances of the case for a husband or wife to receive, whether or not that provision is required for his or her maintenance', whereas, in the case of other applicants under the Act, s 1(2)(b) limits the financial provision which can be made for them to such 'as it would be reasonable in all the circumstances of the case for the applicant to receive for his maintenance'. Oliver LJ (at 465–466), put it thus:

> This [subs (2)] is a subsection of particular importance in the present context. The Inheritance (Family Provision) Act 1938, which first introduced the concept of reasonable testamentary provision to English law, was an Act to provide for the *maintenance* of dependants. The present Act remains such an Act in relation to dependants other than surviving spouses, but this section expressly provides that in the case of a surviving spouse the governing criterion is to be what the court considers to be 'reasonable' provision unqualified by any such consideration. There may, of course, be cases where that reasonable

> provision in all the circumstances might be restricted to maintenance, but the subsection makes it clear that the court, in making such reasonable provision, is not to be inhibited by what I may call 'the Act of 1938 concept' that maintenance is the only criterion or, indeed, even that that is the dominant consideration.

In *Stead v Stead* [1985] FLR 16 Purchas LJ delivering the leading judgment in the Court of Appeal, said that the principles set out in *Re Besterman* were applicable though the facts of the present case were very different. The plaintiff was a widow of 80 who claimed further provision out of her deceased husband's estate of £66,000, including the matrimonial home, which was valued at £29,000. The marriage had lasted for 24 years, but both parties had been previously married and the deceased had two adult children by his former marriage. He gave the plaintiff a life interest in the matrimonial home on condition that she paid all the outgoings, and settled a sum of £6,000 on trust to be invested in order to produce an income for her for life. He gave the residue of his estate to his children. Sir John Arnold P awarded the plaintiff a lump sum of £2,500 and periodical payments of £1,500 per annum backdated to the day following the deceased's death, and he ordered that she might continue to reside in the matrimonial home in accordance with the terms of the will, provided that, with her consent to a sale, another house should be purchased out of the proceeds of sale. His Lordship further directed that when the plaintiff no longer desired to reside in any house the trustees should have the discretion to increase the income provision out of the retained proceeds of sale. The plaintiff's appeal asking that the lump sum should be substantially increased was dismissed, the Court of Appeal finding that the effect of the order, together with the provisions of the will, was at least equal, if not advantageous for the plaintiff, to the provision which she might reasonably have expected to be made had the marriage ended by dissolution rather than by the death of the deceased. The effect of the order was to retain half of the estate for the plaintiff in one way or another, that is, as an income-producing asset or, at the trustee's discretion, as an asset available for partial realisation to produce further income in later years. In addition, the plaintiff could come back under s 6 of the Act for further provision out of the estate (see pp 87–90).

The Court of Appeal thus took due account in that case (and also in *Re Besterman*) of s 3(2) of the Act. Paragraph (a) of that subsection requires that the court shall, in the case of an application by a surviving spouse or a former spouse who has not remarried, have regard to the age of the applicant and the duration of the marriage—as in practice the court always has done as being clearly a relevant matter within s 1(6) of the Act of 1938 or s 26(4)(d) of the Matrimonial Causes Act 1965. Nor, under the former law, did the court ignore the fact that the applicant had contributed to the welfare of the family of the deceased whether by looking after the home or caring for the family or otherwise, a matter which it is now required to ignore by s 3(2)(b).

What is new and of much importance as altering the whole basis of provision in the case of a surviving spouse is the requirement which follows s 3(2)(b) that in the case of an application by such a person the court shall also, unless at the date of death a decree of judicial separation was in force and the separation was continuing, have regard to the provision which the applicant might reasonably have expected to receive if on the day on which the deceased died the marriage, instead of being terminated by death, had been terminated by a decree of divorce. This reflects the opinion of the Law Commission (Law Com No 61, paras 27–28) that as a general principle the surviving spouse should have a claim upon the family assets at least equivalent to that of a divorced spouse and accordingly that for the surviving spouse the standard set by family provision legislation should no longer be confined to maintenance, but should be more generally expressed.

In considering that requirement guidance has in earlier editions of this Book been sought from cases decided by reference to s 25(1) of the Matrimonial Causes Act 1973 or its predecessor, s 5(1) of the Matrimonial Proceedings and Property Act 1970. It is considered right to retain such references, although for a full analysis of the position relating to financial provision on divorce reference should be made to the specialist text books on that subject. Attention is drawn to the fact that s 25 of the Matrimonial Causes Act 1973 as it presently applies was substituted by the Matrimonial and Family Proceedings Act 1984 to give effect to the Law Commission's recommendation (Law Com No 112) that seeking to place the parties in the financial position in which they would be had the marriage not broken down should cease to be a statutory objective. That requirement has therefore been excluded from the present section and the distinction drawn between s 25 and the provisions of the Act (see *Re Besterman, Besterman v Grusin* [1984] Ch 458 at 469 and *Re Crawford* (1983) 4 FLR 273) is no longer fully justified. Many of the cases on s 25 (as originally enacted) remain relevant as the factors to be taken into account are largely the same but it should be noted that the court is now concerned wherever possible to effect a clean break between the parties. It should also be noted that under s 25(1) the court is directed to give first consideration to the welfare (while a minor) of any child of the family who has not yet attained the age of 18. There is as yet no authority as to the effect, if any, of this requirement on an application under the Act.

The starting point is *Wachtel v Wachtel* [1973] Fam 72 where Lord Denning MR said (at 93–94):

> If the court comes to the conclusion that the home has been acquired and maintained by the joint efforts of both, then, when the marriage breaks down, it should be regarded as the joint property of both of them, no matter in whose name it stands. Just as the wife who makes substantial money contributions usually gets a share, so should the wife who looks after the home and cares for the family for twenty years or more.

Lord Denning then went on to consider the so-called 'one-third' rule, which originated in the practice of the ecclesiastical courts in awarding an innocent wife a sum equal to one-third of the joint income of the parties. He said that the so-called rule never was a rule and must never be so regarded, although (at 94–95):

> 'a starting point at one-third of the combined resources of the parties is as good and rational a starting point as any other, remembering that the essence of legislation is to secure flexibility to meet the justice of particular cases, and not rigidity, forcing particular cases to be fitted into some so-called principle within which they do not easily lie. There may be cases where more than one-third is right. There are likely to be many others where less than one-third is the only practicable solution. But one-third as a flexible starting point is in general more likely to lead to the correct final result than a starting point of equality, or a quarter. There is this, however, to be noted. Under the old dispensation, the wife, out of her one-third, had to provide her own accommodation. If she was given the right to occupy the matrimonial home, that went to reduce the one-third. Under the new dispensation, she will get a share of the capital assets; and, with that share, she will be able to provide accommodation herself, or, at any rate, the money to go some way towards it.'

Lord Denning concluded that if a wife was to get periodical payments for her maintenance and support the fairest means of providing for her was to give her one-third of the husband's future earnings and one-third of the capital assets which she had helped to create. 'She will certainly in this way be as well off as if the capital assets were divided equally—which is all that a partner is entitled to' (at 95). Lord Denning added (at 96) that when the husband had available capital assets sufficient for the purpose, the court should not hesitate to order a lump sum, and that a wife's share in capital assets should not be reduced merely because she might remarry. The limitations of the so-called 'one-third' rule were emphasised by Oliver LJ in *Re Besterman*, where he said (at 473) that Judge Mervyn Davies 'was referred to *Wachtel v Wachtel* [1973] Fam 72 as an authority for the proposition that a lump sum payment following divorce may well amount to a third or even a half of the family assets, although it is accepted that this can now be considered as no more than a possible guide-line or cross-check'.

In *Trippas v Trippas* [1973] Fam 134 (decided by the Court of Appeal a week after *Wachtel v Wachtel*) Scarman LJ (at 144) said that he believed it essential that the court should retain the complete flexibility of approach which the statute (that is, now s 25(1) of the Matrimonial Causes Act 1973 and cf s 3(1) of the Act) emphasised, and he referred to the fact that in that case the wife, while she made no specific contribution to the business life or business earnings of her husband, had for over 25 years of marriage maintained the home; she had brought up the children, and she provided general and moral support to a man sometimes hard-pressed by business worries. Scarman LJ pointed out (at 146) that there was nothing in the so-called one-third rule or in the language of the statute which precluded the court from doing rough justice on the basis of approximate equality provided that it was, on the whole, fair to both parties.

Under s 25 (as amended) conduct will only be taken into account if it is such that the court considers it would be inequitable to disregard it. However, it is thought that cases on s 25 before substitution may still be relevant. From the decision of the Court of Appeal in *Harnett v Harnett* [1974] 1 WLR 219 it appears that conduct (see s 25(1) of the Matrimonial Causes Act 1973 and cf s 3(1)(g) of the Act) is something which should be taken into account only in a very broad way; that is to say, only where there is something in the conduct of one party which would make it quite inequitable to leave that out of account having regard to the conduct of the other party as well in the course of the marriage; conduct should be considered only if there is some misconduct of a gross and obvious nature (see per Cairns LJ at 224–225). From this it appears that a spouse will forfeit his or her share of the family assets only when he or she has been guilty of very grave misconduct. In *Re Snoek* (1983) 13 Fam Law 18 the behaviour of the applicant, the widow of the testator, had during the latter part of their marriage been atrocious, but Wood J nevertheless ordered that she should have £5,000 out of an estate of £40,000 (see also *Bateman v Bateman* [1979] Fam 25, a case under s 25(1) of the Matrimonial Causes Act 1973, in which Purchas J held that, although the conduct of the applicant, the wife, had substantially contributed to the breakdown of the marriage by both her violence and her damaging attitude towards the husband and his career, she should by no means be deprived of all financial provision but would be granted reduced orders).

In cases under the divorce legislation involving large assets the one-third rule has little application. *Preston v Preston* [1982] Fam 17 was such a case and in it Ormrod LJ in the Court of Appeal considered three earlier cases which had reached that court, *O'D v O'D* [1976] Fam 83, *S v S* (1980) 10 Fam Law 240 (Balcombe J) (CAT (Civil) No 664 of 1980), and *Page v Page* ((1981) *The Times*, 30 January). The facts of those three earlier cases need not be considered here: it will suffice to set out the six general propositions which Ormrod LJ said in *Preston v Preston* (at 24–25) could be extracted from them when assessing a lump sum payment to a wife. Attention is again drawn to the changes to s 25 of the Matrimonial Causes Act 1973 but it is thought that in general the principles remain the same.

(1) The court should approach the problem by following the directions set out in s 25(2) of the Matrimonial Causes Act 1973, that is, by considering all the circumstances of the case and, in particular, the factors set out, before deciding on the order which will most nearly satisfy the objective set by Parliament, namely, 'to place the parties, so far as it is practicable and, having regard to their conduct, just to do so, in the financial position in which they would have been if the marriage had not broken down and each had properly discharged his or her financial obligations and responsibilities towards the other'. It is, therefore, wrong in principle to adopt a purely arithmetical approach by considering what proportion of the total assets should be allocated to the wife. The judgments of all three of the cases are agreed on that point and the change of objective has not changed this. The suggestion in *Wachtel v Wachtel* [1973] Fam 72 of one half or one third of the total assets is, therefore, no more than a guideline, though it may be a useful check on the tentative figure which emerges from working through the considerations set out in the section. See also *Harnett v Harnett*

[1974] Fam 156 (upheld on the facts by the Court of Appeal [1974] 1 WLR 219) where Bagnall J said (at 164) that, as the total value of the husband's assets increased, the proportion to which the wife was entitled was likely to be lower, and *Potter v Potter* [1982] 1 WLR 1255, where the Court of Appeal found the one-third guideline inappropriate for capital. Both were cases under the divorce jurisdiction. It seems, however, that the court in considering an application by a surviving spouse will, in order to arrive at a figure, approach s 3(1) of the Act in a manner broadly similar to that in which in the divorce jurisdiction the court approaches s 25(2) of the Matrimonial Causes Act 1973.

(2) The word 'needs' in s 25(2)(b) of the Matrimonial Causes Act 1973 in relation to the other provisions in the subsection is equivalent to 'reasonable requirements', having regard to the other factors and the objective set by the concluding words of the subsection (see *O'D v O'D*, followed by *S v S* and *Page v Page*).

(3) The powers of the court ought not to be exercised for the benefit of adult children, by enabling the wife to set up a child in business (*S v S*) or to provide by will for a child who is unlikely to benefit under the husband's will or otherwise (*Page v Page*).

(4) Active participation by the wife, either by working in her husband's business or by providing finance, will greatly enhance her contribution to the welfare of the family under para (f) of s 25 (2) of the Matrimonial Causes Act 1973, and may lead to a substantial increase in the lump sum over and above her 'reasonable requirements'. This, in effect, recognises that she has 'earned' a share in the total assets, and should be able to realise it and use it as she chooses (*S v S*).

(5) The acceptance by the wife of a frugal standard of living throughout the marriage, enabling the husband to plough back into his business a large proportion of the profits and so develop it into a considerable enterprise, is a factor which can properly be reflected in the lump sum awarded (*S v S* and *Page v Page*). The same effect is produced where the wife's earnings contribute to the husband's success, especially in the early stages where they may be an important element in it. Para (c) of s 25(2) of the Matrimonial Causes Act 1973 requires the court to have regard to the standard of living of the family during the marriage, but it would be

anomalous if this were taken as an indication for reducing the lump sum for a wife who has accepted a lower standard of living in the hope that she and the family will benefit later.

(6) Advanced age may be an important factor in that the wife's fullest requirements may be provided for by a smaller capital sum (*Page v Page*).

In *Preston v Preston* Ormrod LJ said (at 28) that on the true construction of s 25 of the Matrimonial Causes Act 1973 there came a point, in cases where the available resources were very large, when the amount required to fulfil its terms levelled off, and re-distribution of capital as such in some unspecified ratio began, which was outside the section. The problem, however, remained to determine where the levelling-off point lay. Obviously, it would shift as the value of money changed, and might be affected, as in *S v S*, by the role played by the wife in the build up of the available resources. These observations seem to be equally applicable to cases of very large estates arising under the Act. Moreover, where the estate is comparatively small, a very different approach may be necessary in determining the size of a lump sum. In *Re Besterman*, Judge Mervyn Davies adopted an 'annuity approach', which the Court of Appeal, on the facts of that case, rejected: but Oliver LJ said (at 479) that, in criticising that approach, he did so only in the context of the particular facts. There might well be circumstances where it was not only a right approach, but it was the only right approach. As appears from that case, the difficulty lies in applying the proposition of law to the facts of any particular case.

In any event when the principles of the cases under the Matrimonial Causes Act 1973 are applied by reference to s 3(2) of the Act to the case of a surviving spouse, there is one modification which must obviously be made: because the other party to the marriage is dead, the question of future earnings does not arise. The court can, of course, order periodical payments (s 2(1)(a)), but there is no particular point in doing this unless it is desirable to retain the capital for reversioners. If there is no need to do that it may be more beneficial to the surviving spouse to have no income payments but a larger slice of capital. Justice may be better done on the basis of approximate equality (see *Trippas v Trippas*, per Scarman LJ).

It should be noted that in *Re Clarke* [1991] Fam Law 364 (the facts of which are referred to on p 52) Scott Baker J said that essentially what was required in both divorce and inheritance was that the plaintiff should be housed, should have an income to live reasonably comfortably and should have something to fall back on to deal with future contingencies. If the estate is sufficiently large to enable such provision to be made, having regard to other matters to which the court is directed to have regard, that formulation (taken from *Re Besterman*) would appear to be as good a rule of thumb as any.

Re Bunning, Bunning v Salmon [1984] Ch 480, in which Vinelott J applied *Re Besterman* provides an illustration of the manner in which the court, while applying the principles of the cases under the Matrimonial Causes Act 1973, modifies those principles to take account of the fact that the other party to the marriage is dead. The plaintiff, then aged 34, married the testator, then aged 56, as his second wife in 1963. Soon afterwards, in order to help the testator in his business, the plaintiff gave up her job, thus losing considerable pension prospects. In 1978 she left the testator and she refused to return to him despite his repeated requests. Between 1968 and 1971 (when he retired) the testator gave the plaintiff £4,200, and in 1973 he transferred to her £40,019 worth of government securities. In the same year he also gave her £3,595. The testator died in 1982, making no provision for the plaintiff by his will. His net estate was £237,000. He gave thirteen pecuniary legacies totalling £26,000 to individuals, two legacies, one of £25,000 and the other of £1,000, to the Royal Society for the Protection of Birds, and £100,000 to the Department of Veterinary Medicine at Cambridge University for the purpose of establishing a fellowship. He gave his residuary estate as to 80 per cent to be added to the legacy given to Cambridge University and as to 20 per cent to be added to the legacies given to individuals. The plaintiff's assets were estimated at £98,000. She had a widow's pension of £32.85 a week, and other pensions of £632 per annum. She had investment income of £2,600. Her prospects of employment were good. There were no other dependants. To maintain her standard of living (which was far from extravagant) the plaintiff would need about £9,000 per annum.

Vinelott J calculated that on an application under the Matrimonial Causes Act 1973 prior to substitution (when the court would have had to take into account the testator's future needs without any foreknowledge of his imminent death) the plaintiff would have received £36,000. This figure took into account the fact that the plaintiff's assets had been largely derived from the testator. His Lordship held, however, that that should not be taken as limiting the amount which it would be reasonable for the plaintiff to receive out of the testator's estate, and he awarded her £60,000. That figure took into account, on the one hand the fact that the plaintiff was comparatively young and was entitled to a reasonable degree of financial security during what was likely to be a lengthy widowhood, and on the other hand the fact that the testator's assets had been built up, largely by his own efforts, before the marriage, so that the court should not interfere with his right to dispose of those assets, save to the extent necessary to make reasonable provision for the plaintiff. Vinelott J directed that the £60,000 be borne by the residue given to Cambridge University and, so far as that was not sufficient, rateably by the legacy given to the University and the legacy of £25,000 given to the Royal Society for the Protection of Birds. The costs were to be borne by residue before the division of the balance into 80 per cent and 20 per cent shares.

An element of confusion in respect of the question of what weight is to be given to the provision which the applicant might have expected to have obtained on divorce has recently been added by the decision of the Court of Appeal in *Moody v Stevenson* [1992] Ch 486, a case in which *Re Besterman* does not appear to have been cited to the court. The applicant was the widower of the deceased and they had been married in 1971 when they were both over 60 and the applicant had gone to live with the deceased in the deceased's home. In 1984 the deceased became ill and went to live in a nursing home after which there was no contact between the applicant and the deceased although the applicant continued to live in the deceased's property. The deceased died in 1988 leaving her estate to her stepdaughter by a previous marriage who was herself in financial need. The stepdaughter took proceedings for possession of the house and the applicant commenced proceedings under the Act. His application was refused and he appealed. The Court of Appeal allowed the appeal directing a settlement of the property giving the applicant the right to live in the house for so long as he wished and was able to do so. Waite J, giving the judgment of the court, stated (at 498) that the objective of 3(2)(b) was that the acceptable minimum posthumous provision for a surviving spouse should correspond as closely as possible to the inchoate rights enjoyed by that spouse in the deceased's lifetime by virtue of his or her prospective entitlement under the matrimonial law. With this statement it appears there can be little argument. However, having held that the minimum was not reached in this case the succeeding parts of the judgment (at 502–504), concerned with what provision ought to be made, may be read as implying that in most cases such provision will not only be the minimum but also the maximum provision which should be made so that if the minimum is achieved no further provision need be made. Certainly the court took such steps as it could to try to bring about a situation which was as close as possible to the situation which would have prevailed had the marriage ended on divorce rather than death (see 503C and G). In the most usual case where the spouses were living together at the date of the death, the application of this approach could give rise to the highly anomalous and surely unintended situation that because on the hypothetical divorce there would have been insufficient assets to have provided a home for both parties the applicant should not be permitted to continue to live in the matrimonial home. However, as was recognised by Vinelott J in *Re Bunning,* (at 498) on an application under the Act the court is not restricted to the amount which the applicant would have obtained on divorce (unless that it is reasonable in all the circumstances of the particular case) as the court no longer needs to provide for the deceased and in *Re Besterman,* (at 469) Oliver LJ emphasised that the figure resulting from what he called the s 25 exercise was only one of the factors to which the court had to have regard. The possibility that *Moody v Stevenson* cannot stand with *Re Besterman,* was raised before the Court of Appeal in *Jessop v Jessop* [1992] 1 FLR 591 but the court considered it unnecessary to decide the point. It is probable however that *Moody v Stevenson* will be held to have been decided on its own special facts or to be authority only for the proposition that except in exceptional circumstances the provision that would have been made on divorce is the minimum that should be made for a surviving spouse.

In two recent cases applications by surviving spouses have been dismissed on the grounds that reasonable financial provision had been made for the applicants. In *Re Clarke* [1991] Fam Law 364 the deceased and the applicant had married in 1976 when they were both aged over 70. They kept their finances separate and there was evidence that the widow had some £60,000 capital of her own. The deceased left the applicant a life interest in the matrimonial home and a life interest in £25,000 and left the remainder of his estate of £179,501 to his children and grandchildren from his first marriage. Scott Baker J held that he was completely satisfied that the deceased had made reasonable financial provision for the applicant. In *Davis v Davis* [1993] 1 FLR 54 the Court of Appeal dismissed the appeal of the applicant widow from an order of Thorpe J dismissing her application under the Act. Again this was the deceased's second marriage and the deceased and the applicant had only been married for seven years before the deceased's death. In the week before his death the deceased had given his wife a capital sum of £15,000 and he left her virtually all his chattels and a life interest in the residue of his estate with remainder to his son by his first marriage. The estate itself was made up of a property purchased by the trustees as a residence for the widow, an interest in a farm which was expected to be sold within a relatively short period, an interest in the estate of an uncle of the deceased and a reversionary interest in the deceased's father's estate: hence there was little actual capital available at the date of the hearing. It was argued that the will failed to make reasonable financial provision for the widow because it failed to give her a capital sum which it was said she would have obtained on divorce. Thorpe J stated that if it could be said that in the circumstances of that case a life interest in the entire residue was not reasonable provision then it could be asserted in almost any case in which the testator elected to make provision for his spouse by that means. The Court of Appeal considered that Thorpe J did not fail to take into account any relevant circumstances and did not err in law and therefore the appeal failed.

It is clear that a second (or later) wife or husband whom the deceased married late in life is likely to be awarded less than a spouse married for many years, the court being specifically required by s 3(2)(a) to have regard to the duration of the marriage. A similar view is taken in New Zealand (see *Re Cunningham, Cunningham v Cunningham* [1936] NZLR Supp 69 and *Re Worms, Worms v Campbell* [1953] NZLR 924).

In the nature of things applications by widows are more common than applications by widowers: quite apart from the fact that the expectation of life of a woman is greater than that of a man, a widower is, even in these days of sex equality, less likely than a widow to need provision from the estate of a deceased spouse. Although in the early years of the Act of 1938 applications by widowers were discouraged, it is now quite clear that a surviving husband has as good a right as a surviving wife to make an application under the Act.

Guidance on the weight to be given to cohabitation before marriage of the deceased and the applicant may be found in *Foley v Foley* [1981] Fam 160, a case under s 25(1) of the Matrimonial Causes Act 1973 in which Eveleigh LJ (with whom Watkins LJ and Sir David Cairnes agreed) said (at 67) that in the great majority of cases public opinion would readily recognise a stronger claim founded upon years of marriage than upon years of cohabitation, but added that, on the other hand, there might be cases where the inability of the parties to sanctify and legitimise their relationship called for a measure of sympathy which would enable the court to take what had happened during the period of cohabitation into account as a very weighty factor. His Lordship referred to *Kokosinski v Kokosinski* [1980] Fam 72 as being one such case, while *Campbell v Campbell* [1976] Fam 347 was certainly not. It is thought that this dictum is applicable to cases under the Act.

7 Spouses living apart without a decree of judicial separation

Obviously the fact that the deceased and the applicant were separated at the date of death is a matter which the court may take into account under 3(1)(g) in assessing whether in all the circumstances of the case reasonable financial provision has been made for the applicant and, if not, what level of provision ought to be made in that particular case. However, the fact of the separation itself does not affect the principles to be applied. Thus in *Re Bunning, Bunning v Salmon* [1984] Ch 480 the deceased and the applicant had been separated for some four years prior to the deceased's death.

8 Judicially separated or former spouse

The court must, in considering an application by a wife or husband of the deceased who was judicially separated at the date of the deceased's death, or by a former wife or husband, have regard not only to the matters specified in subs (1) of s 3 of the Act but also to (a) the age of the applicant and the duration of the marriage and (b) the contribution made by the applicant to the welfare of the family of the deceased, including any contribution made by looking after the home or caring for the family (s 3(2)). However, the status of such an applicant in making a claim is no higher than that of any other applicant under s 1 (save for an applicant under s 1(1)(a)) that is to say, the applicant is entitled only to such financial provision as it would be reasonable in all the circumstances of the case for her or him to receive for her or his maintenance (s 1(2)(b)). The Act thus gives effect to the recommendations of the Law Commission which pointed out (Law Com No 61, para 60) that in the case of a former or judicially separated spouse the financial position of the parties will normally have been considered at the time of the decree and any adjustments then appearing to be necessary will, as a general rule, have been made. This position is modified by s 14 of the Act if the deceased dies within the period of 12 months following the date on which the decree absolute or decree of judicial separation was granted and either no application for ancillary relief under ss 23, 24 or 24A of the Matrimonial Causes Act 1973 has been made, or such an application has been made but had not been determined at the date of death. In such cases the court has a discretion, if it thinks just to do so, to treat the applicant as if he or she was an applicant within s 1(1)(a) of the Act.

It seems likely that an application by a judicially separated or former spouse will now seldom be justified, and before an application is launched careful consideration should be given to the decision of the Court of Appeal in *Re Fullard, Fullard v King* [1982] Fam 42, the first case of an application by a former spouse to reach that court (which dismissed the plaintiff's appeal from the dismissal of her claim by Bush J). Having referred to s 3 of the Matrimonial Causes (Property and Maintenance) Act 1958, whereby a former wife was first enabled to apply for provision out of her deceased husband's estate (and doubtless bearing in mind that s 5 of that Act afforded a similar right to a former husband), Ormrod LJ, said (at 45–46):

> It is very important to remember that, at the time that section first came into existence, the court had no power to deal with capital adjustments between spouses. At that period the court's powers were greatly restricted in relation to ancillary relief because they could not deal adequately with the situation when (usually) a husband came into a substantial capital sum, either because he earned it or inherited it or for some other reason, after the ancillary relief order had been made. So there were many cases in and around that time where ex-wives were in receipt of periodical payments which ceased on the death of their former husbands and were placed in a position of extreme difficulty. There is no doubt that that section was passed originally to give the court power to deal with that sort of situation when it arose. With the coming into effect of the Matrimonial Proceedings and Property Act 1970 with the new powers to make property adjustment orders and very much freer power to order lump sums, the court now has power to make appropriate capital adjustments as between spouses after divorce and those powers, although they are not necessarily comprehensive—and that is plain from s 15 of the Act of 1975 which clearly contemplates that proceedings may be taken under [the Act] after divorce—nonetheless the number of cases in which it would be possible for an applicant to bring himself (or herself) within the

> terms of s 2 of the Act in my judgment, would be comparatively small. Where the estate—like this one—is small, in my view the onus on an applicant of satisfying the conditions of s 2 is very heavy indeed and these applications ought not to be launched unless there is (or there appears to be) a real chance of success, because the result of these proceedings simply diminishes the estate and is a great hardship on the beneficiaries if they are ultimately successful in litigation. For that reason I would be disposed to think that judges should reconsider the practice of ordering the costs of both sides in these cases to be paid out of the estate. That is probate practice; this is something quite different. I think judges should look very closely indeed at the merits of each application before ordering that the estate pays the applicant's costs if the applicant is unsuccessful.

His Lordship said (at 46–47) with reference to s 3(1)(g) of the Act, which requires the court to have regard to any other matter, including the conduct of the applicant or any other person, which in the circumstances of the case the court may consider relevant, that the fact that the parties had been divorced and the result of that divorce in financial terms was highly relevant.

Ormrod LJ referred (at 49) to two cases where an application by a former spouse might succeed; that in which a periodical payments order had been going on for a long time and the deceased was found to have a reasonable amount of capital in his estate; and that in which a substantial capital fund such as insurance or pension policies, was unlocked by the death of the deceased.

That the existence of policy moneys will not necessarily justify an application is exemplified by *Brill v Proud* (1984) 14 Fam Law 59, in which the plaintiff was the former wife of the deceased. Their marriage had been dissolved in 1978, when a consent order was made in full and final settlement of the claims of the parties for financial provision. The deceased agreed to transfer the matrimonial home (worth £12,750) and its contents to the plaintiff for the sum of £1,000. The deceased had a wage of £50 a week. The plaintiff was a dancing instructress and her weekly earnings, together with her old age pension, exceeded those of the deceased. He died in 1980, leaving his entire estate, worth some £12,000, to the defendant, who had been kind to him after the divorce. The main asset of the estate was the proceedings of an insurance policy, £10,000, which was maintained by the deceased's employers and the payment of which was subject to several contingencies. The deceased did not disclose to the plaintiff the existence of the policy, and she claimed that she was no longer bound by the agreement made on the divorce and should have the entire sum. Following the divorce settlement, she had assets of over £16,000 after selling the matrimonial home and buying another property for £19,000, which she had later sold for £27,000, leaving her with net proceeds of £23,000. She had spent £4,000 on a cruise, bought a flat for £13,000, and bought a car for £2,795. Most of the remainder of her money she had spent on living expenses, and she had only some £400 left, but she had the flat and the car and her pension. The defendant had a house worth £25,000, capital of £6,000 and a pension of £3,600 per annum. The judge of the Brighton County Court dismissed the plaintiff's claim, finding that the deceased had no legal or moral obligation to make provision for the plaintiff by his will and that the divorce and the financial settlement had concluded the question of making provision for her. The Court of Appeal dismissed her appeal and was critical of the fact that the small estate had been much depleted by costs (see p 32).

In *Re Crawford* [1983] 4 FLR 273, however, a claim by a former wife succeeded. The plaintiff had been divorced from the deceased, after 24 years of marriage, in 1968, so there had been no adjustment of property (the court having no power at that time to make such an order), and at his death the deceased was paying her £4,371 per annum. On the deceased's premature retirement he received a lump sum of £69,767, which was paid into joint accounts in the name of the deceased and his second wife. The second wife and the children of the second marriage were in receipt of substantial index-linked pensions from the deceased's employer and the second wife also received from the pension trustees £72,402. The net value of the deceased's estate was £30,892. The deceased made no provision by his will for the plaintiff. She was in receipt of supplementary benefit. She owned the house in which she lived and had £1,500.

Four issues arose:

(a) whether the court should take into account financial benefits to the beneficiaries which did not form part of the deceased's estate;

(b) what principles applied to the court's discretion under s 9 in relation to property held on a joint tenancy;

(c) if the deceased's share of such property was ordered to be treated as part of his estate, whether it should be treated differently; and

(d) if the needs of the plaintiff remained the same, whether it was reasonable for her to receive the same provision after the deceased's death as was agreed or ordered during his lifetime.

Eastham J, held as to (a) in the affirmative, having regard to s 3(1)(c) of the Act; as to (b) that no specific principles applied to the exercise of the court's discretion, since the appropriate guidance was clearly stated in s 9 (see pp 81–83); as to (c) in the negative, that is, that joint property should not be treated differently; and as to (d) that, having regard to ss 1(2) and 3(1), (2), it could not be assumed that 'reasonable financial provision' was the same as periodical payments (during life) ordered under the Matrimonial Causes Act 1973, because under s 25(1) of that Act the court was required, so far as practicable, to put the parties in the same position as if the marriage had not broken down, whereas under s 1(2)(b) of the Act the court had to provide only such sum as was reasonable for the former wife's maintenance. It has already been pointed out that this is no longer the case (see p 44 and *Re Farrow* [1987] 1 FLR 205). In connection with the fourth issue, Eastham J considered (at 281–282) the judgment of Lane J in *Re Eyre* [1968] 1 WLR 530, a decision under the Matrimonial Causes Act 1965, where her Ladyship said (at 541):

> As to the former wife receiving as much after as before the death of the husband: assuming that her needs and her means apart from the estate remain as they were before the husband's death, and assuming further that the net estate is sufficient for the purpose, then, to my mind, it is reasonable that she should continue to receive the same provision as that agreed or found to be appropriate during the husband's lifetime. The sufficiency of the estate for this purpose is to be determined having regard to what is provided for, or needed by, other claimants on the deceased's bounty.

Eastham J said that he could not regard that passage as establishing a general proposition that on the assumed facts reasonable financial provision under the Act was the same as periodical payments during life if those payments were either agreed or fixed by the court. On the facts of the case before him, however, and having considered the matters set out in s 3(1), (2) (see pp 25–26), Eastham J ordered that the deceased's half share of the lump sum of £69,767 be treated as part of the net estate, and that a lump sum of £35,000 be paid to the plaintiff.

Re Fullard was not cited in *Re Crawford*, a fact pointed out by Hollings J in *Re Farrow*, a case where the applicant was also successful. In that case the applicant and the deceased had separated in 1968 after 19 years of marriage and the decree nisi was made in 1973. On 14 June 1978 Eastham J made an order in the ancillary relief proceedings consequent on the divorce giving the applicant a lump sum of £50,000 and periodic payments of £5,500 per annum. The deceased died on 5 May 1979 and the periodic payments came to an end on his death. In giving judgment on the applicant's application under the Act, Hollings J considered the judgment of Eastham J which had been given after a full hearing, but made it clear that he had to consider the facts as at the date of the hearing before him and whether on those facts the intestacy of the deceased failed to make reasonable financial provision for the applicant. One of the problems was that the bulk of the estate was represented by a farm which had passed on his intestacy to the deceased's two sons and from which they made their livelihood. However, having considered *Re Fullard* and *Re Crawford*, Hollings J awarded a lump sum of £15,000 to take into account the fact that the applicant was without periodic payments for some seven years and ordered periodic payments of £5,000 per annum from the date of the order.

Having regard to the approach to applications by former spouses which must now be made in the light of the decision of the Court of Appeal in *Re Fullard*, it is thought that earlier decisions on such applications will now seldom provide much guidance.

Sections 15, 16, 17 and 18 of the Act also give effect to recommendations of the Law Commission relating to cases of divorce, nullity and judicial separation.

Section 15 (as amended) gives the court power to restrict the rights of a former spouse to apply for provision under the Act on the death of the other spouse on an application during the lifetime of both spouses. Section 15 (1) provides that on granting a decree of divorce, a decree of nullity of marriage or a decree of judicial separation or at any time thereafter, the court may, if the court considers it just to do so order that either party to the marriage shall not be entitled on the death of the other party to apply for an order under s 2. Prior to 12 October 1984 both parties had to agree before the order could be made but such an order can now be made in the face of opposition (s 15(1) as substituted by s 18 of the Matrimonial and Family Proceedings Act 1984). Section 15A of the Act, which was inserted by s 25(3) of the Act of 1984 and came into force on 16 September 1985 (*ibid* s 47(1)(b) and the Matrimonial and Family Proceedings Act 1984 (Commencement No 2) Order 1985 (SI 1985 No 1316)) confers on the court the power to make a similar order on making an order under s 17 of that Act for financial provision and property adjustment following the termination of a marriage in an overseas country (see p 9).

By empowering the court to bar an application for provision under s 2, the Act inferentially excludes the possibility of contracting out while the marriage is continuing and there has been no decree of judicial separation, or by consent, but without the court's express approval, at the time of or subsequent to a decree. As to the impossibility of ousting the jurisdiction of the court, see *Re M, deceased* [1968] P 174; also *Hyman v Hyman* [1929] AC 601.

An application under s 15(1) was considered by the Court of Appeal in *Whiting v Whiting* [1988] 1 WLR 565. The court dismissed the husband's appeal against the dismissal of his application for an order under the section preventing his former wife making an application under the Act. Balcombe LJ, with whom Stocker and Slade LJJ agreed, stated that before the court could consider it just to make an order depriving a divorced spouse of any opportunity to claim financial provision from the estate of the other spouse it should be given some indication of what that estate is likely to consist of and some details of the persons whom the applicant considers to have a prior claim on his estate in the event of his decease. As such evidence was not before the court the appeal was dismissed.

Sections 16, 17 and 18 of the Act implement the recommendations contained in Part VII of the Law Commission's Report (Law Com No 61). Section 28(1)(b) of the Matrimonial Causes Act 1973 empowers the court when it grants a decree of divorce, nullity or judicial separation to make in favour of one of the spouses or in favour of a child of the family an order for secured periodical payments which will remain in force after the death of the person against whom it is made. In that event, where the person able to make payments under the order dies, s 31 of that Act empowers the court to vary or discharge the order. The existence of any such order in favour of a surviving spouse or former spouse or child and the question whether it should remain in force with or without variation will be relevant matters on an application for family provision, so that it is desirable that the court, in considering such an application, should have power to review any orders for maintenance made in matrimonial proceedings and continuing in force after the death of the person liable to make the payments. Section 16(1) of the Act accordingly provides that where an application for an order under s 2 is made to the court by any person who was at the time of the death of the deceased entitled to payments from the deceased under a secured periodical payments order made under the Matrimonial Causes Act 1973, s 23(1)(b), then, in the proceedings on that application, the court shall have power, if an application is made under s 16 by that person or by the personal representative of the deceased, to vary or discharge that periodical payments order or to revive the operation of any provision thereof which has been suspended under s 31 of the Matrimonial Causes Act 1973. Section 16(2) provides that in exercising the powers conferred by the section the court shall have regard to all the circumstances of the case, including any order which it proposes to make under s 2 or under s 5 (which relates to interim payments) and any change (whether resulting from the death of the deceased or otherwise) in any of the matters to which the court was required to have regard when making the secured periodical payments order. Section 16(3) provides that the powers exercisable by the court under the section in relation to an order shall be exercisable also in relation to any instrument executed in pursuance of the order. Section 31 of the Matrimonial Causes Act 1973 remains in force and will still have to be relied upon by the personal representatives of a deceased person who wish to take the initiative to have a secured periodical payments order varied or discharged where there is no application under the Act. Moreover, the powers of s 31 may also be useful in cases where a simple variation of an order against a deceased person is required, or where the applicant under s 31 is a person barred from applying for an order for family provision under the Act.

Section 36 of the Matrimonial Causes Act 1973 (amended by s 26(1) of the Act) empowers the court, on the death of one of the parties to a marriage, to entertain applications for the alteration of a maintenance agreement which they have made during their joint lives and which is expressed to continue in force after the death of one of them. For this purpose a maintenance agreement means an agreement in writing between the parties to a marriage containing financial arrangements (Matrimonial Causes Act 1973, s 34(2)).

The Law Commission recognised that the existence of a maintenance agreement expressed to continue after the death of one of the parties will, whether or not the agreement is or is not alterable under s 36, be a relevant factor in determining what order should be made under the Act for family provision in favour of the surviving spouse.

Section 17 implements the Law Commission's recommendations (Law Com No 61, para 264–265) that a wider power to vary maintenance agreements, whether falling within s 36 of the Matrimonial Causes Act 1973 or not, should be available to a court considering an application for provision under s 2 of the Act. Subsection (1) provides that where an application for an order under s 2 is made to the court by any person who was at the time of the death of the deceased entitled to payments from the deceased under a maintenance agreement which provided for the continuation of payments under the agreement after the death of the deceased, then, in the proceedings on that application, the court shall have power, if an application is made under s 17 by that person or by the personal representative of the deceased, to vary or revoke that agreement. Subsection (4) provides that in the section 'maintenance agreement', in relation to a deceased person, means any agreement made, whether in writing or not and whether before or after the commencement of the Act, by the deceased with any person with whom he entered into a marriage, being an agreement which contained provisions governing the rights and liabilities towards one another when living separately of the parties to that marriage (whether or not the marriage has been dissolved or annulled) in respect of the making or securing of payments or the disposition or use of any property, including such rights and liabilities in respect of the maintenance or education of any child, whether or not a child of the deceased or a person who was treated by the deceased as a child of the family in relation to that marriage. Subsection (2) provides that in exercising the powers conferred by the section the court shall have regard to all the circumstances of the case, including any order which the court proposes to make under s 2 or s 5 (interim orders) of the Act and any change (whether resulting from the death of the deceased or otherwise) in any of the circumstances in the light of which the agreement was made. Subsection (3), which corresponds to subs (4) of s 36 of the Matrimonial Causes Act 1973, provides that if a maintenance agreement is varied by the court under s 17 the like consequences shall ensue as if the variation had been made immediately before the death of the deceased by agreement between the parties and for valuable consideration.

Where an application has been made under s 31 of the Matrimonial Causes Act 1973 for the variation of an order made under that Act or is made under s 36 of that Act for the variation of a maintenance agreement, the applicant may find that the court's power to make the variation desired has been defeated by a disposition made by the deceased, although this disposition might have been successfully challenged had the application been one for family provision made under the Act (see Chapter 7). Accordingly s 18(1) of the Act provides that where (a) a person against whom a secured periodical payments order was made under the Matrimonial Causes Act 1973 has died and an application is made under s 31(6) of that Act for the variation or discharge of that order or for the revival of the operation of any provision thereof which has been suspended, or (b) a party to a maintenance agreement within the meaning of s 34 of that Act has died, the agreement being one which provides for the continuation of payments thereunder after the death of one of the parties, and an application is made under s 36(1) of that Act for the alteration of the agreement under s 35 thereof, the court shall have power to direct that the application made under s 31(6) or s 36(1) as the case may be shall be deemed to have been accompanied by an application for an order under s 2 of the Act. Section 18(2) provides that where the court gives a direction under subs (1) it shall have power, in the proceedings on the application under s 31(6) or as the case may be s 36(1) of the Matrimonial Causes Act, to make any order which the court would have power to make under the provisions of the Act if the application under s 31(6) or as the case may be s 36(1) had been made jointly with an application for an order under s 2 of the Act. The court is empowered to give such consequential directions as may be necessary for enabling the court to exercise any of the powers available to it under the Act in the case of an application for an order under s 2.

However, s 18(3) provides that where an order made under s 15(1) of the Act is in force with respect to a party to a marriage the court shall not give a direction under s 18(1) with respect to any application made under s 31(6) or as the case may be s 36(1) of the Matrimonial Causes Act by that party on the death of the other party.

9 Applications by children and persons treated as children of the family

In the case of an application by a child of the deceased (s 1(1)(c) of the Act) or any person (not being such a child) who, in the case of any marriage to which the deceased was at any time a party was treated by the deceased as a child of the family in relation to that marriage (s 1(1)(d)) the court must have regard in addition to the matters set out in s 3(1) to those in s 3(3). These include the manner in which the applicant was being or in which he might expect to be educated or trained. Moreover,where the application is made by virtue of s 1(1)(d) the court must also have regard (a) to whether the deceased had assumed any responsibility for the applicant's maintenance and, if so, to the extent to which and the basis upon which the deceased assumed that responsibility and to the length of time for which the deceased assumed that responsibility; (b) to whether in assuming and discharging that responsibility the deceased did so knowing that the applicant was not his own child; and (c) to the liability of any other person to maintain the applicant. The wording of s 3(3) reflects to some extent that of s 25(3) of the Matrimonial Causes Act 1973, which contains guidance to the court in the exercise of its powers to make financial provision for a child of the family in the case of divorce. While it is essential to take into account the liability of any other person to maintain the applicant child (see *Roberts v Roberts* [1962] P 212), the fact that that person can be found does not, if his capacity to maintain the child is limited, extinguish the liability of a person who has once assumed responsibility for the child's maintenance by treating him as a child of the family (see *Snow v Snow* [1972] Fam 74).

It seems that the position of a child who applies under s 1(1)(d) will often be closely equated to that of a child applying under s 1(1)(c), since the deceased may have made little if any distinction in his attitude towards his own children and those treated by him as children of his marriage. On the other hand, it was pointed out by Slade LJ in *Re Leach, Leach v Lindeman* [1986] Ch 226 (at 231) that s 3(3) shows that where an application is made by virtue of s 1(1)(d), the legislature did not regard the applicant as being necessarily disqualified from applying, merely because the deceased had never assumed any responsibility for his or her maintenance, though it contemplated that this would be an obligatory factor for the court to take into account when deciding what, if anything, to award in the exercise of its discretion.

The position of an illegitimate child will not, it seems, be any less favourable than that of one who is legitimate. In *CA v CC* (1978) *The Times*, 18 November (reported *sub nom In the Estate of McC* (1979) 9 Fam Law 26) the deceased's illegitimate minor son was awarded half the residuary estate, sharing it with the deceased's legitimate son, to whom it had been left. (The deceased's mistress also made a successful claim: see p 76).

A parent has a legal as well as a moral obligation to maintain a minor child. The overriding importance of the welfare of children is recognised in s 25 of the Matrimonial Causes Act 1973, sub s (1) of which states that it shall be the duty of the court in deciding whether to exercise its powers to make financial provision or property adjustment orders on divorce or judicial separation and, if so, in what manner, to have regard to all the circumstances of the case, first consideration being given to the welfare while a minor of any child of the family who has not attained the age of 18. Providing the estate is sufficient to enable provision to be made, an application under the Act on behalf of a minor child is likely to be viewed favourably as would an application on behalf of a young adult for whom it might be said that the deceased still had a moral obligation to provide at the date of his or her death. Thus in *Re Collins* [1990] Fam 56 Hollings J made an award of £5,000 to the daughter of the deceased who was aged 19 and unemployed at the date of the hearing. However, the position of an adult child, particularly if the child is independent and capable of earning his or her own living is much more difficult. In those circumstances the approach of the court is similar to that under the Act of 1938 and it is clear from the cases that although it is possible for an adult to make a successful application such a child must show not only that he or she reasonably requires further provision for his or her maintenance but also that there is some special circumstance other than merely the fact of the blood relationship which makes it reasonable that he or she should be maintained out of the estate of the deceased.

The leading case is *Re Coventry, Coventry v Coventry* [1980] Ch 461. This was an application by a son of the deceased, who was living with the deceased at the date of death. The estate, which was not large, passed to the widow who had been separated from the deceased for some 18 years and was in poor financial circumstances. Oliver J said (at 465) that applications for maintenance by able bodied and comparatively young men in employment and able to maintain themselves must be relatively rare and needed to be approached with a degree of circumspection. Although later (at 474) his Lordship made it clear that an application by a male plaintiff of full age ought not to be approached with any preconceived notion that there is some especially heavy burden on him beyond that which must, as a practical matter, necessarily exist when a person who applies to be maintained by somebody else is already capable of adequately maintaining himself and he made it equally clear (at 475) that it was not enough for the applicant to rely on his blood relationship with the deceased, there had to be something more which made it unreasonable that no further provision was made for him. Of s 3(3) Oliver J in *Re Coventry* said (at 476) that it pointed to the sort of circumstances in which it would be appropriate for an adult capable of earning his own living to seek provision under the Act—a case, eg, in which the deceased died whilst his adult son was being supported in the process of acquiring some occupational qualification and in which no provision was made by the deceased for its completion. It appears that if a son gives up work and disables himself from earning an adequate living in order to devote himself to his father, a moral duty to provide for the son's maintenance may be placed on the father (see per Oliver J at 477, per Goff LJ at 489–490 and per Buckley LJ at 495). See also as to applications by adult sons *Re Christie, Christie v Keeble* [1979] Ch 168 and *Re Dennis, Dennis v Lloyds Bank Ltd* [1981] 2 All ER 140.

There are some decisions under the Act of 1938 (all of them applications by daughters) which may remain of relevance, and it is appropriate to preview them first before turning to the decisions under the Act. However, as with all decisions under the Act of 1938 they should be treated with caution.

The applicant in *Mastaka v Midland Bank Executor and Trustee Co Ltd* [1941] Ch 192 was the daughter of the testatrix. This daughter was born in 1920 and had lived since infancy at the charge and in the care of a person other than her mother; she had accepted a relationship of friendship and no more with her mother, and had never attempted to obtain financial assistance from her. Her mother made no provision for her in her will, and Farwell J refused to make an order in her favour, holding that, as the daughter had acquiesced in a state of affairs in which the ordinary relationship of mother and daughter did not exist, it was not a proper case for the court to make an order. This application also failed on another ground, namely, the applicant's failure to prove that the testatrix died domiciled in England (see p 4).

Re Andrews, Andrews v Smorfitt [1955] 1 WLR 1105 was another case where a daughter was an unsuccessful applicant. She had lived at the testator's house till 1911, when she had left to set up a permanent home with *P*, a married man. After she left home the plaintiff and the testator were estranged, but subsequently they were reconciled and on occasions she stayed with him and looked after him when he was ill. The testator had made no provision for her. She never married and at the time of the application was 69 years of age and receiving constant medical attention; neither she nor *P* had any means of support other than national assistance. Holding that the court had no right to interfere with the testator's dispositions, Wynn Parry J said that a most important, if not the most important consideration was the extent to which, if at all, the testator was under a moral obligation to the plaintiff. No doubt when she had left the parental home she had relied on *P* providing her with the companionship and protection, financial or otherwise, which she would have had a right to expect from him if they could have been and had been joined in wedlock. It followed that thenceforward the testator had no moral obligation to the plaintiff with regard to her maintenance and no moral obligation to provide for her by his will.

In *Re Sivyer, Sivyer v Sivyer* [1967] 1 WLR 1482, an application by the infant daughter of an intestate by his second marriage, the defendant being the intestate's third wife, who succeeded to the whole of the estate on his intestacy, Pennycuick J took into account the fact that the principal asset of the deceased's estate was derived from the applicant's mother and awarded her a larger lump sum than he would have given her had this not been the case. See also pp 31–34.

It seems that if an unfriendly relationship has existed between the deceased and any of his children, due to the fault of the latter, the court will probably refuse to upset the will on an application by the child concerned. Furthermore, if a dependant has been wildly extravagant, and the deceased, by his will, disposes of his property in favour of grandchildren, the court may well have cause to refuse an application by the dependant. In *Re Ducksbury, Ducksbury v Ducksbury* [1966] 1 WLR 1226 (see p 29) on the other hand, Buckley J held that the testator had not been justified in allowing his bitterness against his first wife to come between him and the applicant, who was the elder of his two daughters by his first marriage.

In *Re Andrews* the plaintiff was clearly in need: yet her claim was unsuccessful. It follows that an application by a daughter who is capable of maintaining herself or who is being maintained by a husband does not seem to be any more likely to succeed than one by a son who is self-supporting. That will ordinarily be the case even when the estate is very large and the daughter is living in very modest circumstances, and even where she has been a dutiful daughter who has cared for her deceased parent. No matter how great the difference between her means and those of the deceased may be, she will not succeed unless she is able to prove that she is positively in need, or at least that she has suffered some financial detriment, for example, from the fact that she has abandoned a means of livelihood to care for her parent, or has by reason of the parent's death lost some benefit such as support in education or training. A child who is the victim of a parent's capriciousness, or for whom a parent has perhaps just accidentally failed to provide, may justifiably feel a sense of grievance; but the purpose of the Act is not to remedy hard cases, but to provide for maintenance in cases of need where maintenance can be, and reasonably should be, but has not been made, out of the deceased's estate. A case under the Act which illustrates the point is *Rann v Jackson* (6 November 1978), reported only in Appendix A to *Tyler's Family Provision Practice* at p 386). A married daughter applied against the estate of her father, the defendant being her unmarried sister, to whom the testator had left his estate worth about £23,000 other than £2,000 which he gave to the plaintiff and one or two other small legacies. The defendant had an income of about £3,000 per annum and capital of about £17,000. His Honour Judge Toyn (sitting as a Judge of the Family Division), dismissed the application, finding that it was not unreasonable on the testator's part to make no further provision than he had for a daughter who was married and had a husband who was working and running his own business. The Court of Appeal dismissed the plaintiff's appeal.

This importance of being able to show need as well as some special circumstance giving rise to a moral obligation on the deceased can also be seen in *Riggs v Lloyds Bank Plc* (CAT (Civil No 1151 of 1992)). The applicant was the daughter of the deceased who died in 1989 leaving his whole estate to his son under a will dated 1974. His Honour Judge Wicks QC found that the applicant and her husband lived within their means, their home was subject to a small mortgage and the husband had a secure job but that the applicant had helped the deceased throughout her adult life both personally and in his business and therefore awarded her £20,000 out of the estate valued £120,000 to be paid in two instalments. The Judge made the award specifically to assist the applicant at a time when her children were minors and therefore her needs would be greatest. The Court of Appeal overturned this decision on the grounds that there was no general need for maintenance and the basis on which the judge had made the award was not one which had been explored before him (see p 21).

In *Re Debenham* [1986] 1 FLR 404 an application by a daughter succeeded. The plaintiff was the daughter of the testatrix, was 58 years of age, and was an epileptic. She was married. Her husband was 63. They owned a small bungalow, but very little other capital. Both had been in employment, but had been made redundant. The plaintiff had a pension of about £500 per annum, but her husband had no pension. They were in receipt of supplementary benefit of £52 a week, and in two years' time they would receive the old age pension (then £57 a week). The estate of the testatrix amounted to £172,000. She left a number of small legacies, including £200 to the plaintiff, and the residue equally among six charities. The applicant was unwanted by her mother and had been sent as a baby to be brought up by grandparents in South Africa. Throughout her life her mother remained aloof and distant from the plaintiff and was very cruel to her.

Having referred to *Re Coventry, Coventry v Coventry* [1980] Ch 461 (see p 65), Ewbank J said (at 408) that, in effect, maintenance meant what was sufficient to enable the applicant to live decently and comfortably according to the station of life to which she had been called. It did not merely mean enough to bring her to subsistence. On the other hand, it did not mean sufficient to give her a life of luxury. The reference to 'station in life' requires some comment. In the case of a married woman it seems to mean the station in life of her husband rather than of her parents; thus a married woman whose husband's income is such that they are able to live decently and comfortably but not luxuriously is not entitled to maintenance from the estate of a father who is a millionaire and whose standard of living is very different from her own. It is also important to note that Ewbank J said (*ibid*) that he had to remember that he was dealing with the applicant and not with her husband, who was not an applicant under the Act, and must beware of making provision which would be directed to his benefit rather than to hers. This approach is to be compared with the approach adopted by the Court of Appeal in *Re Besterman, Besterman v Gresin* [1984] Ch 458 when awarding a lump sum to a surviving spouse (see p 41).

Re Callaghan [1985] Fam 1 and *Re Leach, Leach v Lindeman* [1986] Ch 226, in which the Court of Appeal approved *Re Callaghan*, were both cases under s 1(1)(d), the former being an application by a stepson and the latter being an application by a stepdaughter. The claim of the plaintiff in *Re Callaghan* was against the estate of his stepfather, who came in 1950 as a lodger to the plaintiff's widowed mother, and lived in a house provided by her late husband's father. Shortly afterwards, the deceased began to live with her and to treat the plaintiff as his son. Eventually, in 1972, the plaintiff's mother and the deceased married, and the plaintiff's mother conveyed her house into the joint names of the deceased and herself. The plaintiff's mother died intestate on 8 May 1980. The deceased was by this time ill and he was a difficult patient. He died intestate on 30 August 1980 having, during his last illness, been cared for by the plaintiff and his wife. The latter gave up her job in order to look after the deceased, and the plaintiff for the same reason took his holiday and compassionate leave. The value of the deceased's estate was £31,000 and the persons entitled on his intestacy were his three married sisters, all persons of moderate means. At the date of the hearing, the plaintiff had an income of approximately £7,850 per annum gross and his wife was in part-time employment earning approximately £3,900 per annum gross. They had no capital and a bank loan of £700. They wanted to buy their council house, the purchase price of which was £13,250, to be found mainly by a mortgage for £13,000. The plaintiff and his wife had two children, who were both in employment.

Having first held that the plaintiff was a 'child of the family' (see pp 14–15) within s 1(1)(d) Booth J went on to consider the question of whether reasonable financial provision had been made for him. Booth J said (at 7) that the obligations and responsibilities which the deceased had to the plaintiff were very considerable indeed; in effect they were the obligations of a widowed parent to a dutiful and responsible only child. To his sisters, on the other hand, the deceased had no further obligations and responsibilities than those brought about by the fact of their blood relationship and by the relationship and by the remembrance of that part of their lives which they had shared together in the past. Booth J took into account the origin of the assets and their devolution through the plaintiff's mother. Her Ladyship found that the effect of the deceased's intestacy was unreasonable inasmuch as it made no financial provision for the plaintiff's needs, and that it would be a reasonable requirement for his maintenance that the plaintiff should have a lump sum to enable him to buy his house without a mortgage. Accordingly, she ordered that the plaintiff should receive £15,000.

The plaintiff in *Re Leach*, claimed against her stepmother's estate. Her own mother died in 1959, and in 1960, when the plaintiff was already 32, her father married the deceased. In 1974, he died, and his estate passed mainly to the deceased. There was a close relationship between the plaintiff and the deceased, who treated the plaintiff as her daughter. In 1981, the deceased died, childless and intestate, leaving as her next-of-kin, two sisters and a brother. Her estate amounted to approximately £34,000. She had encouraged the plaintiff to believe that she would be left by will a half interest in the dwelling house which the deceased owned. This was a matter which, as the Court of Appeal found, could properly be taken into account by virtue of s 3(1)(g) of the Act. At the date when the matter came before the Court of Appeal on appeal from Mr Michael Wheeler, QC (sitting as a Deputy Judge of the Chancery Division), the plaintiff was 55 and faced with retirement in the near future. She had a half-share in a house which she shared with a friend, some £1,200 in a building society account, and a salary of about £6,250 per annum. Her commitments were considerable, including a half share of a £14,000 mortgage, an indebtedness to her friend of £8,000, and a bank loan. In acquiring the house jointly with her friend the plaintiff had been encouraged by the belief that she would be a beneficiary under the deceased's will.

The Court of Appeal having rejected an argument that the plaintiff was not within s 1(1)(d) found that there was evidence to support the Deputy Judges's conclusion that the law of intestacy did not make reasonable provision for the plaintiff, but reduced the award which he made to her (£19,000) to £14,000, purely because at the hearing at first instance the size of the estate had, by reason of an error, been over-estimated.

In *Williams v Johns* [1988] 2 FLR 475 the applicant was unsuccessful. His Honour Judge Micklem sitting as an additional judge of the High Court dismissed an application by the adult adopted daughter of the deceased on the grounds that although the applicant was in need, her own impecuniosity and the deceased's continued affection for her did not give rise either to an obligation to be maintained by the deceased or to a reason why it would be reasonable for the deceased to make provision for her. The judge took into account (at 488) not only the fact that the applicant was independent and capable of maintaining herself but that she had done nothing to care for the deceased and had in fact in the past caused shame and distress to the deceased (see p 37).

In *Re Jennings, Harlow v National Westminster Bank plc* [1994] 3 WLR 67 the Court of Appeal allowed an appeal by the residuary legatees (all of whom were charities) against an order of Wall J awarding £40,000 to the applicant who was the son of the deceased.

The estate was of the order of £300,000. The deceased and the applicant's mother had separated in 1945 and were divorced in 1947 and the deceased made no financial provision for the applicant or for his mother who eventually remarried. The deceased had no contact at all with the applicant after 1947 (when the applicant was four). The applicant enjoyed a reasonable standard of living funded from his remuneration from two companies owned by himself and his wife. The matrimonial home was valued in 1991 at £400-£450,000 subject to a mortgage of £43,000 and a second charge to secure borrowing by one of the applicant's companies. Wall J considered that he was entitled under s 3(1)(d) of the Act to take into account moral and legal obligations owed by the deceased to the applicant during his childhood and that if he was wrong on that point he was still entitled to take into account the fact that the deceased had failed in legal obligations to the applicant during his childhood which therefore gave rise to a special circumstance within *Re Coventry*. The Court of Appeal held that Wall J had been wrong in law in considering that s 3(1)(d) included moral and legal obligations which the deceased had at any time and stated that only obligations and responsibilities owed by the deceased immediately before his death were within that sub-section and dismissed the suggestion that the deceased's failure to discharge his legal and moral responsibilities at the time imposed a continuing moral obligation on him to provide for the applicant (per Nourse J at 74). The Court of Appeal further held that the applicant did not require financial provision for his maintenance.

It will be seen that in all the cases under s 1(1)(c) and s 1(1)(d) where an application has succeeded, the applicant has been able to point to some immediate or threatened financial need for the relief of which a parent or quasi-parent might have been expected to provide by will. It may be thought to be unfortunate that a child, or someone treated as a child, who has lavished care and affection upon a parent or quasi-parent, possibly at considerable personal sacrifice, and for whom no, or no substantial, provision is made by will or the operation of the intestacy rules, has no recourse under the Act because he or she, though far from affluent, cannot point to some indebtedness or other pressing need which has to be met but it has been consistently held that rewarding meritorious conduct is not the function of the Act.

Where the deceased has in his lifetime provided for a child, or a person treated by the deceased as a child of the marriage, (for example, by large sums paid to set the child up in business or for some articles of partnership, or simply by making gifts of capital) the court might well find it perfectly reasonable for the deceased to make no further provision by his will for that child.

10 Applications by persons maintained by the deceased

With regard to the wide category of persons permitted by s 1(1)(e) to make a claim (any person (not being a person included in the foregoing paragraphs of s 1(1)) who immediately before the death of the deceased was being maintained, either wholly or partly, by him), s 3(4) provides that the court must have regard to the extent to which and the basis upon which the deceased assumed responsibility for the maintenance of the applicant and to the length of time for which the deceased discharged that responsibility. The applicant must prove that the deceased 'assumed responsibility' for the applicant's maintenance, but the bare fact of maintenance generally raises the presumption that responsibility for it has been assumed. It may be that the presumption can be rebutted by circumstances, including a disclaimer of any intention to maintain. There is a distinction to be drawn between an intention to maintain during the lifetime of the giver who has something to offer and an intention to provide continuing support after death (see *Jelley v Iliffe* [1981] Fam 128 per Stephenson, LJ at 137 and per Griffiths LJ at 142).

In *Jelley v Iliffe* Griffiths LJ said (at 141) that if a man and a woman were living together as husband and wife, with the man providing the home and all the money for their living expenses, the woman would clearly be dependent on the man, and it would not be right to deprive her of her claim by arguing that she was in fact performing the services which a housekeeper would perform, and that it would cost more to employ a housekeeper than was spent on her and indeed perhaps more than the deceased had available to spend on her. His Lordship said that each case must be looked at carefully on its own facts to see whether common sense led to the conclusion that the applicant could fairly be regarded as a dependant.

Jelley v Iliffe illustrates well the difficulties surrounding applications under s 1(1)(e). The deceased was the widow of the applicant's brother, and his wife, who had also died, was her sister. In 1971 the applicant, then aged 64, went to live with the deceased, who was about three years younger, in her house, and, whatever the exact arrangements between them, they agreed to share the accommodation of the house and did so for eight years until the deceased's death in 1979. The district registrar struck out the originating summons on the ground that the evidence in support disclosed no reasonable cause of action, and Bush J dismissed the applicant's appeal. The Court of Appeal, however, allowed the applicant's further appeal on the basis that he had an arguable case and said that it was only in plain cases that such an application should be dismissed.

Griffiths LJ continued (at 141–142):

> The difficulty I have is to know what significance to attach to the words 'assumed responsibility for the maintenance of the applicant' in s 3(4). s (1)(e) appears to me to be aimed at giving relief to persons where the relationship to the deceased is such that it is highly unlikely that any formal arrangements will have been made between them. Obvious examples are the elderly but impoverished relative or friend who is taken into the deceased's household and given free board and lodging and treated as a member of the family. Or a man living with a woman out of wedlock but supporting her as he would a wife. In such circumstances I would not as a general rule expect to find any formal declaration of assumption of responsibility, but it cannot have been the intention that such cases should fail for want of some such formality. I read 'assumed responsibility for' as being equivalent to 'has undertaken' . . .

The Court of Appeal disagreed with Sir Robert Megarry V-C, who in *Re Beaumont, Martin v Midland Bank Trust Co Ltd* [1980] Ch 444 (at 458) had held that there must be some act or acts which demonstrate an undertaking of responsibility, or the taking of responsibility on oneself, the bare fact of maintenance not being enough. The Vice-Chancellor went on to say (*obiter*) that it might be that would-be benefactors who wish to protect their families ought to obtain from anyone to whose maintenance they propose to contribute, an acknowledgement that they are undertaking no responsibility for his or her maintenance. Griffiths LJ in *Jelley v Iliffe* appears to have had the possibility of such a disclaimer in mind.

The passage in the judgment of Griffiths LJ in *Jelley v Iliffe* (at 141–142) quoted above was referred to by Dunn LJ giving the leading judgment in the Court of Appeal in *Harrington v Gill* (1983) 4 FLR 265 (at 270). In that case, the plaintiff and the deceased had lived together as man and wife for over seven and a half years in the deceased's house. The deceased died intestate. The net estate was £65,000, of which £22,000 was accounted for by the house. The defendant was the deceased's daughter and the only person entitled to his estate. The financial position of her family was reasonably comfortable. The plaintiff had only a state pension and capital of about £1,400. The house was described as a typical two-down and three-up house. Hollings J awarded the plaintiff a lump sum of £5,000 and the income during her life for a further sum of £5,000. He said that the house was too large and expensive for her to keep up and he ordered that she should vacate it within six months and avail herself of council or other accommodation.

The Court of Appeal, while confirming the lump sum and income provisions, held that the judge was wrong as regards the house, and that it was unlikely that the plaintiff (who had by then given up a council flat which she had retained during the whole time when she was living with the deceased) would get council accommodation. A reasonable man in the deceased's circumstances would have wanted the plaintiff to remain in the house for her lifetime, and accordingly it should be settled on her for her life; and she should have its contents subject to any small articles of family or sentimental value which it was reasonable for the defendant to have. Dunn LJ said (at 271) that the relevance of s 3(4) was that, in considering reasonable requirements or reasonable financial provision under s 1(1), the court would, amongst other things, consider the extent to which the deceased had undertaken responsibility for the maintenance of the plaintiff; that is to say, the court would consider as a relevant factor the standard of living enjoyed by the plaintiff during the deceased's lifetime and the extent to which the deceased contributed to that standard of living.

Malone v Harrison [1979] 1 WLR 1353 was a successful application by a mistress whom the deceased, a rich man, had wholly supported for 12 years, but for whom he made no provision in his will. He took her frequently to Malta, where he bought a flat in their joint names, and provided her with a flat in London, also in their joint names. He objected to her working, but provided her with a nominal position in one of his companies, for which she received some £60 a month. She received at least £4,000 a year from him during his lifetime and shares valued at £15,000. By his will he provided for his wife and his brother and for another mistress and her son. Hollings J held that the applicant was entitled to provision because the deceased had made himself responsible for her maintenance. On the basis that her loss of income was £2,000 a year (her earning capacity being assessed at £2,000) and applying a multiplier of 11, she was awarded £22,000 plus a capital sum of £20,000 (making £42,000) from which was deducted £23,000 (representing her capital resources), leaving £19,000.

The plaintiff in *Williams v Roberts* [1986] 1 FLR 349 was 68 and had first met the deceased in 1969. From 1971 until his death in 1981, they lived together as man and wife. Wood J found that the deceased had helped the plaintiff to run a guesthouse which she owned, had made four lump sum payments totalling £7,500 over a period of years, had provided her with various assets in kind, including a motor car, had paid for joint holidays, and had made regular weekly payments to her. The plaintiff was thus a dependant and his Lordship said that he must look at s 3 of the Act and fix a figure which was fair, just and reasonable. He awarded the plaintiff £20,000 out of the deceased's estate valued at between £110,000 and £120,000 gross, which he had left to be divided between his unmarried twin sisters, aged 64.

Possibly the existence of a child of the association may help a mistress' claim. In *CA v CC* (1978) *The Times*, 17 November (reported *sub nom In the Estate of McC* (1979) 9 Fam Law 26) Sir George Baker P ordered that the first applicant, whom he described as the testator's '*de facto* wife', should have a lump sum of £5,000 out of his estate of between £25,000 and £35,000 and (see p 65) that the remainder of the estate should be divided between the first applicant's son (and the second applicant) and the testator's legitimate son, to whom the whole estate had been left by the testator's will. His Lordship spoke of the relationship between the testator and the first applicant as having been a stable one. It is thought that the stability of the arrangements between the deceased and the applicant will always be relevant in the case of claims under s 1(1)(e).

It appears that where the testator has maintained the applicant unwillingly the court will not award greater provision than that provided by the testator (see *Re Viner, Kreeger v Cooper* [1978] CLY 3091, a decision of Master Chamberlain).

At present all applications by cohabitees have to be made under s 1(1)(e). This means that a cohabitee can only make an application if he or she was being maintained by the deceased. The Law Commission has recognised that this often works unfairly in cases where the cohabitees pooled their resources and neither provided considerably more than the other and has recommended that a separate category of applicant be inserted into the Act being a person who lived with the deceased as man and wife for a period of at least two years immediately preceding the death. If that recommendation is accepted, cases under s 1(1)(e) will cease to be relevant to applications by cohabitees (see also pp 15–18).

Chapter 4

What Provision May Be Made

1 The basis of the court's powers

When an application is made to the court under s 1(1) and the court is satisfied that the applicant is within one of the categories of applicant set out in s 1(1)(a)—(e) of the Act (see Chapter 2) and that on a consideration of the matters listed in s 3 of the Act that the deceased's will or the law relating to intestacy (or the combination of both) has not made reasonable financial provision for the applicant it can make any one or more of the orders referred to in s 2 of the Act in the applicant's favour (see *Re Debenham* [1986] 1 FLR 404 where the applicant received a lump sum and periodical payments). In deciding what order to make the court is expressly required to consider the matters listed in s 3 of the Act.

The powers conferred on the court by the Act are more extensive than those which existed under the previous legislation. Under the Act of 1938 those who could apply for provision were restricted to surviving spouses, unmarried daughters or those lacking capacity (whether through age or disability) and sons lacking capacity (whether through age or disability) (s 1(1)(a)—(d)). These persons were collectively referred to as 'dependants'. The court had power under the Act of 1938 (as originally enacted) to order periodical payments for the maintenance of a dependant to terminate on the date, if any, that such an individual ceased to be a dependant. A surviving spouse, for example, ceased to be a dependant on remarriage and an infant son or daughter on attaining majority (s 1(1) and (2) of the Act of 1938). The amount of income available to maintain a dependant was restricted by reference to the annual income produced by the estate (ss 1(3) and 5). The court also had the power to order provision by way of a lump sum payment if the estate was valued at less than £2,000 (on the basis of s 1(3)) (s 1(4)). The court had a limited power (after the expiration of the limitation period) to vary orders made (s 4(1)(a)) or order provision for the maintenance of other dependants (s 4(1)(b)), but only in respect of property the income of which was applicable for the maintenance of a dependant (s 4(1)). It is therefore clear that the court could not increase the total sum of maintenance to be paid out of the deceased's estate. The Act of 1938 was amended by the Act of 1952 and the Family Provision Act 1966 but the Act brought sweeping changes to the court's powers. The present provisions reflect the recommendations of the Law Commission (Law Com No 61, paras 110–125). The Law Commission took the view that the effective enforcement of family provision law required that the court should have powers over the property of the deceased similar to those which it was able to exercise when dealing with financial provision on divorce, nullity or judicial separation. In the result, s 2(1) of the Act lists in paragraphs (a) to (f) six kinds of order, any one or more of which the court may make.

2 The net estate

Save where an order is to be made by the court under s 2(1)(f) of the Act (varying an ante-nuptial or post-nuptial settlement) the court can only order provision to be made for an applicant from the 'net estate' of the deceased. By s 25(1) the 'net estate' is defined as meaning:

(a) all property which the deceased had power to dispose of by will (otherwise than by virtue of a special power of appointment) less funeral, testamentary and administration expenses, debts and liabilities, including any inheritance tax payable out of the deceased's estate on his or her death;

(b) any property in respect of which the deceased held a general power of appointment (not exercisable by will) which has not been exercised;

(c) any sum of money or other property which is treated for the purposes of the Act as part of the net estate of the deceased by virtue of s 8(1) or (2) of the Act (see pp 79–81);

(d) any property which is treated for the purposes of the Act as part of the net estate of the deceased by virtue of an order made under s 9 of the Act (see pp 81–83);
(e) any sum or other property which is, by reason of a disposition or contract made by the deceased, ordered under s 10 or s 11 of the Act to be provided for the purpose of making financial provision under the Act (see Chapter 7).

'Property' includes any chose in action (s 25(1)). The proceeds of any life assurance policy on the deceased's life will be included under (a) above unless the deceased created a trust of the proceeds prior to the date of his death so that he was not competent to dispose of those proceeds by will. It is worth noting that the proceeds of a life assurance policy, for example, or other death benefits, which do not form part of the deceased's net estate will nevertheless be regarded (where relevant) as part of an applicant or beneficiary's resources if a claim is made under the 1975 Act: *Jessop v Jessop* [1992] 1 FLR 591 (see p 30).

(i) Nominations

Section 8(1) of the Act provides that where a deceased person has in accordance with the provisions of any enactment nominated any person to receive any sum of money or other property on his death and that nomination is in force at the time of his death, that sum of money, after the deduction of any inheritance tax payable in respect thereof, or that other property, to the extent of the value thereof at the date of the death of the deceased after deducting any inheritance tax so payable, is treated for the purposes of the Act as part of the deceased's net estate.

Subsection (1) of s 8 expressly states that nothing within the subsection renders any person liable for having paid that sum or transferred that property to the person named in the nomination in accordance with the terms of the nomination. It therefore provides protection to trustees of pension schemes, for example, who distribute benefits pursuant to a nomination.

The deceased's 'net estate' will therefore include any sum of money or other property (less the inheritance tax payable thereon) which is subject to a nomination in force at the deceased's death made pursuant to an enactment. Disputes as to the effect of s 8(1) are common where the deceased had a pension and questions arise as to whether the benefits under that pension are to be included in the deceased's 'net estate'. Unless the deceased had power under the pension scheme to nominate those to benefit on his death and the nomination is made pursuant to an enactment (see below), s 8(1) is not applicable. If the pension benefits automatically pass to the deceased's widow or widower or their destination is in the absolute control of the pension scheme trustees, for example, then they are not included within the deceased's 'net estate' pursuant to s 8(1). If a nomination is made it must be in force at the date of the deceased's death. Whether this is the case will to a large extent depend upon the rules of the scheme (see *Re Cairnes, Howard v Cairnes* (1983) 4 FLR 225 where the nominee was the deceased's wife at the date of the nomination but not at the date of his death. However, at the date of the deceased's death she qualified as a dependent under the rules of the scheme and this was sufficient for the nomination to take effect).

Even where the deceased is able to and has made a nomination in force at the date of their death, unless that nomination is made pursuant to the provisions of an enactment, s 8(1) will not apply. The rules of private sector pension schemes are not made pursuant to an enactment and so will not qualify under s 8(1) of the Act: *Re Cairnes* per Anthony Lincoln J at 231. The rules of public sector pension schemes may be but it is open to question whether, if they are created by statutory instrument, this is sufficient (see *obiter dicta* in *Re Cairnes* per Anthony Lincoln J at 231 for the view that it is).

If the deceased was a member of a private sector pension scheme and had made a nomination which was in force at the date of his death or a member of a public sector pension scheme (not created pursuant to an 'enactment') but again where a qualifying nomination had been made it is possible that the benefits arising could be treated as part of the deceased's 'net estate' pursuant to s 10 of the Act (see Chapter 7).

(ii) *Donationes mortis causa*

Section 8(2) of the Act provides that where any sum of money or other property is received by any person as a *donatio mortis causa* made by a deceased person, that sum of money, after deducting therefrom any inheritance tax payable thereon, or that other property, to the extent of the value thereof at the date of the death of the deceased after deducting any inheritance tax so payable, shall be treated for the purposes of the Act as part of the net estate of the deceased with the same provisions as to the protection of persons who have paid that sum or transferred that property as exists in relation to s 8(1) of the Act (see p 79).

A *donatio mortis causa* is a gift of property in contemplation of the donor's death made upon the condition that the gift is not to be absolute and complete until the donor's death. There are four essential requirements for an effective *donatio mortis causa*:

(a) the gift must be made in contemplation of the donor's death;
(b) the gift must be made on the condition (express or implied) that it is not absolute and complete until the donor's death;
(c) there must be delivery of the subject-matter of the gift or the essential *indicia* of title to it to the donee (or somebody acting on the donee's behalf);
(d) the subject-matter of the gift must be capable of passing by a *donatio mortis causa* and anything which can be transferred by mere delivery can be so given as can other property if there is delivery of a suitable document.

Prior to *Sen v Headley* [1991] Ch 425, it was considered that a *donatio mortis causa* could not be made in respect of land. In *Sen v Headley* the Court of Appeal, overturning the decision at first instance, held that unregistered land, namely the deceased's dwelling house, passed by *donatio mortis causa* to his companion in circumstances where he had made clear his intention to give the said property to her and had given her the key to a steel box which contained the title deeds to the said land. The title deeds were the essential *indicia* of title to the unregistered land and the *donatio mortis causa* was effective

(iii) Property held on a joint tenancy

Section 9(1) of the Act provides that, where a deceased person was, immediately before his death, beneficially entitled to a joint tenancy of any property, then if, before the end of the period of six months from the date on which representation with respect to the estate of the deceased was first taken out, an application is made for an order under s 2 of the Act, the court for the purpose of facilitating the making of financial provision for the applicant may order that the deceased's severable share of that property, at the value thereof immediately before his death, shall, to such extent as appears to the court to be just in all the circumstances of the case, be treated for the purposes of the Act as part of the net estate of the deceased. In determining the extent to which any severable share is to be treated as part of the net estate by virtue of an order under s 9(1), the court is to have regard to any inheritance tax payable in respect of that severable share (s 9(2)). Where an order is made under s 9(1), the provisions of the section do not render any person liable for anything done by him before the order was made (s 9(3)) thereby extending the similar protection available under subs (1) and (2) of s 8 of the Act (see pp 79–81). For the purposes of s 9 there may be a joint chose in action (s 9(4)).

There is no discretion for a court to extend the time within which an application under s 9 must be made as exists for other applications under the Act (s 4 and see Chapter 5).

In *Re Crawford* (1983) 4 FLR 273 Eastham J said (at 280) that there were no specific principles which ought to guide the court in deciding whether to exercise its discretion under s 9. Section 9 contained everything which was necessary for the purpose of guiding the court in deciding whether or not to exercise its discretion and property which fell to be treated as part of the deceased's net estate pursuant to s 9 was to be treated no differently from any other property comprised in the deceased's net estate. The applicant in the case was the deceased's former wife. It was common ground that this was a case where an order under s 2 was appropriate and that a lump sum would be the most appropriate provision to make. The applicant was provided with a lump sum of £35,000 (intended to purchase an annuity providing an income of £4,000 per annum). The deceased's severable shares in a bank and a building society account were treated as part of his net estate pursuant to s 9 in order to achieve this provision. The wide nature of the discretionary power available to the court under s 9 has been emphasised in *Jessop v Jessop* [1992] 1 FLR 591 where the applicant was the deceased's widow and an order was made pursuant to s 9 to treat £10,000 of the proceeds of a property estimated to have a value of £42,000 (and in the joint names of the deceased and his companion) as part of the net estate of the deceased in order to facilitate the making of provision for the widow.

Section 9 expressly states (in contradistinction to s 8) that it is the deceased's severable share 'at the value thereof immediately before [the deceased's] death' to such extent as appears just that is to be treated as part of the deceased's net estate. This was confirmed in *Powell v Osbourne* [1993] 1 FLR 1001 per Dillon LJ at 1005. In that case the applicant was the deceased's widow although there was a decree nisi in existence. For some two years prior to his death the deceased had been cohabiting with the defendant and two months prior to his death they purchased a property for £91,000 in their joint names subject to a mortgage (again in their joint names) securing borrowing of £85,000 and supported by a life policy. The deceased's severable share in this property was the only asset that could be comprised in the deceased's net estate and the widow had applied under s 9. At first instance the widow received £5,750 which accounted for the larger part of the equity of redemption in the property on the basis that the life policy had no real sale or surrender value. In the Court of Appeal this was raised to £15,000. The Court of Appeal emphasised that the deceased's net estate was potentially comprised of the deceased's severable share in the property (subject to the mortgage) plus a half-share in the proceeds of the life policy so that if the deceased had in fact severed the beneficial joint tenancy in the property immediately prior to his death, his net estate would have comprised his half share in the property (free from incumbrance).

Note that s 9 is intended to 'facilitate the making of financial provision' and no more.

3 Periodical payments

Section 2(1)(a) provides that, subject to the provisions of the Act, the court may make an order for the making to the applicant out of the net estate of the deceased of such periodical payments and for such term as may be specified in the order. Section 19(2) provides that an order for periodical payments in favour of an applicant who was the former spouse of the deceased, or the spouse of the deceased in a case where the marriage with the deceased was the subject of a decree of judicial separation and at the death the decree was in force and the separation was continuing, shall cease to have effect on the remarriage of the applicant, except in relation to any arrears due under the order on the date of the remarriage (see the similar provision in the case of an order under s 5, p 114).

Subsections (2) and (3) of s 2 of the Act deal with the method by which provision for periodical payments is to made. The order may provide for (a) payments of such amount as may be specified in the order thereby securing payment of a specific sum to the applicant, or (b) payments equal to the whole of the income of the net estate or such portion thereof as may be so specified, or (c) payments equal to the whole of the income of such part of the net estate as the court may direct to be set aside or appropriated for the making out of the income thereof of payments under the section; or may provide for the amount of the payments or any of them to be determined in any other way the court thinks fit (s 2(2)). As stated, the order may direct that such part of the net estate as may be so specified shall be set aside or appropriated for the making out of the income thereof of those payments; but no larger part of the net estate is to be set aside or appropriated than is sufficient, at the date of the order, to produce by the income thereof the amount required for the making of those payments (s 2(3)). That limitation may be overcome by ordering provision to be made from a future date, as Wynn Parry J did in *Re Franks, Franks v Franks* [1948] Ch 62. An application was made on behalf of an infant child of the testatrix. This child was born in 1946, and it was admitted that no immediate provision for such child was required, though some provision would be required later. In the meanwhile provision was required to be made for a child of the testatrix by an earlier marriage. Wynn Parry J accordingly directed that the summons should stand over until the last Friday in January 1950 (shortly before the child of the first marriage came of age), with a view to considering then, first, the quantum of the provision, and, secondly, the date in the future from which it was to run, with liberty to all parties to apply in the meantime if circumstances should so require. In the meantime the trustees of the testatrix's will would not be prevented from dealing, in accordance with the terms of the will, with income accruing under it, but they would be unable to advance capital.

It is not possible to define the circumstances in which a periodical payments order will be made in an applicant's favour as opposed to an order for any other form of financial provision under s 2. However, it is clear that periodical payments are likely to be ordered where the applicant is elderly or has a short life expectancy (*Stead v Stead* [1985] FLR 16 and *Re Debenham* [1986] 1 FLR 404 per Ewbank J at 410) and are less likely to be ordered where the estate is small and periodical payments will delay the administration of the deceased's estate or a substantial part of it for many years (*Re Collins* [1990] Fam 56). Further, if the deceased was making regular payments to the applicant (or was supposed to have been doing so) these may serve as some indication of the provision that ought to be ordered and (where appropriate) periodical payments at a similar level may be ordered (*Re Farrow* [1987] 1 FLR 205).

When considering periodical payments it is to be noticed that, first, whereas generally provision is ordered as from the date of the deceased's death, the court has a discretion and may, for example, order provision as from the date of the judgment; secondly, that the court can now order payments without limit of time; and, thirdly, that s 6 provides for the variation, discharge, suspension and revival of orders for periodical payments (see p 87).

Askew v Askew [1961] 1 WLR 725, a case under the Matrimonial Causes (Property and Maintenance) Act 1958, seems to be the first one in which the question arose as to the date from which periodical payments should begin. Marshall J said that the court in its discretion would, if the circumstances of any particular case warranted, order payment from the date of the death, but that there was not a right arising immediately after death in all circumstances. On the facts Marshall J ordered payment from the testator's death and ignored the fact that the applicant, who had no financial resources, had been in receipt of national assistance. In *Re Lecoche, Lecoche v Barclays Bank Ltd* (1967) 111 SJ 136, however, Plowman J ordered that payments to the testator's infant sons should run from the date of judgment. His Lordship observed that had he made the order retrospective a house occupied by the testator's mistress and his illegitimate son, to whom he had left the house, would inevitably have had to be sold. As it was, he hoped that the mistress would find it possible to arrange for the applicant sons to be paid without the necessity of selling the house.

In *Re Goodwin, Goodwin v Goodwin* [1969] 1 Ch 283, Megarry J ordered that the award which he made to the testator's widow should run from the testator's death, his *ratio decidendi* being that that was the date from which any provision made by the will would normally have taken effect, and so it was right for the court to do in this respect what the will would have done had it made reasonable provision for the plaintiff. She had been in receipt of social security payments, but Megarry J said that any consequent adjustment between the plaintiff and the social security authorities was a matter for them. In *Lusternik v Lusternik* [1972] Fam 125 the Court of Appeal, considering a claim under the Matrimonial Causes Act 1965, held that whether there should be any backdating of the award and its extent was a matter entirely within the discretion of the court. There was no prima facie rule that an award should be backdated to the date of death. While ordinarily it might well be backdated to the date of the application, that should not be done where (as in the present case) the proceedings were unduly protracted, unless there was some fault on the part of those representing the estate. The backdating of an order for periodical payments has the effect of adding an order for a lump sum. The trial judge, Hollings J had limited the backdating to a period of 15 months prior to the date of his order, and the Court of Appeal held that this was right. Cairns LJ rejecting a contention that there was any rule that prima facie the payment should be backdated to the death, said that this was certainly not laid down as a rule in *Askew v Askew*. The Court of Appeal did not consider *Re Goodwin*. Mention was made in argument of *Re Eyre* [1968] 1 WLR 530, a decision of Elizabeth Lane J under the said Act of 1965, in which payments were ordered to run from the date of the plaintiff's summons.

In *Stead v Stead* periodical payments were ordered to be made, backdated to the day after the deceased's death and (more recently) in *Re Farrow* the applicant received periodical payments at a similar level to maintenance payments she ought to have received during the deceased's lifetime of £5,000 per annum and a lump sum of £15,000 per annum to compensate her for the seven year period between the commencement of her proceedings under the Act and final determination (see p 58).

Although Megarry J in *Re Goodwin* was not prepared to consider the effects of his order upon the social security being received by the applicant this is not always the case. In *Re Debenham* Ewbank J (at 410) expressly decided not to backdate his order for periodical payments to the date of the deceased's death due to the social security problems that would be created. Similarly, advisers ought to consider whether any inheritance tax problems will arise on the backdating of an order for periodical payments (see pp 130–132).

While there is no longer any statutory requirement (as there was originally under the Act of 1938) limiting the provision which the court may see fit to order to an estimated or notional income of the estate, Buckley J said in *Re Blanch, Blanch v Honhold* [1967] 1 WLR 987 that in order to reach a just apportionment of the benefits of a deceased's estate an estimate of its probable income yield might still be relevant. In *Re F* ((1965) *The Times*, 26 February) Cumming-Bruce J held that on an application under the Matrimonial Causes (Property and Maintenance) Act 1958 the court had jurisdiction to order periodical payments at a rate in excess of the income from the estate.

If the court decides to make an order for periodical payments it may impose conditions or restrictions. When, for example, an order is made in favour of a widow as against infant children, a condition requiring her to maintain them will normally be imposed, and it can be imposed even if no application has been made by or on behalf of the children. The testator in *Re Lidington, Lidington v Thomas* (*No 2*) [1940] Ch 927 left nothing to his wife and the greater part of his estate in trust for his two children on their attaining the age of 28 years. Farwell J making an order that the income of two-thirds of the testators's estate should be paid to the widow, required that she should undertake to maintain the testator's two children during their infancy. In *Re Hills, Hills v Foote* [1941] WN 123 Morton J made an order that two-thirds of the actual income of the testator's estate be paid to his widow during her widowhood, but this was not to give her any power to require realisation of any part of the estate (reversionary or otherwise) by the trustee nor to affect the provisions of the will as regards the trustee's powers and duties to realise or postpone the realisation of any part of the property. Furthermore, the order was made subject to the widow informing the trustee of any income to which she might become legally entitled and of any property to which she might become legally entitled in possession, except property not exceeding £100 in value vesting at the same time and from a single source, accumulations of income belonging to her, property purchased for value by her out of her own moneys, and movables, chattels and effects of household, domestic or personal use or ornament. See also *Re Pointer, Pointer and Shonfield v Edwards* [1941] Ch 60.

4 Variation, discharge, etc of orders for periodical payments

Where the court has made an order, the original order, under s 2(1)(a) of the Act for the making of periodical payments to a person, the original recipient, it can, on application, for that purpose vary or discharge such an order, or suspend any provision of it temporarily and revive the operation of any provision so suspended (s 6(1)). Without prejudice to the generality of subs (1) of s 6, an order made on an application for the variation of the original order may:

(a) provide for the making, out of any relevant property (as defined in s 6(6)), of such periodical payments and for such term as may be specified in the order to any person who has applied, or would but for s 4 (which is concerned with the time limit for applications: see Chapter 5) be entitled to apply, for an order under s 2 (whether or not, in the case of any application, an order was made in favour of the applicant);
(b) provide for the payment out of any relevant property of a lump sum of such amount as may be specified to the original

recipient or to any such person as is mentioned in (a) above; and

(c) provide for the transfer of the relevant property, or such part thereof as may be specified, to the original recipient or to any person as is so mentioned (s 6(2)).

This gives effect to the recommendations of the Law Commission (Law Com No 61, para 181) that where an order for periodical payments is varied or discharged the court should have power to order out of the property set aside to provide the periodical payments, the payment of a lump sum to any person entitled to apply for provision out of that property and to order the transfer to any such person of the whole or part of such property.

Where the original order provides that any periodical payments payable thereunder to the original recipient are to cease on the occurrence of a specified event (other than the remarriage of a former spouse) or on the expiration of a specified period, then if, before the end of a period of six months from the date of the occurrence of that event or on the expiration of that period, an application is made for an order under the section, the court shall have power to make any order which it would have had power to make if the application had been made before that date (whether in favour of the original recipient or such person as has applied, or would but for s 4 be entitled to apply, for an order under s 2, and whether having effect from that date or from such later date as the court may specify) (s 6(3)).

Any reference in s 6 to the original order includes a reference to an order made under that section and any reference in the section to the original recipient includes a reference to any person to whom periodical payments are required to be made by virtue of an order under the section (s 6(4)): that is to say, the court may exercise its powers under s 6 in respect of an order which was itself made under that section.

An application under s 6 may be made by:

(a) any person who by virtue of s 1(1) has applied, or would but for s 4 be entitled to apply, for an order under s 2;
(b) the personal representatives of the deceased (see *Re Lidington, Lidington v Thomas (No 2)* [1940] Ch 927);
(c) the trustees of any relevant property; and
(d) any beneficiary of the estate of the deceased (s 6(5)).

'Beneficiary' is defined in s 25(1) to include both (a) a person who under the will of the deceased or under the law relating to intestacy is beneficially interested in the estate or would be so interested if an order had not been made under the Act and (b) a person who has received any sum of money or other property by way of nomination or by a *donatio mortis causa* which, by virtue of s 8(1) or s 8(2) as the case may be, is treated as part of the net estate of the deceased; or who would have received that sum of money or other property if an order had not been made under the Act. Persons interested in dispositions in respect of which orders are made under s 10 or s 11 of the Act are not 'beneficiaries'. Personal representatives are included because they might not technically at the date of an application have become trustees and so might not, unless expressly included, be eligible to apply.

It is provided by subs (6) of s 6 that an order under the section may only affect (a) property the income of which is the date of the order applicable wholly or in part for the making of periodical payments to any person who has applied for an order under the Act, or (b) in the case of an application under s 6(3) in respect of payments which have ceased to be payable on the occurrence of an event or the expiration of a period, property the income of which was so applicable immediately before the occurrence of that event or the expiration of the period, as the case may be. Such property is 'relevant property' for the purposes of subs (2) and (5).

Section 6(7) provides that in exercising the powers conferred by the section the court is to have regard to all the circumstances of the case, including any change in any of the matters to which the court was required to have regard when making the order to which the application relates. The powers of variation and discharge contained in s 6 are applied by s 26(4) to orders under the former law. As to the matters to which the court was required to have regard when making the order, see s 3 which is considered in Chapter 3.

Section 6(8) requires the court when making an order under the section to give such consequential directions as it thinks necessary or expedient having regard to the provisions of the order. For example, the effect of an order under s 6 may be to release or reduce the amount of capital or property on which the periodical payments are charged and subs (8) permits the court to direct the destination of any property released.

Paragraphs (d), (e) and (f) of s 2(1) (see pp 93–95) permit the court to make orders for the settlement of property, for the acquisition of property, and for the variation of an ante-nuptial or post-nuptial settlement, but s 6(9) provides that no such order may be made under s 6. Subsection (9) also makes it clear that s 6 has no application in respect of the court's discretionary powers to make orders under s 9 in respect of property held jointly by the deceased and another or other persons; under s 10 in regard to certain dispositions *inter vivos* made by the deceased; or under s 11 in regard to contracts made by the deceased (see as to s 9, pp 81–83 and as to ss 10 and 11, Chapter 7).

Two cases under the Act of 1938 illustrate how use may be made of the power to vary periodical payments orders. The testator in *Re Bateman, Bateman v Simpson* (1941) 85 SJ 454 left an estate valued at approximately £500, and made no provision for his widow. He gave his residuary estate on trust for his daughter M, on her attaining 21 years, with power to apply 10s a week for her maintenance, with a gift over to his other children on M dying under the age of 21. The testator's widow, who was 40 years of age, applied for maintenance; she had no property of her own, but was earning £2 a week. Uthwatt J said that M had a first claim on the estate, and he did not see that it was possible to make an order for an immediate payment to the widow, though some change in the future might justify a provision in her favour; for example, M might die under the age of 21, and disaster might overtake the widow, so that she could not earn her living. Having recourse to s 4(1) of the Act of 1938 the learned judge accordingly ordered the summons to stand over with liberty to restore not later than six months after M attained the age of 21 or on any change of circumstances.

If the income received by an applicant under an order of the court substantially increases, the court may reduce that income. This happened in *Re Gale, Gale v Gale* [1966] Ch 236. In 1957, when Wynn Parry J made the original order, giving the widow the whole of the income of the net estate, most of the testator's property was tied up in houses producing very low rents owing to the Rent Restrictions Act, and the income was only about £500 a year. It remained at this figure until March 1958, but in the next year, following the release of the houses from the operation of the Rent Restrictions Act, it increased to a figure over £1,000. The widow had, by the time the matter came before Cross J in 1964 on an application by the executors, to save £6,000. Cross J varied the provision made for the widow to £600 a year, reducible to £500 so long as she received the income of a house, belonging to the estate but lived in by her daughter, direct from the daughter. The Court of Appeal dismissed the widow's appeal from that order. *Re Dorgan, Dorgan v Polley* [1948] Ch 366 is the only reported case where a person other than the original applicant, applied to vary a periodical payments order. However, it is a case on s 4(1) of the Act of

1938 and failed due to the particular provisions of that section which were not satisfied.

5 Lump sum payment

Section 2(1)(b) confers an unrestricted discretion to order maintenance by way of a lump sum and, as in the case of provision by way of periodical payments, it is made clear by s 25(3) that the court's order may extend to the whole of the net estate. An order may be made, not only on an original application, but also on an application made under s 6 for the variation or discharge of an order for periodical payments (s 6(2)(b), see pp 87–90).

There is no power to vary an order for provision by way of a lump sum payment (cf the power conferred by s 6(1) to vary an order under s 2(1)(a), see pp 87–90). It is, however, provided by s 7(1) that such an order whether made under s 2(1)(b) or s 6(2)(b), may provide for payment of the lump sum by instalments of such amount as may be specified in the order; and where an order is made by virtue of s 7(1) the court has power, on an application made by the person to whom the lump sum is payable, by the personal representatives of the deceased, or by the trustees of the property out of which the lump sum is payable, to vary that order by varying the number of instalments payable, the amount of any instalment and the date on which any instalment becomes payable (s 7(2)).

An order for the payment of a lump sum has the advantage from the point of view of the parties that it means that the applicant's claim is disposed of once and for all and the administration of the deceased's estate can be completed. For that reason it is the usual basis of settlement in the numerous cases under the Act which never come to trial. It has, however, inherent disadvantages. On the one hand a lump sum may have the effect of enabling the applicant to make provision for someone else who is not a dependant of the deceased and who accordingly benefits fortuitously at the expense of the beneficiaries. In *Re Besterman, Besterman v Grusin* [1984] Ch 458 (see p 41), however, Oliver LJ (at 466) rejected any suggestion that the court should start with a bias against making provision which might, ultimately, have the effect of enabling the applicant to make provision for somebody else who was not an applicant: that was something which was inherent in a lump sum order.

On the other hand, a spouse who accepts a lump sum forgoes the right conferred by s 6 to apply to the court for a variation of the order so as to make further provision. The importance of that consideration was referred to by Oliver LJ in *Re Besterman* where he said (at 477) that the extent of the lump sum 'ought (at any rate where, as here, the estate is ample for the purpose and scarcity of funds is not an inhibiting factor) to take account of the fact that the plaintiff is (whether or not of her own volition) giving up the right to return to the court for a variation of the provision in the event of unforeseen contingencies.' His Lordship referred to *Robinson v Robinson* (*Practice Note*) [1982] 1 WLR 786 (a case under the Matrimonial Causes Act 1973) where the importance of this consideration in relation to provision under s 25 of that Act was referred to, and said that it equally applied to the Act (see also *Preston v Preston* [1982] Fam 17, another case under the Matrimonial Causes Act 1973, where Ormrod LJ said (at 27) that the value of the applicant's claim to periodical payments, which she had offered to forgo, must be taken into account, but discounted for the advantage of an immediate payment of capital. Later (at 478) Oliver LJ in *Re Besterman* referred to the need for the court, in making a lump sum order, to take account of inflation).

The court will sometimes award a lump sum for a specific purpose. For example, in *Re Callaghan* [1985] Fam 1 a lump sum was awarded to assist in the purchase of a property. Lump sum awards have also been made in order to assist an applicant in purchasing an annuity thereby securing an income: *Re Crawford* (1983) 4 FLR 273.

6 Transfer of property

Paragraph (c) of s 2(1) of the Act permits an order to be made for the transfer to the applicant of such property comprised in the net estate of the deceased as may be specified in the order, where 'property' includes for this purpose any chose in action (see s 25(1)). While there is no power to vary an order for the transfer of property, it is possible to apply under s 6(1) for an order for the transfer of property by way of variation of an existing order for periodical payments (see s 6(2)(c)). In such a case, however, the order can affect only 'relevant property' (see s 6(6) and p 89). An order for the transfer of property may also be made on an application made under s 6(3) (see p 88).

In *Re Christie, Christie v Keeble* [1979] Ch 168 Mr Vivian Price QC (sitting as a Deputy Judge of the Chancery Division) on finding that reasonable financial provision had not been made for an adult son by his mother's will ordered that a property (which the deceased had undoubtedly intended to give to the son) be transferred to him. This is an unusual case given the clear indications of the deceased's wishes on which the learned judge appeared to place great weight. In *Rajabally v Rajabally* [1987] 2 FLR 390 the court ordered the matrimonial home to be vested in the widow on her husband's death and ordered payment of £7,500 to the deceased's eldest son (to be raised, if necessary, by a mortgage on that property). By his will, the deceased had left the home equally amongst his wife and his three sons, the eldest being his son by his first marriage. That son was mentally ill, he lived in council accommodation with security of tenure but his employment prospects were poor. It was found that the widow had contributed to the house through her earnings and her labour and that the will had not made reasonable financial provision for her.

Where a dwelling house is purchased from a local authority, whether pursuant to the authority's right to dispose of land conferred by Part II of the Housing Act 1985 or pursuant to the right to buy conferred by Part V of that Act, an early disposal (see ss 35 and 155 of that Act) by the purchaser usually entitles the authority to repayment of a proportion of the discount allowed to the purchaser on the sale. But a disposal of the whole of the house in pursuance of an order made under s 2 of the Act is exempt from the repayment provision (see the Housing Act 1985, ss 39(1)(c) and 160(1)(c)).

7 Settlement of property

Paragraph (d) of s 2(1) enables the court to make an order for the settlement for the benefit of the applicant of property comprised in the deceased's estate. Section 6 has no application to an order made under para (d) of s 2(1) (see s 6(9) and p 89). As, therefore, an order once made cannot be varied or discharged, it is clearly important for the order itself to contain power to vary the interest created or the property affected so far as the need for variation can be foreseen.

In *Re Mason, Mason v Mason* (1975) 5 Fam Law 124 the court ordered settlement of the matrimonial home on the applicant within the Settled Land Act 1925 thereby giving her the extensive powers of sale and leasing, for example, available thereunder.

8 Acquisition of property

Paragraph (e) of s 2(1) enables the court to make an order for the acquisition out of property comprised in the net estate of the deceased of such property as may be specified in the order and for the transfer of the property acquired to the applicant or the settlement of it for his benefit. What has been said above with regard to a settlement ordered under para (d) of s 2(1) has equal relevance here: that is to say, while there is no power to vary or discharge under s 6 (see subs (9) of that section and p 89), the property acquired can be settled in such a way as to permit interests in it to be varied. The power to acquire property is clearly a useful one, since it not infrequently happens that the deceased's estate includes a house which, by reason of size or otherwise, is unsuitable for occupation by the applicant: the power now under discussion enables that house to be sold and a more suitable dwelling to be purchased in its place. If the estate does not include a house, then one may be acquired for the applicant.

9 Variation of ante-nuptial or post-nuptial settlement

Finally, para (f) of s 2(1) enables the court to make an order varying any ante-nuptial or post-nuptial settlement (including such a settlement made by will) made on the parties to a marriage to which the deceased was one of the parties, the variation being for the benefit of the surviving party to that marriage, or any child of that marriage, or any person who was treated by the deceased as a child of the family in relation to that marriage: unlike the powers conferred by the earlier paragraphs of the subsection, this power cannot be exercised on behalf of the applicants in other categories and it is not limited to the deceased's net estate. In connection with para (f) of s 2(1) there should also be borne in mind the provisions of s 17, which provide for the variation and revocation of maintenance agreements (see pp 61–62). There is no power under s 6 to vary or discharge an order made under para (f) of s 2(1) (see s 6(9)).

The Act contains no definition of ante-nuptial or post-nuptial settlement. It seems that any document which makes provision for one or both of the parties to a marriage may constitute such a settlement (see *Prinsep v Prinsep* [1929] P 225; *Smith v Smith* [1945] 1 All ER 584; *Prescott (formerly Fellowes) v Fellowes* [1958] P 260). In *Hargreaves v Hargreaves* [1926] P 42, Hill J (at 45) held that the settlement must have been made 'in contemplation of, or because of, marriage and with reference to the interests of married people, or their children'.

In the context of the matrimonial legislation potential benefits given to the spouse of an employee under the employee's pension scheme were capable of rendering that scheme a post-nuptial settlement liable to be varied under s 24(1)(c) of the Matrimonial Causes Act 1973: *Brooks v Brooks* [1994] 2 FLR 10. In that case the scheme was varied at first instance to give the wife a modest pension. The husband appealed and a majority of the Court of Appeal (Waite and Neill LJJ with Hoffmann LJ dissenting) dismissed his appeal. Leave has been given for this case to be heard by the House of Lords but no decision has yet been released.

10 Consequential directions

Subsection (4) of s 2 reflects the recommendations of the Law Commission (Law Com No 61, paras 118, 119, 154) and provides that an order made under the section may contain such consequential and supplemental provisions as the court thinks necessary or expedient for the purpose of giving effect to the order or for the purpose of securing that the order operates fairly as between one beneficiary of the estate of the deceased and another. Without prejudice to the generality of the subsection, three specific powers are conferred:

(1) The court may order any person who holds any property which forms part of the net estate of the deceased to make such payment or transfer such property as may be specified in the order. That power takes account of the fact that the definition of 'net estate' in s 25(1) includes property which may be in the hands of persons other than the personal representatives; such persons may be required by the order to transfer the property which they hold either to the personal representatives or to someone else, as the court directs (see further ss 8 and 9 (which are concerned with property available for financial provision, see pp 79–83)) and ss 10–13 (which confer on the court powers in relation to transactions intended to defeat applications for financial provision (see Chapter 7)).

(2) The court may vary the disposition of the deceased's estate effected by the will or the law relating to intestacy, or by both the will and the law relating to intestacy, in such manner as the court thinks fair and reasonable having regard

to the provisions of the order and all the circumstances of the case. It appears that this power enables the court to provide that a beneficiary of specific property which is diverted to an applicant can be recompensed out of some other part of the estate.

(3) The court may confer on the trustees of any property which is the subject of an order under s 2 such powers as appear to the court to be necessary or expedient. Those powers might include discretionary powers.

Subsection (4) of s 2 perpetuates and makes clear the discretion of the court to decide what part of the testators estate is to be used for providing maintenance and if appropriate, to order it to be paid out of pecuniary legacies as well as residue. In *Re Bunning, Bunning v Salmon* [1984] Ch 480 the court at first instance ordered that provision to be made for a widow was to be found primarily from a gift of residue to Cambridge University and then rateably from the University and the RSPB as pecuniary legatees (see also *Malone v Harrison* [1979] 1 WLR 1353). It is now absolutely clear that maintenance can be ordered to be paid out of pecuniary legacies as well as residue.

The existence of this discretion was recognised at least as early as *Re Simson, Simson v National Provincial Bank Ltd* [1950] Ch 38. The testator in that case left to his housekeeper property valued at approximately £6,000, to his wife, whom he married in 1910 and from whom he separated in 1929, £1,000 together with £1,600 payable under insurance policies, to two nephews £500 each, and the residue of his estate (approximately £3,000 in value) to his two children equally. His widow, to whom during his life he had paid £200 a year, applied for maintenance. Vaisey J calculated that the widow would receive £104 a year from the bequests made to her, and considered that that amount should be brought up to £200 a year by an award, under the Act of 1938, of £96 a year. He held that he was empowered to order that amount to come out of the pecuniary legacies as well as the residue, and that the correct allocation of the amount was £55 a year from the housekeeper's legacy, £9 a year from the nephew's legacies, and £32 a year from the residue payable to the children.

In *Re Jackson, Jackson v Nottidge* [1952] WN 352 the testator's estate amounted to over £93,000. To his widow, whom he had married in 1910 and from whom he had been separated in 1919, he gave an annuity for life of £150. He bequeathed certain legacies, amounting in total to £4,250 (to be paid in priority to other legacies) further legacies, charitable in nature and amounting to £59,000 and the residue of his estate, which amounted to £6,000, to 14 charitable institutions in equal shares. The widow made an application under the Act of 1938 and Roxburgh J made an order giving her an additional annuity of £450 for her widowhood. The learned judge said that bequests of chattels in the will must be discharged in full and that the legacies to which priority was given must be paid in full. He ordered that the burden of the fund required to pay the plaintiff the additional annuity during her widowhood should be borne as to fifty-nine sixty-fifths by the other legacies, and as to six sixty-fifths by the residue and that when the fund ceased to be required it should be divided between those legacies and the residue in those proportions. Payment of maintenance out of a pecuniary legacy was also ordered in *Re Westby* (1946) 62 TLR 458, by Romer J.

Re Simson was considered by Burgess V-C in the Court of Chancery of the County Palatine of Lancaster in *Re Preston, Preston v Hoggarth* [1969] 1 WLR 317. In that case the testator by his will dated 18 May 1958 gave as his reason for making no provision for his wife the fact that she had returned to Australia, where they had been married, with their infant daughter without his consent. She applied for maintenance under the Act of 1938 and Burgess V-C accepted her evidence that she understood and believed that the testator would follow her, and he found that the testator had not made reasonable provision for her. The testator died on 5 December 1966. By his will he provided that if his widow should take any action to recover any part of his estate for herself, then he desired that any award made to her should be taken out of the part which he had given to his two grandchildren and that their share should be reduced accordingly. He gave half his estate to a friend, H, and the other half equally between two nieces and the two grandchildren. Burgess V-C awarded the widow £2,600 out of an estate of approximately £4,600. He held that s 3(1), (2) of the Act of 1938 enabled him not only to apportion the burden of the award as regards respective classes of beneficiaries, but also to throw the burden unequally between beneficiaries in the same category or class. He directed that the burden should be borne by H as to twenty-eight forty-eighths, by each of the two nieces as to seven forty-eighths, and by each of the two grandchildren as to three forty-eighths.

Re Doring, Doring v Clark [1955] 1 WLR 1217 illustrates how the court may vary the incidence of payments without altering the size of the provision made by the will. The plaintiff was the testator's second wife and at the time of the marriage was 39, he being then 56 years of age. He bequeathed her his personal chattels, £250, and half of his residuary estate. After payment of liabilities and legacies his estate was approximately £30,000, and half of the residue generated £600 a year. The testator gave the other half of his residue as to one-sixth to his brother and as to two-sixths to his sister. He had carried on a partnership with his brother, and under the terms of the partnership deed was given an option, which he exercised, making his brother liable to pay the plaintiff an annuity of £500 during their joint lives, but subject to the proviso that if in any year the net profits of the business should be less than £3,000, the annuity for the year next following should abate proportionately. The plaintiff's real complaint was not as to the quantum of the provision but as to the manner in which it was made. Wynn Parry J held that in so far as the quantum—an aggregate sum of about £1,100—was concerned, he could not interfere, but that it was not reasonable to make £500 of that subject to contingencies. Accordingly he ordered that there should be paid to the applicant out of the income of the residue an annuity of £500 during widowhood, with a proviso that neither the annuity nor any part of it be payable except to the extent that it was not received under the provisions of the partnership deed. (His lordship distinguished *Re Franks, Franks v Franks* [1948] Ch 62 (see p 84) because in the case before him he was able to say that the widow ought to have £1,100 a year, and all he was designing to do was to set up the necessary machinery whereby she would receive it during widowhood, whereas in *Re Franks* it was not possible at the date of the hearing to quantify the amount of provision which should be made.)

Chapter 5

Time Limit for Claims

1 The time limit

Applications for an order under s 2 of the Act must (save with the court's permission) be 'made' on or before the end of the period of six months from the date on which representation with respect to the deceased's estate is first taken out (s 4).

The period of six months from the date on which representation is first taken out means the period of six calendar months. A reference to a month in a statute is to be understood as a calendar month (Interpretation Act 1978, s 5 and Sched 1). In calculating a period of months, the corresponding date rule is applied. For example, if probate is granted on 30 April, the six month period will expire on 30 (not 31) October. The rule will be modified where necessary: for example, six months from 31 May expires on 30 November (not 1 December) (see *Dodds v Walker* [1981] 1 WLR 1027).

If proceedings are commenced in the High Court, the application is 'made' when the originating summons is issued: *Re Chittenden, Chittenden v Doe* [1970] 1 WLR 1618. *Re Chittenden* concerned an application in the High Court under s 2(1) of the Act of 1938 (as originally enacted): ' . . . an order under this Act shall not be made save on an application made within six months from the date on which representation in regard to the testator's estate . . . is first taken . . . ' Ungoed-Thomas J held that service of the originating summons was merely procedural and not a part of the substantive application under the Act of 1938. The application was therefore 'made' when the originating summons was issued. The editors' view is that an application in the county court is 'made' on the date that proceedings are issued. It is clear that an application can therefore be made within the limitation period but not notified to the personal representatives until the expiry of that period when distribution could have taken place. In this situation s 20(1) of the Act will not protect the personal representatives.

A person who is considering commencing proceedings under the Act may apply to be sent an office copy of any grant of representation to the deceased's estate which either was issued within the previous 12 months or issues within the following six months (see NCPR 1987, Rule 43). This method of ensuring that time does not run unobserved against a potential applicant is much more convenient than the entry of a caveat, a course which has sometimes been followed in the past.

Applicants and their advisers ought to be aware that there is no discretion to extend the six month time limit in relation to an application under s 9 of the Act under which the court can extend the property available to the applicant to include the deceased's severable share of property in which immediately before death the deceased was a beneficial joint tenant (see pp 81–83).

2 Determination of date when representation first taken out

In considering the question when representation was first taken out, a grant limited to settled land or to trust property is to be left out of account and a grant limited to real estate or to personal estate is to be left out of account unless a grant limited to the remainder of the estate has previously been made or is made at the same time (s 23). A grant of letters of administration *ad colligenda bona* for the purpose of preserving property forming part of the estate will not affect the running of time. However, time will run where there is a grant *durante absentia* or to an attorney administrator. In such a case the representation extends to the whole of the deceased's estate.

In *Re Johnson* [1987] CLY 3882, Latey J held that a grant of representation limited to pursuing a negligence claim arising out of a road accident in which the deceased had died was not the 'first taking out of representation'. A limited grant in 1983 had merely enabled the personal representatives to undertake a particular course of action, not to distribute the deceased's estate. Distribution could only take place after an unlimited grant in 1987 and it was from this date that time began to run under the Act. An application under the Act had been made within six months of the 1987 grant which was obviously out of time if the six month period began in 1983. Latey J indicated that even if time had begun to run in 1983 he would have exercised his discretion under s 4 to extend the time allowed for making an application.

In *Re Bidie, Bidie v General Accident Fire and Life Assurance Corporation Ltd* [1949] Ch 121 the Court of Appeal (Lord Greene MR, Somervell and Evershed LJJ) held (reversing the decision of Jenkins J [1948] Ch 697) that where letters of administration were granted and subsequently a will was found, the period of limitation ran from the later grant of probate. In reaching this decision the Court of Appeal was guided by the original wording of s 2(1) of the Act of 1938, which could only have been construed as referring to representation under a will, and Somervell and Evershed LJJ thought that it was possible than when after a will was proved a later will was discovered and proved, the period of six months would run only from the date of proof of that later will. *Re Bidie* was distinguished in *Re Miller, Miller v de Courcey* [1969] 1 WLR 583. In the latter case it was argued, in reliance on *Re Bidie*, that time ought to run from the date of a grant in solemn form and not from the date of an earlier grant in common form in the deceased's estate. Pennycuick J distinguished *Re Bidie* which he said was an entirely different case. The grant in solemn form was not a new grant and time ran from the original grant in common form.

Consistent with the dictum in *Re Bidie*, Judge Thomas (sitting as a Judge of the Chancery Division) in *Re Freeman, Weston v Freeman* [1984] 1 WLR 1419 held that where a grant of probate was revoked and then there was a grant of letters of administration on an intestacy the words 'first taken out' in s 4 must be taken as a reference to the first valid grant, in that case the grant of letters of administration. A literal reading of s 4 indicated that the period of limitation ought to run from the date of the original (now revoked) grant. That led to an absurdity. The plaintiff was perfectly satisfied with the dispositions made by the testator, yet, in order to preserve her position, she would have had to issue proceedings under the Act within six months of that grant just in case the will should (as happened) be set aside. It was necessary to construe the word 'representation' in s 4 as meaning 'effective' or 'valid' representation. His Lordship said that he took the expression 'first taken out' to be a reference to a case where there was an original valid grant followed on a subsequent date by another valid grant. Examples were to be found in cases of cessate grants or grants of double probate. In such cases the date of the original grant was the relevant date for the purpose of s 4.

3 Extension of time

The Act of 1938 (as originally enacted) did not permit the court to extend the time allowed for the making of an application. A restricted discretionary power was introduced by Sched 4 of the Act of 1952, Sched 4 (s 2 (1A) of the Act of 1938) so that where the deceased died after 31 December 1952 but before 1 January 1967 the court could extend the six-month limit where it was shown that the limitation period of six months would operate unfairly in consequence of:

(a) the discovery of a will or codicil involving a substantial change in the deceased's estate, or
(b) a question whether a person had an interest in the estate, or as to the nature of an interest in the estate, not having been determined at the time when representation was first taken out, or
(c) some other circumstance affecting the administration or distribution of the estate.

Section 5 of the Family Provision Act 1966 introduced the unfettered discretion now contained in s 4 of the Act for deaths on or after 1 January 1967. Decisions prior to that date remain of some value as indicating the circumstances in which the court will exercise its discretion. The Act gives no guidance whatever, as Sir Robert Megarry V-C pointed out in *Re Salmon, Coard v National Westminster Bank Ltd* [1981] Ch 167 (at 173). There is no reported decision on an application based on para (a) of s 2(1A) of the Act of 1938. It is, however, clear that the discovery of a testamentary document which does not affect the substance of the existing dispositions would provide no ground for a belated application, even under s 4 of the Act.

Re Bone, Bone v Midland Bank Ltd [1955] 1 WLR 703 is the only authority solely on para (b) of s 2(1A) of the Act of 1938. The deceased's widow issued an originating summons under the Act of 1938 which was two days out of time. Danckwerts J extended the time, exercising his discretion on the ground that the plaintiff's solicitors had been kept waiting by the executor's solicitors, who had led them to suppose that a construction summons would be issued. His Lordship was satisfied that it was on the whole a case where it would be a hardship if the time were not extended.

However, the plaintiff could have made an application under the Act of 1938 and had it adjourned pending a decision on the construction summons. While it seems likely that *Re Bone* would be followed today it is clear that the precautionary step of issuing a summons under the Act should be taken even where a construction summons is being taken out and in spite of the wider discretion now possessed by the court. This is underlined by *Re Miller, Miller v de Courcey* [1969] 1 WLR 583 (see p 101) where an extension of time under s 2(1A) of the Act of 1938 was refused. The plaintiff sought revocation of a grant of probate in common form made on 24 May 1963 on the basis that the deceased lacked testamentary capacity. The grant was pronounced for in solemn form on 14 November 1967. Only after the grant in solemn form did the plaintiff make an application under the Act of 1938. Pennycuick J found there had been no new grant after that in common form and 24 May 1963 was the date on which representation was first taken out. The learned judge further refused to extend the limitation period. The currency of the probate action did not cause the limitation period to act unfairly as the plaintiff could have made an application under the Act of 1938 irrespective of that action.

Para (c) of s 2(1A) of the Act of 1938 created problems. The wide discretion available under s 4 now renders these problems redundant but the case law under para (c) provides some useful illustrations. *Re Greaves, Greaves v Greaves* [1954] 1 WLR 760 is the earliest case. Roxburgh J dismissed the application taking the view that although circumstances existed which did affect the administration or distribution of the deceased's estate, the limitation period did not operate unfairly as a result of those circumstances. The plaintiff did not know the true value of the estate; negotiations with the defendants, who were both executors and beneficiaries, for a compromise had been suspended but not ended when, eight months after probate, the summons was issued, and the estate had not been distributed. Possibly the case would have been decided differently today. It was distinguished both in *Re Bone* and in *Re McNare, McNare v McNare* [1964] 1 WLR 1255. In the latter case Ungoed-Thomas J held that the period should be extended because the fact that the plaintiff widow lacked information of the true value of the testator's estate and that her solicitors were in negotiation with the executor were circumstances affecting the distribution of the estate and matters in consequence of which the limitation period would operate fairly. *Re McNare* was itself distinguished by Russell LJ (sitting as an additional judge of the

Chancery Division) in *Re Kay, Kay v West* [1965] 1 WLR 1463, where the application was only one day too late, due to the plaintiff's solicitors overlooking the time limit and postal delays; but the decision turned on the narrow limits of para (c). His Lordship, having drawn attention to the fact that, had the application been made under the Matrimonial Causes (Property and Maintenance) Act 1958 the court could have extended the limit, said that the double standard (then in existence) in relation to spouses and former spouses was undesirable. This indicates that his Lordship would have extended the time had he thought it open to him to do so, and that the case would have been decided differently today.

Re Hodgkinson, Hodgkinson v Jones [1967] Ch 634 (Note) (CAT (Civil) 27 May 1957) was not cited in *Re McNare* or *Re Kay*. The plaintiff knew that the testator, her husband, whom she had not seen for many years, had died but believed he had no estate and did not apply until she was sent an advertisement asking for creditors of his estate. The Court of Appeal, dismissing an appeal from Vaisey J (*The Times*, 26 October 1956), refused to extend the time limit. Partial distribution had taken place, the plaintiff knew that the testator had died and her erroneous beliefs had no effect on the administration or distribution of the deceased's estate. *Re Hodgkinson* was applied and *Re McNare* not followed by the Court of Appeal (reversing the decision of Cross J) in *Re Bluston, Bluston v Davis* [1967] Ch 615. The testator gave the net income arising from certain property to his widow, the plaintiff, for her life, and the executors told her that the income from the property was 'in the region of £1,000 to £1,100 per annum'. This estimate made no allowance for tax, and when, after the expiration of the time limit the plaintiff learned this, she sought an extension, alleging that she had been misled. The Court of Appeal held that her erroneous belief that 'net income' meant income remaining after payment of tax was not a 'circumstance affecting the administration or distribution of the estate' and dismissed the application. In *Re John, John v John* (1966) 111 SJ 15, however, the plaintiff, the widow of the testator, relied on promises which her step-children made to her as to the provision which they would make for her. Those promises were broken and Cross J extended the time limit. The learned judge regarded the promises, on which the applicant had acted, as a circumstance affecting the administration of the estate.

In *Re Trott, Trott v Miles* [1958] 1 WLR 604 a summons was issued on behalf of a daughter who was *en ventre sa mère* at the date of the testator's death. She was born within six months of probate, but the summons was not issued until after the six month period had expired. Upjohn J ordered that the time within which the summons might be issued should be extended so as to make it valid, holding that the daughter's birth was itself a circumstance affecting the administration of the estate.

Turning to the Act, the court's discretion under s 4 of the Act is not restricted. In *Re Salmon*, Sir Robert Megarry V-C identified six points which should guide the court in exercising its discretion under s 4, while disclaiming any intention to lay down principles and emphasising that he was far from saying that the six considerations which he stated were exhaustive, for plainly they were not.

The first point is that the discretion of the court is unfettered. No restrictions or requirements of any kind are laid down in the Act. It follows that, as Ungoed-Thomas J said (at 93) in *Re Ruttie, Ruttie v Saul* [1970] 1 WLR 89, the discretion is plainly one which is to be exercised judicially, and in accordance with what is just and proper.

Secondly, the onus lies on the applicant to establish sufficient grounds for taking the case out of the general rule, and depriving those who are protected by it of its benefits. That consideration, too, derives from *Re Ruttie*. The time limit is a substantive provision laid down by the Act itself, and is not a mere procedural time limit imposed by rules of court which will be treated with the indulgence appropriate to procedural rules. The burden on the applicant is thus no triviality: the applicant must make out a substantial case for it being just and proper for the court to exercise its statutory discretion to extend the time. In *Re Ruttie* Ungoed-Thomas J in allowing an extension of time where the application was out of time by some six weeks, bore in mind that there had been negotiations for a settlement, and an inquiry into the question whether the plaintiff had the benefit of community of property (she and her deceased husband having had and retained Polish nationality), that the plaintiff had been ill, that there had been no distribution of the estate, and that there had been no hardship to the defendant, except what was inevitably involved in any extension of time, namely, the loss of the advantage which a rigid time limit would give to the defendant, a loss inevitably contemplated by the Act by giving a discretion for the extension of time at all.

Thirdly, it must be material to consider how promptly and in what circumstances the applicant has sought the permission of the court after the time limit has expired. The learned Vice-Chancellor said that this is not, of course, a crude matter of simply looking at the length of time which has been allowed to elapse. It was not a mere matter of comparing, for instance, the six weeks of *Re Ruttie* with the two and a half years of *Re Gonin, Gonin v Garmeson* [1977] 2 All ER 720, in which Walton J refused to extend the time when the only real suggestion why time should be extended was that the plaintiff alleged that her solicitors had given her the wrong advice. The learned judge took the view that the plaintiff was to blame for a large part of the delay before the making of an application. It was contended that there would be no prejudice to the defendants if time were to be extended; but Walton J said that it was always prejudicial to anybody not to receive money which they were due to receive at the earliest possible moment (at 736). Sir Robert Megarry V-C in *Re Salmon* said that the whole of the circumstances must be looked at, and not least the reasons for the delay, and also the promptitude with which, by letter before action or otherwise, the claimant gave warning to the defendants of the proposed application. Thus if the warning was given within time but for some good reason the proceedings were not commenced until a short while after time had run, his Lordship would expect the applicant's task to be relatively simple. Where there has been some error or oversight, an obvious question is whether the applicant has done all that was reasonably possible to put matters right promptly, and kept the defendants informed.

Fourthly, it is obviously material whether or not negotiations have been commenced within the time limit; for it they have, and time has run out while they are proceeding, this is likely to encourage the court to extend the time. Negotiations commenced after the time limit might also aid the applicant, at any rate if the defendants have not taken the point that time has expired. The Vice-Chancellor said that if while time is running out one negotiates with a claimant on a basis which accepts liability but disputes quantum, one must not be surprised if the court refuses to allow one to rely on the expiry of time, or if, having power to extend the time, the court exercises it.

Fifthly, it is relevant to consider whether or not the estate has been distributed before a claim under the Act has been made or notified. The end of the six month period marks a change from a period when any distribution by the personal representatives is made at their own risk (s 20(1)) to a period where there is some statutory protection for a distribution. The learned Vice-Chancellor pointed out that so far as the beneficiaries are concerned, there will usually be a real psychological change when the estate is distributed. Before the distribution they would have only the expectation of payment; and if they are entitled to a share of residue, they will often have a considerable degree of uncertainty as to the amount. After the distribution, they have the money itself, and know the exact amount. If an order is made under the Act, money already distributed can if necessary be recovered (see s 20(1)). From the beneficiaries' point of view there is a difference between receiving in due course less than they had hoped to receive, and having something which they have already received and regarded as their own taken away from them. In addition, beneficiaries are more likely to have changed their position in reliance on the benefaction if they have actually received it than if it lies merely in prospect. If it is always prejudicial to beneficiaries not to receive money which they are entitled to receive at the earliest possible moment, it is likely to be even more prejudicial to have taken away from them money which they have actually received and begun to enjoy.

Sixthly, it is relevant to consider whether a refusal to extend the time would leave the claimant without redress against anybody. In *Re Gonin* Walton J considered the possibility that the plaintiff might sue her solicitors in negligence if in fact it was due to their faulty advice that her claim was not made in time. In *Re Salmon* Sir Robert Megarry V-C said that, although the subject matter was different, there seemed to him to be considerable force in the approach to be found in the line of cases associated with *Allen v Sir Alfred McAlpine & Sons Ltd* [1968] 2 QB 229, on dismissing actions for want of prosecution. Even if the plaintiff personally is completely blameless, the delays of his or her solicitors must be treated as the delays of the plaintiff, though injustice to the plaintiff will often be avoided by the existence of the plaintiff's right to sue the solicitors for negligence (*ibid*, at 256–257, per Diplock LJ). The learned Vice-Chancellor said that there might appear to be some logical difficulty in making the decision whether the defendants should escape liability under the Act depend in any degree on whether the responsibility for the delay was that of the plaintiff personally or was that of the plaintiff's solicitors: the liability of the defendants, it might be said, ought not to depend upon the distribution of fault between the plaintiff and his or her solicitors. Nevertheless, however logic might affect the defendants' position, there was a real and plain difference to a plaintiff between having a claim against his or her solicitors instead of against the defendants, and having no claim against anybody. It is thought, however, that the relevance of negligence by the applicant's solicitors must be approached with caution as it was said in the Court of Appeal in *Adams v Schofield* (1981) CLY 504 (CAT (Civil) 22 July 1981) that it was wrong in principle to attach decisive importance to the fact that the plaintiff will have a claim against his solicitors and see *Birkett v James* [1978] AC 297.

On the facts of *Re Salmon* an extension of time was refused. The delay was substantial: it was some four and a half months before the executor was warned of the proceedings and a further month expired before they were commenced. The fault was wholly on the plaintiff's side and there were no extraneous factors over which she had no control. The explanations of the delay were inadequate and insubstantial. The plaintiff's solicitors had failed to act promptly even when they realised that they would have to seek an extension or warn the executor that they intended to do so. There were no negotiations either within or out of time. Nearly all the estate had been distributed during the period of delay. In the circumstances it was probable that proceedings against the solicitor for negligence lay to hand.

In *Re Dennis, Dennis v Lloyds Bank Ltd* [1981] 2 All ER 140 Browne-Wilkinson J held that on an application for leave to issue proceedings out of time the court, in deciding whether to extend the time limit, was entitled to consider (by analogy with applications for summary judgment, RSC Ord 14 and CCR Ord 14, r 9) whether the applicant would have an arguable case in the proceedings. His Lordship found that the plaintiff son's claim was bound to fail as it was not a proper claim for maintenance, and part of the delay in the making of an application was unexplained and refused to extend the time limit. However, in the more recent case of *Polackova v Sobolewski* (CAT (Civil) 28 October 1985) the Court of Appeal refused the defendant's appeal against an order extending the time within which a former spouse could make a claim. The delay of three and a quarter months was admittedly not significant, there had been no distribution and the appellate court said that if the former spouse established the facts as set out in her supporting affidavit she would have an arguable case and she ought therefore to be able to make an application. Again, in *Clifford v Tanner* (CAT (Civil) No 616 of 1986) the Court of Appeal allowed the plaintiff former spouse's appeal against a refusal to extend the time within which she could apply for provision to be made for her. The court found that if the plaintiff could establish the facts presented in her supporting affidavit she would have an arguable case under s 10 of the Act and an extension of time to cover the seven-month delay outside the six-month time limit was ordered. In *Re Longley, Longley and Longley v Longley* [1981] CLY 2885 Blackett-Ord V-C refused to extend the time limit because the claim was formulated 14 months after the expiration of the time limit and there was a good claim in negligence against the plaintiff's solicitors.

Smith v Loosely (CAT (Civil) 18 June 1986) was a clear case for the grant of an extension of time under s 4. The plaintiff widow's application was one and a half months out of time and the accepted explanation was that she was financially unsophisticated and had failed for some time to fully appreciate the consequences of her deceased husband's will which gave her an interest for life in the whole of his estate. However, prompt action was taken once she had instructed solicitors, there had been no distribution and it was not challenged that she had an arguable claim. The court here once more emphasised that the discretion available under s 4 is entirely unfettered and is not in the nature of a series of hurdles to be successfully negotiated by an applicant. This approach was adopted in *Stock v Brown* [1994] 1 FLR 840. The plaintiff widow's application was five years and five months out of time. On death the deceased had left his wife a life interest in the whole of his estate, namely, the matrimonial home and certain investments. The deceased's nephews and nieces and certain charities were interested in remainder. None of the latter opposed the plaintiff's application or sought to make an appearance in the proceedings. The deputy district judge in granting leave to apply out of time relied on the fact that there had been no capital distribution and no prejudice was caused to those interested in remainder by the delay in the making of the application (which was admittedly meritorious) under the Act. Further, the plaintiff had not received any independent legal advice at the relevant time. On appeal from the deputy district judge (an appeal by way of a rehearing) His Honour Judge Thorpe, dismissing the appeal, placed weight on the fact that the application was necessitated by the dramatic interest rate fall in 1992, a matter entirely beyond the plaintiff's control. The plaintiff's income had dropped from between £8,000 to £9,000 per annum to £4,101 per annum.

Although there was a long delay in *Stock v Brown* the plaintiff had a meritorious claim under the Act and had not received advice to this effect until a later date. No distribution had taken place, no prejudice would be suffered by those interested in remainder and the application only became necessary due to factors beyond the plaintiff's control. In these exceptional circumstances leave was given. In *Re Escritt* (1982) 3 FLR 280 on the other hand legal advice was received and ignored within the limitation period and therefore leave to apply out of time was refused).

It seems likely that the court would be more ready to exercise its discretion under s 4 of the Act in favour of minors and other persons not *sui juris* since failure to issue a summons within the normal time would not be the fault of the potential applicant and if the time were not extended they would suffer hardship through no fault of their own. Sometimes (as in *Re Franks, Franks v Franks* [1948] Ch 62) no immediate provision is required for a minor; but if there is likely to be a future need a summons should be issued without delay.

4 Application before grant

In *Re Searle, Searle v Siems* [1949] Ch 73 Roxburgh J held that an application was not invalidated by reason of the originating summons having been issued prior to the date of probate; inasmuch as it was made within six months after the date of probate, it satisfied the requirements of s 2(1) of the Act of 1938 (see now s 4 of the Act). An application had been made to set aside the proceedings under the Act of 1938 for irregularity due to the fact that the summons was issued prior to a grant of representation. The learned judge said that to do so would offend the rules of natural justice as the plaintiff was now out of time to commence fresh proceedings (there being no discretion at that time to extend the six-month time limit). Further, the learned judge considered that s 2(1) (as originally enacted) was designed to stop late applications and no consideration had been given to the possibility of early applications. As stated, s 2(1) of the Act of 1938 originally contained no discretion for extension of the six-month time limit and importantly, there was no procedural requirement at that time that the grant of representation be exhibited with the supporting affidavit (see now RSC Ord 99, r 3). Production of the grant of representation was only required at the hearing of the summons.

It is now essential for a grant of representation in a deceased's estate to have been obtained before an application under the Act is made if the application is not be set aside for irregularity: *Re McBroom* [1992] 2 FLR 49. In *Re McBroom* the applicant was the son of the deceased. The deceased had died in a car accident with his younger partner. The deceased and his partner had two assets in their joint names, a property and cash in a building society account. The younger partner was deemed (by operation of the law of survivorship) to have survived the deceased and the property and cash therefore formed part of her estate. Letters of administration in her estate had been granted but there had been no grant in the deceased's estate. The son applied for reasonable financial provision to be made for him from the estate of his deceased father and for an order under s 9 of the Act to facilitate the making of that provision. Eastham J considered the provisions of ss 4 and 9 of the Act and the terms of s 19 requiring a memorandum of any order under the Act to be endorsed on or permanently annexed to the grant of representation in the estate. Reference was also made to RSC Ord 99, rr 3 and 7 (Appendix III). The former rule provides that an official copy of the grant of representation in the deceased's estate be exhibited to the applicant's supporting affidavit thereby implying that a grant must exist at the commencement of proceedings.

It is submitted that *McBroom* was correctly decided (see *G Harrap and M Allardice* (1993) 137 SJ 41 for a different view and *Dawkins v Judd* [1986] 2 FLR 360 for a case prior to *McBroom* where no grant of representation to an insolvent estate had been made but a successful application under s 10 of the Act was made; no point seems to have been taken on the lack of a grant) but advisers ought to be aware that leave was given in the case for an appeal to the Court of Appeal and no decision has yet been released. Although not cited or referred to in *McBroom*, *Re Searle* is no longer to be regarded as correctly stating the law.

5 Protection for personal representatives after expiry of time limit

Section 20(1) of the Act protects personal representatives who distribute any part of the estate after the six-month period has expired and no application under the Act has been made. The personal representatives are not rendered liable for having distributed any part of the estate of the deceased after the expiration of six months from representation first being taken out on the ground that they ought to have taken into account the possibility that the court might permit an application under the Act after the end of that period, or, where an order has been made under s 2, that the court might exercise its powers of variation conferred by s 6. This provision is without prejudice to any power to recover any part of the estate so distributed by virtue of the making of an order under the Act: that is to say, the equitable right to follow trust assets is preserved.

6 Grant of representation to proposed applicant

Section 116 of the Supreme Court Act 1981 gives the High Court a discretionary power to appoint administrators of a deceased's estate. In granting administration, it shall have regard to the rights of all persons interested in the deceased's estate or the proceeds of sale thereof, and the object of this provision is to allow a person otherwise entitled to a grant to be passed over where it is considered expedient. Surprisingly, the Act, unlike its predecessors, does not deem the applicants referred to in s 1 to be persons interested in the estate of the deceased; but there seems to be no doubt that, as an applicant clearly is so interested, a grant can be made to him. There has never been any requirement that the deceased's executors shall be cited or requested to prove before a potential applicant is allowed to take out a grant under this section. Where there is no person either entitled or willing to apply for a grant the Official Solicitor has agreed to consider acting on a request being made.

In *Re F* ((1965) *The Times*, 26 February) an application under s 3 of the Matrimonial Causes (Property and Maintenance) Act 1958, Cumming-Bruce J revoked a grant of letters of administration with the will annexed which had been made to the testator's widow and, pursuant to s 162 of the Supreme Court of Judicature (Consolidation) Act 1925 (as amended, now s 116) appointed as administrators one solicitor from the firm acting for the applicant, the testator's former wife, and one from the firm representing the widow.

Chapter 6

Interim Orders

1 The statutory provision

Where, on an application for an order under s 2 of the Act, it appears to the court

(a) that the applicant is in immediate need of financial assistance, but it is not yet possible to determine what order (if any) should be made under s 2, and

(b) that property forming part of the net estate of the deceased is or can be made available to meet the needs of the applicant,

s 5(1) of the Act, enables the court to order that, subject to such conditions or restrictions, if any, as the court may impose and to any further order of the court, there shall be paid to the applicant out of the deceased's net estate such sum or sums and (if more than one) at such intervals as the court thinks reasonable; and the court may order that, subject to the provisions of the Act, such payments are to be made until such date as the court may specify, not being later than the date on which the court either makes an order under s 2 or decides not to exercise its powers under that section.

While subs (1) of s 5 is in wide terms, it does restrict the orders that the court can make to an order for periodical payments or an order for payment of a lump sum: 'such sum or sums and (if more than one) at such intervals as the court thinks reasonable'. The court will usually make a periodical payments order, as referred to in para (a) of s 2(1), but it might sometimes find it proper to order a lump sum payment, as permitted by para (b).

Subsection (2) of s 5 provides that subs (2), (3) and (4) of s 2 shall apply to an order under s 5 as they apply to an order under s 2 (see pp 83–87).

Subs (2) and (3) of s 2 contain provisions relevant to the making of periodical payments orders under s 2(1)(a) including the setting aside or appropriation of such part of the deceased's net estate as will generate sufficient income to satisfy the payments ordered (s 2(3)). Subs (4) of s 2 provides for the making of such consequential and supplemental provisions as may be necessary or expedient for giving effect to the order made or securing its fair operation.

Subsection (3) of s 5 requires the court, in determining what order, if any, should be made under the section, to have regard, so far as the urgency of the case permits, to the same matters as those to which it is required to have regard under s 3 (see Chapter 3).

Importantly, by subs (4) of s 5, an order made under s 2 may provide that any sum paid to the applicant by virtue of s 5 shall be treated to such an extent and in such manner as may be provided by that order as having been paid on account of any payment provided for by that order. The amount of any interim order can therefore be deducted from the final order and as a matter of practice this is the usual course.

Section 19 (2) of the Act provides that an order for periodical payments made under s 5 in favour of (a) an applicant who was the former spouse of the deceased, or (b) the spouse of the deceased in a case where the marriage with the deceased was the subject of a decree of judicial separation and at the death the decree was in force and the separation continuing, shall cease to have effect on the applicant's remarriage, except in relation to any arrears due under the order on the date of the remarriage.

Section 20(2) of the Act provides that a personal representative who pays any sum directed by an interim order under s 5 shall not be under any liability by reason of the estate not being sufficient to make the payment, unless at the time of making the payment he has reasonable cause to believe that the estate is not sufficient. In that case, of course, it will have been his duty to inform the court to this effect at the time of the making of the application. The existence of a reasonable cause to believe and of the belief founded upon it is ultimately a question of fact to be tried on evidence, and the grounds on which a person acts must be sufficient to induce in a reasonable person the required belief: *IRC v Rossminster Ltd* [1980] AC 954 per Lord Wilberforce at 1000 and per Lord Diplock at 1011.

2 Practice

The power to order interim provision was introduced as a result of *Re Ferrar's Application, Ferrar v Roberts* [1966] P 126 and Lord Denning's dissenting judgement therein (see Conroy, 'Interim Orders and Family Provision' [1994] 24 Fam Law 26). In parliamentary debate on the introduction of the power, Viscount Colville of Culross said:

> We want the interim power to deal with an emergency situation, in circumstances where it obviously will not do any appreciable harm to the bulk of an estate (HL Vol 276 (1967) at col 13).

It was stated then and later emphasised that the power to order interim provision was particularly valuable where, for example, a widow needed money to live on or to pay rent or satisfy mortgage repayments (see HL Vol 276 (1967) at col 11 and Law Com No 61, para 147). Although the example of a widow is commonly used, all categories of applicant under the Act can apply for interim provision. If they are to do so they must, of course, first establish that they are within one of the categories contained in s 1(1) of the Act. This will usually be straightforward but does mean that an applicant who claims to have been maintained by the deceased (s 1(1)(e)) will first have to satisfy the court as to that state of affairs.

Once the court is satisfied that the applicant is within the Act, that applicant must satisfy the three requirements of s 5. Firstly, the applicant must show that at the date of the hearing of their interim provision application they are in 'immediate need' of financial assistance (s 5(1)(a)). An applicant is in immediate need when their need is most pressing or urgent. In the case of *Re Ralphs, Ralphs v District Bank Ltd* [1968] 2 WLR 1522 the testator, who died in April 1965, by his will and codicil bequeathed £3,000 and the income from £12,000 to his daughter, the income of £8,000 to his widow, and the residue to his son. The widow made an application under the Act of 1938 and interim provision approximately equal to the income she was to receive from the deceased's estate in any event was ordered on 18 July 1967: *Re Ralphs* (1967) *The Times*, 19 July. When the substantive application came on for hearing on 25 June 1968 it emerged that the widow and the daughter had suffered hardship prior to the order for interim provision. The widow had been forced to resort to borrowing from the bank and the daughter, who had a dependent child, to state assistance. There had clearly been 'immediate need'. In *Barnsley v Ward* (CAT (Civil) No 19 of

1980), the applicant claimed to have been maintained by the deceased. She was found to be in 'immediate need' of financial assistance and periodical payments of £53 per week were ordered to be paid to her until judgment of further order. The applicant was unemployed and had an income shortfall of £53 per week. She was unable to satisfy the mortgage repayments on the property in which she lived which formed part of the deceased's net estate.

Secondly, the applicant must show that property forming part of the deceased's net estate is or can be made available to meet their needs (s 5(1)(b)). Property is available if it is cash in the net estate of the deceased or if it is readily saleable property. In *Re Ralphs* the income from a legacy bequeathed to the applicant (in any event) was available. In *Barnsley v Ward* the deceased had a half share valued at £35,000 in property which was let and subject to a rent review. This property was available to meet the applicant's needs.

Finally, the applicant must show the court that it is right in all the circumstances of the case for the court to exercise its discretion and make an order in the manner sought. The court must have regard, so far as it is able, to the matters listed in s 3 of the Act (see Chapter 3) and to the fact that if an interim order is made, its 'whole purpose . . . is to hold the situation as reasonably and fairly as possible pending final determination': *Barnsley v Ward* per Ormrod LJ.

A deceased's personal representatives ought to consider the position of a needy beneficiary. In *Re Ralphs* the executors had made no payments to the widow and the daughter in respect of their benefits under the will until ordered to do so. In withholding benefits the executor had been influenced by *Re Simson, Simson v National Provincial Bank Ltd* [1950] Ch 38, in which Vaisey J had said that an executor should make no distribution to beneficiaries while proceedings under the Act of 1938 were pending, or while there was any possibility or expectation of such proceedings. Cross J said in *Re Ralphs* (at 1525) (after consulting with the other Chancery judges) that in the great majority of cases where some benefit was given to the applicant by the will there could be no good reason for withholding it pending the substantive hearing. The executors should form their own view as to the payments which could properly be made and, if necessary, ask beneficiaries who might be affected for their consent, and, if that were withheld, an application could be made to the court for leave to make the payments in question. The court, if it thought the withholding of the consent unreasonable, could throw the costs of the application on the party to blame. An applicant who receives some benefit from the deceased's estate, but seeks further provision by an application under s 2, should first request the executor to make some payment to them pending the hearing of their application under s 2. An application under s 5 should be made only if the necessary consents are not forthcoming.

In *Barnsley v Ward* the Court of Appeal on an appeal from an order under s 5 made by Vinelott J deprecated appeals from orders under the section.

3 Procedure and Legal Aid

Proceedings under the Act can be brought in the High Court or county court and the relevant provisions and the advantages of each jurisdiction are discussed elsewhere (Chapters 2 and 9). There is no need for an applicant to specifically request interim relief in their originating summons or originating application. The facts supporting such a claim should, however, be set out in the supporting affidavit or within the body of the originating application. In the High Court the application for interim relief can be made on notice in accordance with RSC Ord 32 and in the county court on notice in accordance with CCR Ord 13, r 1. Applications under s 5 do not have to be heard in chambers but the vast majority are.

The statutory charge created by s 16(6) of the Legal Aid Act 1988 does not apply to any sum or sums ordered to be paid under s 5 (see the Civil Legal Aid (General) Regulations 1989 (SI 1989 No 339), reg 94(b)).

Chapter 7

Statutory Prevention of Evasion

Sections 10, 11, 12 and 13 of the Act provide a means of circumventing actions taken by the deceased during his or her lifetime with a view to avoiding claims under the Act which might be made after his or her death. Prior to the Act a person could defeat or at least prejudice rights of his dependants after his death by two types of transactions effected by him whilst he was yet alive: he might dispose of his property elsewhere, and he might make a contract to leave the property elsewhere in his will as happened in *Schaefer v Schuhmann* [1972] AC 572, an appeal to the Privy Council from the Supreme Court of New South Wales in a matter arising under the Testator's Family Maintenance and Guardianship of Infants Act 1916–1954 (New South Wales).

The principal objection to legislation to prevent transactions designed to defeat family provision must it is thought be the uncertainty introduced into *inter vivos* transactions, coupled with the difficulty in the case of a deceased person of producing evidence of an intention to defeat the claims of members of his family. The donee who may have accepted a gift quite innocently may later find it impeached; though there must be cases in which the donee ought to be suspicious of the donor's intentions. When considering the problem, the Law Commission, while recognising the difficulties, found it to be a matter of overriding importance to ensure that the laws relating to family provision were effective (Law Com No 61, para 191), and the Act gives effect to the measures which the Law Commission recommended. The case for reform was supported by the fact that s 37 of the Matrimonial Causes Act 1973 empowers the court to avoid transactions made with the intention of defeating a claim for financial provision in the analogous case of matrimonial proceedings. There is the further point that the very existence of measures to prevent a person from defeating family provision by dispositions in his lifetime is likely to discourage a testator from acting to his dependant's prejudice.

1 Section 10: Inter vivos dispositions

Section 10 of the Act is concerned with dispositions made during the deceased's lifetime other than for full valuable consideration, principally gifts and 'sales' at an undervalue. The approach to the problem of dispositions *inter vivos* differs from the approach adopted in s 37 of the Matrimonial Causes Act 1973, which simply empowers the court to set aside dispositions made with the intention of defeating a claim to financial relief under that Act. The general principle now established and contained in s 10 of the Act is that a person who receives property from the deceased during his lifetime may, in certain circumstances, be required by the court to provide money or property from which a claim for such provision can be satisfied.

It is a pre-requisite to a claim against a donee that there should be an application to the court under s 2 (s 10(1)). Section 10 is not available where the court has before it an application under s 6 to vary or discharge an order for periodical payments made under s 2(1)(a) (see s 6(9)).

Section 10(2) provides that where on an application under subs (1) the court is satisfied:

(a) that, less than six years before the date of the death of the deceased, the deceased with the intention of defeating an application for financial provision under the Act made a disposition, and
(b) that full valuable consideration for that disposition was not given by the donee or by any other person, and
(c) that the exercise of the powers conferred by s 10 would facilitate the making of financial provision for the applicant,

then (subject to the provisions of s 10 itself (see especially s 10(6)) and of ss 12 and 13) the court may order the donee (whether or not at the date of the order he holds any interest in the property disposed of to him or for his benefit by the deceased) to provide, for the purpose of the making of that financial provision, such sum of money or other property as may be specified in the order. As to the condition that, before an order under subs (2) can be made, there must have been a disposition by the deceased with the intention of defeating an application under the Act, it is provided by s 12(1) that the condition shall be fulfilled if the court is of the opinion that, on a balance of probabilities, the intention of the deceased (though not necessarily his sole intention) in making the disposition was to prevent such an order being made or to reduce the amount of the provision which might otherwise be granted by such an order. In *Re Kennedy, Kennedy v The Official Solicitor to the Supreme Court* [1980] CLY 2820 Judge Willis held in the Shoreditch County Court that it was not essential to show that the deceased had the existence of the provisions of the Act present to his mind when the impugned transaction was made, but there must be evidence that the deceased intended to defeat a claim made after his death against his estate. It seems that the standard of proof used in fraud cases is irrelevant (cf s 37(2)(a) of the Matrimonial Causes Act 1973 and see *K v K* ((1982) *The Times*, 16 February)).

The approach to be adopted on an application under s 10 is apparent from the judgment of Bush J in *Re Dawkins, Dawkins v Judd* [1986] 2 FLR 360. In that case the applicant, who was the widow of the deceased, applied for an order that the defendant, the daughter of the deceased by his first marriage, should pay to the applicant part of the proceeds of sale of the former matrimonial home which had been transferred to the defendant by the deceased for the sum of £100 in May 1981. The deceased died in July 1982 and there was no other estate out of which provision for the widow could be made. Bush J considered that the first matter he had to decide was whether provision for the widow would have been ordered had there been no disposition of the matrimonial home prior to the death of the deceased. It being largely conceded by the defendant that the court would have made such provision Bush J then went on to consider whether the defendant should be ordered to provide the proceeds of sale of the matrimonial home for the purpose of making provision for the widow. The question which Bush J (at 366) considered that he had to answer was 'On balance is it my opinion that when the husband sold [the matrimonial home] to the defendant for £100 he did so with the intention, though not necessarily the sole intention, of preventing an order for financial provision being made under the Act, or reducing the amount of the provision which might otherwise have been granted?' and he answered this question in the affirmative. Finally Bush J considered whether he should therefore make an order that the defendant provide money for the purposes of making provision for the widow and concluded having regard to s 10(6) of the Act (see p 122), which lays down certain matters to which the court is to have regard, that the widow should receive £10,000 and the funeral expenses out of the proceeds of sale of £27,000.

'Disposition' in subs (2) of s 10 does not include (a) any provision in a will, any such nomination as is mentioned in s 8(1) or any *donatio mortis causa*, or (b) any appointment of property made, otherwise than by will, in the exercise of a special power of appointment, but, subject to these exceptions, includes any payment of money (including the payment of a premium under a policy of assurance) and any conveyance, assurance, appointment or gift of property of any description, whether made by an instrument or otherwise (subs (7)). Paragraph (a) of s 10(7) has to be read in the context of the definition of 'net estate' in s 25(1): any property disposed of by will (otherwise than in exercise of a special power of appointment), property subject to nomination by the deceased (s 8(1)) and *donationes mortis causa* (see s 8(2)) are within the definition of 'net estate', and for this reason do not fall to be included within the definition of 'disposition' in s 10(7). 'Valuable consideration' does not include marriage or a promise of marriage (s 25(1)).

The court's power is unaffected by a subsequent disposal of the relevant property or of any interest in it by the donee. However, where the disposition is made by the deceased to any person as a trustee the powers of the court to order that trustee to provide a sum of money or other property is subject to the limitation that the amount of any sum of money or the value of any property ordered to be provided:

(i) in the case of an application in respect of a disposition which consisted of a payment of money, shall not exceed the aggregate of so much of that money as is at the date of the order in the hands of the trustee and the value at that date of any property which represents that money or is derived therefrom and is at that date in the hands of the trustee;

(ii) in the case of an application in respect of a disposition which consisted of the transfer of property (other than a sum of money), shall not exceed the aggregate of the value at the date of the order of so much of that property as is at that date in the hands of the trustee and the value at that date of any property which represents the first-mentioned property or is derived therefrom and is at that date in the hands of the trustee (see s 13(1)).

Furthermore, where an application is made in respect of a disposition made to any person as a trustee, the trustee is not liable for having distributed any money or other property on the ground that he ought to have taken into account the possibility that an application under s 10 would be made (13(2)). Section 13(3) enables the court to exercise its powers under s 10 against the persons who are the trustees for the time being, even though they were not the original trustees, but affords to them also the protection given by s 13(1) and (2).

Subsection (2)(a) of s 10 limits the power of the court to re-open dispositions made by the deceased to those made within the period of six years before the death. There is a further limitation in s 10(8), which provides that the section shall not apply to any disposition made before the commencement of the Act on 1 April 1976 (s 27(3)).

The power of the court under s 10 is a discretionary power, though the court is required by subs (6), in determining whether and in what manner to exercise its powers, to have regard to the circumstances in which any disposition was made and any valuable consideration which was given therefor, the relationship, if any, of the donee to the deceased, the conduct and financial resources of the donee and all the other circumstances of the case. The amount which a donee of money may be ordered to pay or the value of any property which he may be ordered to transfer is limited by subs (3) to the amount of the payment made by the deceased after deducting therefrom any inheritance tax borne by the donee in respect of that payment; and the amount which a donee of property other than money may be asked to pay or transfer is limited by subs (4) to the value at the date of the death of the deceased of the property disposed of by him to or for the benefit of the donee, or if that property has been disposed of by the donee or (as provided by s 12(4)) by the donee's personal representative, the value at the date of that disposal, after deducting in any case any inheritance tax borne by the donee in respect of the transfer of that property by the deceased. See also as to the inheritance tax consequences s 146 of the Inheritance Tax 1984 and pp 130–132.

The Law Commission recognised that once an application has been made for the review of a disposition made by the deceased, a situation may arise in the proceedings in which the applicant or applicants for provision or the donee under the transaction which is being challenged may wish to challenge some other disposition which the deceased has made, and accordingly recommended that the court should, at the instance of any such party, have power to review such other dispositions (Law Com No 61, paras 216–217). Effect is given to this recommendation by s 10(5) which provides that where an application is made for an order under subs (2), then, if on an application by the donee or by any applicant for an order under s 2 the court is satisfied:

(a) that, less than six years before the date of the death of the deceased, the deceased with the intention of defeating an application for financial provision under the Act made a disposition other than the disposition which is the subject of the original application; and
(b) that full valuable consideration for that other disposition was not given by the person to whom or for the benefit of whom that other disposition was made or by any other person,

the court (after consideration of the matters referred to in s 10(6)) may exercise in relation to the person to whom or for the benefit of whom that other disposition was made the powers which it would have had under subs (2) if the original application had been made in respect of that other disposition and it had been satisfied as to the matters set out in paras (a), (b) and (c) of that subsection; and it is provided that, where any application is made under subs (5), any reference in s 10 (except in subs (2)(b)) to the donee is to include a reference to the person to whom or for the benefit of whom that other disposition was made.

By virtue of s 12(4) references to the donee include the personal representative of the donee, but the court has no power to make an order in respect of any property forming part of the estate of the donee which has been distributed by the personal representative; and the personal representative is not liable for having distributed any such property before he has notice of the making of an application under s 10 on the ground that he ought to have taken into account the possibility that such an application would be made.

Where the court makes an order under s 10 it may give such consequential directions as it thinks fit (including directions requiring the making of any payment or the transfer of any property) for giving effect to the order or for securing a fair adjustment of the rights of the persons affected thereby (s 12(3)).

2 Section 11: Contracts to leave property by will

Section 11 of the Act is concerned with contracts to leave property by will other than for full valuable consideration. In considering the question of such contracts the Law Commission thought that a distinction should be drawn between a contract where the intention of the promisor was to defeat a claim for family provision and a contract to leave property by will where there was no such intention. In the latter case the Law Commission could see no ground for giving the court power to interfere (Law Com No 61, para 226).

Section 11 of the Act gives effect to the Law Commission's recommendations (Law Com 61, paras 227–232). Provided that there is in existence an application to the court under s 2, the applicant may apply to the court under s 11(1) for an order under s 11(2). To make an order under subs (2), the court must be satisfied:

(a) that the deceased made a contract by which he agreed to leave by his will a sum of money or other property to any person or by which he agreed that a sum of money or other property would be paid or transferred to any person out of his estate;

(b) that the deceased made that contract with the intention of defeating an application for financial provisions under the Act;

(c) that when the contract was made, full valuable consideration for that contract was not given or promised by the person with whom or for the benefit of whom the contract was made (who is referred to in s 11 as 'the donee') or by any other person; and

(d) that the exercise of the powers conferred by s 11 would facilitate the making of financial provision for the applicant.

Then, if so satisfied, and subject to the provisions of the section (see especially s 11(4)) and ss 12 and 13, the court may make any one or more of the following orders, that is to say:

(i) if any money has been paid or any other property has been transferred to or for the benefit of the donee in accordance with the contract, an order directing the donee to provide, for the purpose of the making of that financial provision, such sum of money or other property as may be specified in the order;

(ii) if the money or all the money has not been paid or the property or all the property has not been transferred in accordance with the contract, an order directing the personal representatives not to make any payment or transfer any property, or not to make any further payment or transfer any further property, as the case may be, in accordance therewith or directing the personal representatives only to make such payment or transfer such property as may be specified in the order.

There is no power to make an application under subs (1) on an application under s 6 to vary or discharge the original order under s 2 (s 6(9)).

The Act contains no definitions of 'a contract' and therefore the question arises as to whether a promise made by the deceased to leave property by will on which the promisee has relied to his detriment, thereby giving rise to a proprietary estoppel as in, for example, *Re Basham* [1986] 1 WLR 1498, could fall within s 11, assuming all other conditions are satisfied. In some cases the estoppel will give rise to an immediate disposition of an interest in property prior to the death of the deceased and those cases will presumably fall within s 10 of the Act. However, where s 10 does not apply such an agreement does not give rise to an enforceable contract in the usual meaning of that term. Having regard to the fact that the Act does contemplate the possibility of a contract for which no valuable consideration has been given (s 12(2)) it may be arguable that 'contract' within the meaning of s 11 of the Act includes any enforceable promise to leave property by will.

As in the case of an application under s 10, so also in the case of an application under s 11, the court must be satisfied as to the deceased's intention to defeat an order for financial provision under the Act and s 12(1) again applies: that is to say, the condition shall be fulfilled if the court is of the opinion that, on a balance of probabilities, the intention of the deceased (though not necessarily his sole intention) in making the contract was to prevent an order being made under the Act or to reduce the amount of the provision which might otherwise be granted by an order thereunder. However, it is provided by s 12(2) that where an application is made under s 11 with respect to any contract made by the deceased and no valuable consideration was given or promised by any person for that contract then it shall be presumed, unless the contrary is shown, that the deceased made that contract with the intention of defeating an application for financial provision under the Act. 'Valuable consideration' does not include marriage or a promise of marriage (s 25(1)). It will be observed that s 11(2) covers both a contract to leave money or other property by will and a contract that money will be paid or property transferred out of the deceased's estate.

A limitation is imposed by s 11(3) which provides that, notwithstanding anything in subs (2), the court may exercise its power thereunder in relation to any contract made by the deceased only to the extent that the court considers that the amount of any sum paid or to be paid or the value of any property transferred or to be transferred in accordance with the contract exceeds the value of any valuable consideration given or to be given for that contract, and for this purpose the court has to have regard to the value of property at the date of the hearing.

The court's powers are discretionary and in determining whether and in what manner to exercise its powers it must have regard to the circumstances in which the contract was made, the relationship, if any, of the donee to the deceased, the conduct and financial resources of the donee and all the other circumstances of the case (s 11(4)). Section 11(5) provides that where the court makes an order under subs (2) in relation to any contract, the rights of any person to enforce that contract or to recover damages or to obtain other relief for the breach thereof shall be subject to any adjustment made by the court under s 12(3) and such right shall survive to such extent only as is consistent with giving effect to the terms of the order. As in the case of an order under s 10, so also in the case of an order under s 11, s 12(3) provides that the court may give such consequential directions as it thinks fit (including directions requiring the making of any payment or the transfer of any property) for giving effect to the order or for securing a fair adjustment of the rights of the persons affected thereby.

Section 12(4) provides that the review of the contract may be instituted or continued against the estate of a deceased donee or promisee; but in such a case the court does not have power to make an order in respect of any property forming part of the estate of the donee which has been distributed by the personal representative; and the personal representative is not liable for having distributed any such property before he has notice of the making of an application under s 11 on the ground that he ought to have taken into account the possibility that such an application would be made.

Section 11(6) provides that the provisions of this section do not apply to a contract made before the commencement of the Act on 1 April 1976 (s 27(3)). (Cf the similar limitation in the case of s 10.) On the other hand, in contrast to s 10, apart from this the date of the contract is immaterial in the sense that it is subject to the provisions of the section however long before the date of the death of the deceased it was made. In this respect the power of the court under s 11 to re-open transactions is wider than its corresponding power under s 10. The reason for this is that the Law Commission took the view (Law Com No 61, para 237) that whereas in the case of a disposition *inter vivos* the donor was immediately divesting himself of property and this must in most cases have a restraining effect upon him, in the case of contracts to dispose of property by will there was no similar disincentive, because the deceased remained in full enjoyment of his property during his lifetime. It followed that any rule rendering such contracts immune from challenge if made more than a specified period before death might be a positive encouragement to make them.

As in the case of dispositions *inter vivos*, so in the case of contracts to dispose of property by will, protection is given to trustees by s 13. Section 13(1) provides that where an application is made for an order under s 11 in respect of any payment made or property transferred, in accordance with a contract made by the deceased, to any person as a trustee, the powers of the court to order the trustee to provide a sum of money or other property shall be subject to the limitation that the amount of any sum of money or value of any property ordered to be provided:

(i) in the case of an application in respect of the payment of money in accordance with a contract, shall not exceed the aggregate of so much of that money as is at the date of the order in the hands of the trustee and the value at that date of any property which represents that money or is derived therefrom and is at that date in the hands of the trustee;

(ii) in the case of an application in respect of the transfer of property (other than a sum of money) in accordance with the contract, shall not exceed the aggregate of the value at the date of the order of so much of that property as is at that date in the hands of the trustee and the value at that date of any property which represents the first-mentioned property or is derived therefrom and is at that date in the hands of the trustee.

Where an application is made in respect of any payment made or property transferred in pursuance of a contract to any person as a trustee, the trustee is not to be liable for having distributed any money or other property on the ground that he ought to have taken account of the possibility that such an application would be made (s 13(2)). Section 13(3) enables the court to exercise its powers under s 11 against the persons who are the trustees for the time being, even though these were not the original trustees, but affords to them also the protection given by s 13(1) and (2).

Section 20(3) is supplemental to s 11. It protects a personal representative who has reason to believe that the deceased has entered into a contract to leave property by his will with the intention of defeating an application for financial provision by enabling the personal representative to postpone completion of the contract until the expiration of six months from the date on which representation to the estate is first taken out, or, if during that period an application is made under s 2, until the determination of the proceedings on that application. Without this protection the personal representative might be bound to perform the contract within the six months period.

Chapter 8

The Final Order

1 The form of the order

It is important that the order, whether made following a full hearing or in normal or in Tomlin form (where the terms of the compromise are set out in a schedule to the order and do not form part of the order itself) on a compromise, contains not only the actual award made but also all necessary and consequential directions including such variations, if any, as are to be read into the will, or how the intestacy rules are to be varied, or how any ante- or post- nuptial settlement is to be varied under s 2(1)(f) as the case may be. This is important from the point of view of inheritance tax, particularly having regard to the exemption accorded to a transfer to a spouse domiciled in the United Kingdom (see the Inheritance Tax Act 1984, s 18). Express directions are also important for regulating the incidence of the order on the beneficiaries. *Re Simson, Simson v National Provincial Bank Ltd* [1950] Ch 38 (see p 96) shows that where a will is varied it is not necessarily fair that the whole burden of the order should fall upon the residuary legatee; it may be fair for it to fall rateably on all the beneficiaries receiving pecuniary legacies (see also *Re Bunning, Bunning v Salmon* [1984] Ch 480 (p 56) and *Re Preston, Preston v Hogarth* [1961] 1 WLR 317 (p 97)). The order may be complicated to work out; the court may have to give effect to such principles as those laid down in *Re Cottrell, Buckland v Bedingfield* [1910] 1 Ch 402 on the abatement of annuities, and in *Re Earl of Chesterfield's Trusts* (1883) 24 Ch D 643 on the respective rights of the tenant for life and remainderman.

In drafting the form of the order consideration must be given (a) to the tax consequences of the order (as to which see below) and (b) to whether any Legal Aid charge will bite and, if so, whether provision should be made for monies to be paid to the solicitor for the applicant in accordance with reg 87 of the Civil Legal Aid (General) Regulations 1989 (SI 1989 No 339). Under reg 94 of those Regulations as amended by the Civil Legal Aid (General Amendment) (No 2) Regulations 1991 (SI 1991 No 2036) the first £2,500 of any money or of the value of any property recovered or preserved by virtue of an order made under s 2 or s 6 of the Act or deemed to have been made under those sections is free from the statutory charge. It is therefore important that any order makes it clear that it is made under the Act or where there is a compromise that the terms of the compromise are such that they could have been made under the Act. Where any monies recovered for the applicant or preserved for a defendant who is an assisted person for the purposes of legal aid are under the order, or the terms of any compromise, to be used for the purpose of purchasing a home for that person or his dependants this should be made clear as this will assist the assisted person in obtaining postponement or enforcement of the Legal Aid charge under reg 96 of the Civil Legal Aid (General Regulations) 1989 as amended by the Civil Legal Aid (General Amendment) (No 3) Regulations 1991 (SI 1991 No 2784). See also reg 97 which provides in similar terms where a house is recovered or preserved to provide a home for the applicant.

2 Effect for purposes of taxation

It is of course impractical to consider all possible tax consequences of orders which could be made under the Act in a book of this nature. The aim of this section is to draw attention to the principal points which arise and to put practitioners on notice of some of the possible tax consequences of an order under the Act. In the case of orders which are not entirely straightforward special consideration must be given to the tax position and in complicated cases involving substantial amounts of money expert tax advice should be obtained. The taking of such advice before the final terms of the order are settled may lead to substantial tax savings.

Section 19(1) of the Act specifically states that for inheritance tax purposes the will or the law relating to intestacy as the case may be shall take effect and be deemed to have had effect from the date of the deceased's death subject to the provisions of the order. This is reiterated in s 146(1) of the Inheritance Tax Act 1984. By s 146(8) of that Act the same applies to an order in the Tomlin form but only in so far as the terms of the settlement could have been included in an order made under s 2. Thus, if the terms set out in the schedule provide for the variation of a settlement other than an ante-nuptial or post-nuptial settlement falling within s 2(1)(f) the fact that such variation is being effected as part of the compromise of proceedings under the Act will have no bearing on the tax consequences and the order will take effect for inheritance tax purposes from the date of the order and not from the date of the deceased's death.

The inheritance tax position on orders which provide for the payment of lump sums or for the settlement or transfer of property in terms expressed to take effect from the deceased's death is straightforward: the dispositions made by the deceased's will or on an intestacy are treated as if they had included the award made by the order and inheritance tax may be refunded or further tax paid accordingly. The position in respect of periodic payments or settlements or variation of settlements which are expressed in the order only to take effect from the date of the order may give rise to more difficulty. Section 146(6) of the Inheritance Tax Act 1984 will prevent any charge to inheritance tax in respect of anything done in compliance with an order under the Act or which occurs on the coming into force of such an order which would give rise to a charge to tax under Part III of that Act (taxation of settled property), other than s 79, or s 52(1) (termination of a life interest during the lifetime of the person entitled) but there will be situations where this does not apply, eg where the order provides (or has the same effect in practice) for the original beneficiary to take the income of the residuary estate to the date of the order and for the applicant to take the income thereafter. In some cases the order may have no effect on the taxation of the deceased's estate on his death but may have tax consequences at the date of the order for the beneficiaries or the trustees of the will or any settlement varied by the order or terms of compromise.

Where an order is made under s 10 of the Act (see Chapter 7) requiring a person to whom the deceased made a disposition prior to his death to make available property for the purposes of an order under the Act, s 146(2) of the Inheritance Tax Act 1984 provides for that property to be treated as property in the estate of the deceased at his death for inheritance tax purposes and for an adjustment in respect of any inheritance tax paid in respect of the original disposition.

Attention is drawn to s 29A of the Inheritance Tax Act 1984 which contains an anti-avoidance provision. This section applies in relation to deaths occurring after 26 July 1989 where a claim (of any type) is made against the deceased's estate. If that claim is satisfied by a beneficiary making a disposition of property which did not form part of the deceased's estate for inheritance tax purposes at his death and that beneficiary was entitled to property under the deceased's will or intestacy which was exempt for inheritance tax purposes under ss 18 and 23–28 of the Inheritance Tax Act 1984, for example, where the beneficiary was the surviving spouse of the deceased (s 18) or was a charity (s 23), then s 29A(2) provides for the tax payable on the deceased's death to be reassessed as if the value of the property transferred in satisfaction of the claim was attributed to a non-exempt gift made by the deceased and not to the exempt gift to the beneficiary. This section would apply for example where the estate passes under the will to the surviving spouse of the deceased and is therefore exempt under s 18 of the Inheritance Tax Act 1984 and a claim is made under the Act by a child of the deceased. Instead of the claim being satisfied by a payment out of the estate which might give rise to a charge to tax on the deceased's death the spouse transfers property to the child out of his or her own estate making use of the potentially exempt transfer provisions (Inheritance Tax Act 1984, s 3). Under s 29A the Inland Revenue can treat the payment to the child as being made out of the deceased's estate on his death and tax it accordingly.

The capital gains tax and income tax legislation contain no special provisions referring to the Act and therefore s 19(1) of the Act is the only statutory provision governing the incidence of tax. Where a compromise is effected within two years of the death of the deceased which is not the subject of an order under the Act it may be possible to rely upon s 62(6) of the Taxation of Chargeable Gains Act 1992.

3 Enforcement

In *Re Pointer, Shonfield v Edwards* [1946] Ch 324 Wynn-Parry J having referred to s 3(1) of the Act of 1938 (the predecessor of s 19(1) of the Act) said (at 326):

> The reference to the enactments relating to death duties shows that [s 3] proceeds on the footing that the provision made by the order is to be treated as a legacy. In my judgment the scheme of the Act [of 1938] involves first, that, assuming the necessary conditions obtain, the court may by order make provision for the defendant applying to it; secondly, if it makes such an order the provision made thereby is to be treated for all purposes as a legacy; and thirdly, the will is for all

purposes to have effect as if that legacy had been contained in it when it was made.

See also *Berkeley v Berkeley* [1946] AC 555, which Wynn-Parry J followed.

Wynn-Parry J's dictum was applied by the Court of Appeal in *Re Jennery, Jennery v Jennery* [1967] Ch 280. An order for payment of a lump sum of £600 had been made by Cross J on 6 July 1964, but no payment had been made under the order by the personal representatives, who were also the beneficiaries under the will. Dismissing an appeal from an order of Stamp J who had dismissed the widow's notice of motion for a four-day order, the Court of Appeal held that the widow's right established by the order for payment out of the testator's estate had no greater effect than to make her the equivalent of a beneficiary under the will and bore no resemblance to an order for payment (see RSC Ord 45, r 1) which could be the subject of a four-day order. The proper procedure was an action for administration of the estate.

However, s 19 of the Act is not in an identical form to s 3(1) of the Act of 1938. In particular the latter section provided that where an order was made under the Act of 1938 the will or the law relating to intestacy or both, as the case might be, should take effect and should be deemed to have had effect from the date of the deceased's death 'subject to such variations as may be specified in the order for the purpose of giving effect to the provision for maintenance thereby made'. It therefore appeared to be envisaged that the terms of the will or the provisions of the Administration of Estates Act 1925 would be varied and that the administration of the estate would proceed on that basis. Section 19 of the Act provides that where an order is made then for all purposes the will relating to intestacy or both, as the case may be, shall have effect and be deemed to have had effect as from the deceased's death 'subject to the provisions of the order'. It is therefore arguable that for the purposes of enforcement there is no reason why the terms of the order should not be enforced in the normal manner so that, for example, an order that a lump sum should be paid within a particular period should be capable of being enforced in one of the ways provided by RSC Ord 45, r 1.

4 Miscellaneous

In earlier editions of this Book it was suggested that s 19 of the Act might cause problems where an order was made in favour of a person or the spouse of a person who had witnessed the will and in whose favour a gift in the will would therefore have been void by reason of s 15 of the Wills Act 1837. The present editors consider that even had that been the case under s 3(1) of the Act of 1938, it is not the case under s 19. Similarly, the present editors do not consider that in a case where the deceased died intestate or without appointing executors and letters of administration are granted to one administrator alone the making of provision for a minor or the creation of a life interest in any part of the estate by an order under the Act will give rise to any difficulties with regard to the fact that had such provision been contained in the will letters of administration would not have been granted to less than two individuals. In such circumstances it may be sensible to ensure that a second trustee is appointed but there is no requirement to that effect.

Chapter 9

Practice on Application for Provision

1 Which court?

There are three possible venues for commencing an application under the Act: the Chancery Division of the High Court, the Family Division of the High Court and the county court.

From 1984 until 1991 the county court jurisdiction in respect of applications under the Act was limited to cases where it was shown to the satisfaction of the court that the net estate of the deceased at the date of death was less than the 'county court limit'. As the 'county court limit' for this purpose was set at £30,000 from 1 December 1981 the number of cases falling within the county court jurisdiction in recent years has been limited. However, s 25 of the County Courts Act 1984 which governs the jurisdiction of the county court under the Act was amended by the High Court and County Courts Jurisdiction Order 1991 (SI 1991 No 724) so as to give the county court jurisdiction in relation to applications under the Act limited only by the provisions as to the general jurisdiction of the county court. Those provisions are to be found in the High Court and County Courts Jurisdiction Order 1991 (SI 1991 No 724) as amended. The effect of art 4 of that Order is that applications under the Act can now be commenced in whichever of the Chancery Division, Family Division or county court is considered most convenient in all the circumstances. However, there are new rules as to where the application ought to be tried as opposed to commenced and, having regard to the practical difficulties in relation to delay and lost files which can arise where a case is transferred from one jurisdiction to the other, it appears sensible to try to commence proceedings in the jurisdiction in which it is likely to be tried, all other things being equal.

Article 7 of that Order deals with the allocation of place of trial and provides that where proceedings have a 'quantifiable value' which is less than £25,000 the proceedings should be tried in the county court unless transferred to the High Court or commenced in the High Court and the High Court considers that it ought to try the action. Similarly, proceedings with a 'quantifiable value' exceeding £50,000 ought to be tried in the High Court unless commenced in the county court which considers that it should not be transferred or commenced in the High Court which considers that it ought to be tried in the county court. Although it is not stated it is presumed that actions with a 'quantifiable value' between £25,000 and £50,000 should be tried in the court in which they are commenced.

Two issues arise from this which are of importance when considering where an application under the Act should be commenced. First, does an application under the Act have a 'quantifiable value' and, secondly, what criteria will be applied by the court in deciding whether or not to transfer the matter to another court?

The quantifiable value of an action is dealt with in art 9 of the Order which provides that the value of an action for a sum of money, whether specified or not, is the amount which the applicant reasonably expects to recover and an action which is for specified relief other than a sum of money has a value equal to the amount of money which the applicant could reasonably state to be the financial worth of the claim to him. Where the action in whole or in part has no financial worth to the applicant it has no quantifiable value. As an application under the Act is for financial provision to be made for the applicant, even if the order sought is to secure accommodation for the applicant, it appears reasonable to assume that most applications under the Act will have a quantifiable value and those advising on quantum of claims will have to consider the likely outcome of the proceedings in deciding where the application ought to be tried. It is important to note that the value of the estate as a whole is no longer the criteria but the value of the application to the applicant. Thus, the deceased may have left a large estate but the county court may still be the most appropriate trial venue if the realistic value of the applicant's claim is low.

Order 99, r 11 of the Rules of the Supreme Court which previously dealt with transfers to the county court in cases under the Act was repealed in 1992 and the general rules as to transfer therefore apply. Transfers from the High Court to the county court and vice versa are now governed by ss 40, 41 and 42 of the County Courts Act 1984 (as substituted by s 2(1) of the Courts and Legal

Services Act 1990). The criteria to be applied by the court when deciding whether or not to order a transfer are set out in art 7(5) of the Order and are:

(a) the financial substance of the action;
(b) whether the action is otherwise important and, in particular, whether it raises questions of importance to persons other than the parties or questions of general public interest;
(c) the complexity of the facts, legal issues, remedies or procedures involved; and
(d) whether the transfer is likely to result in a more speedy trial of the action (but no order can be made on this ground alone).

The other considerations likely to affect the initial choice of starting place are the consequent place of trial (county court applications must be commenced in the court for the area in which the deceased was resident at the date of death which may not be convenient for the parties) and whether there are any concurrent applications, eg for declarations as to beneficial interests in property, which are the subject of separate proceedings and are outside the county court jurisdiction.

Attention is drawn to Practice Direction: Chancery Division (24) which provides that on the summons for directions the Master should consider whether the case is suitable for transfer to a county court under s 40 of the County Courts Act 1984 and states that, inter alia, applications under the Act will normally be considered suitable for transfer unless they raise any important question of law or fact. Cases will normally be transferred to the Mayor's and City of London Court (which now operates a separate chancery section) unless the parties specifically request otherwise.

Where an application is transferred from the county court to the High Court the order must state whether it is desired that the proceedings be assigned to the Chancery Division or the Family Division (CCR Ord 48 r 9 as amended by the County Court (Amendment No 2) Rules 1983 (SI 1983 No 1716) and the County Court (Amendment) Rules 1992 (SI 1992 No 793)).

2 Applications in High Court

The practice in the High Court is regulated by RSC Ord 99, as substituted by Rules of the Supreme Court (Amendment) 1976 (SI 1976 No 337) and operative from 1 April 1976. The old Ord 99 and r 103 of the Matrimonial Causes Rules 1973 remain in force as appropriate in respect of deaths before that date, but are not here considered: by now they can probably be considered to be obsolete. The new Ord 99 made some fundamental changes in practice, to which attention is drawn in *Practice Note* (*Inheritance: Family Provision*) [1976] 1 WLR 418, issued by the Chief Chancery Master and the Senior Registrar of the Family Division jointly. This Note was not included in the 1993 edition of the Rules of the Supreme Court but still provides valuable guidance.

The most noticeable feature of Ord 99 is that it assigns applications in the High Court to the Chancery Division or to the Family Division (r 2) and provides a code of procedure common to both Divisions. Proceedings are begun by originating summons which may be issued out of Chancery Chambers the principal registry of the Family Division or any district registry of the High Court (r 3(1)). This leaves it to the plaintiff to decide upon both Division and venue (subject always to the power of the court subsequently to give directions as to venue, if it thinks that the case can more conveniently be tried at a place different from that selected by the plaintiff (Ord 25, r 3)). An action is assigned to a division by the issue of proceedings therein: *Saunders v Beevor* [1971] 1 WLR 383. Where the applicant is a spouse or former spouse it seems that the Family Division will generally be the appropriate Division in which to proceed and this may also be the case with a minor child. In other cases the Chancery Division may be preferable and this will be so in any case in which the taking of accounts is necessary since special facilities for doing this exist in that Division. Under Ord 99, proceedings in the Chancery Division may be issued in any district registry and not only in the Chancery District Registries (Birmingham, Bristol, Cardiff, Leeds, Liverpool, Manchester, Newcastle-upon-Tyne and Preston). However, where an application is issued in the Chancery Division in a district registry which is not a Chancery District Registry attention is directed to Practice Direction: Chancery Division (9B) which sets out the practice where it is desired that the trial should be held other than in London or a Chancery District Registry.

The originating summons should follow Form No 10 in Appendix A to the Rules of the Supreme Court. In the event of separate applications in the same estate being made by separate plaintiffs in different courts, it appears that the best course is for the personal representatives (who will have been made defendants) to apply for consolidation and for transfer to a suitable venue, or for the applications to be heard together.

Under the former law, where there were two or more claimants whose interests conflicted, difficulties arose as to the presentation of their claims since two or more plaintiffs could not be separately represented by counsel at the hearing. On the other hand, the Act of 1938 required that the application should be 'by or on behalf of' the dependant, and it was, therefore, not possible for one claimant to initiate the proceedings, making the other claimant a defendant. Accordingly, all claimants whose interests were in conflict had to be made plaintiffs and an application had then to be made to strike out one or more of them as plaintiffs and to add them as defendants (see *Practice Note* [1954] 1 WLR 778, where the appropriate form of order will be found). Every such defendant had then to enter appearance by a solicitor other than the plaintiff's solicitor. It appears that that practice may still properly be followed, and the old form of order used (if necessary together with an order for consolidation), but r 6 of Ord 99 introduced an entirely new concept by providing that where an application under the Act is made jointly by two or more applicants and the originating summons is accordingly issued by one solicitor on behalf of all of them, they may, if they have conflicting interests, appear on any hearing of the summons by separate solicitors or counsel or in person, and where at any stage of the proceedings it appears to the court that one of the applicants is not, but ought to be, separately represented, the court may adjourn the proceedings until he is.

This practice is of most use where separate applications are made by closely connected persons such as a widow and her minor child who may initially consult the same firm of solicitors. In other cases separate sets of proceedings are likely to be commenced, followed by an order that they should be heard at the same time or one immediately following the other.

Order 80 of the Rules of the Supreme Court applies to applications under the Act by or against minors and patients as it does to other High Court matters. Thus, an application on behalf of a minor or patient must be made by his or her next friend and a defendant who is a minor or patient must act by a guardian ad litem. At the time proceedings are commenced an applicant may be unaware that a defendant beneficiary is a minor or patient but the position should become clear when the personal representative files his or her affidavit under Ord 99, r 5.

The personal representatives and all beneficiaries (whether specific, general or pecuniary legatees or specific devisees or residuary legatees) whose interests may be affected by the application should be made parties: *Re Lidington* [1940] WN 279 and *Re Simson* [1950] Ch 38. Except in small estates or where the bulk of the estate is distributed in the form of small pecuniary legacies, specific and pecuniary legatees are less likely to be affected by the application and can be omitted. Where there is any doubt as to who should be joined the best practice is probably to commence proceedings solely against the personal representatives and consider which beneficiaries should be joined at the first hearing of the summons. Without prejudice to its powers under Ord 15, the court may at any stage of proceedings under the Act direct that any person be added as a party to the proceedings or that notice of the proceedings be served on any person (Ord 99, r 4(1)). If the beneficiaries are numerous and their interests apparently identical or they cannot be found or ascertained the originating summons can ask for a representation order under Ord 15, r 13 which applies specifically to applications under the Act (Ord 99, r 4(2)). However, as the court has jurisdiction to apportion the burden of any award which may be made between the various beneficiaries (see *Re Preston, Preston v Hogarth* [1969] 1 WLR 317 and pp 95–98) this course is probably not suitable where beneficiaries who receive substantial amounts under the deceased's will or intestacy may be in very different financial circumstances. An alternative course is to serve notice on beneficiaries under Ord 15, r 13A of the Rules of the Supreme Court on the basis that an application under the Act is an action relating to the estate of a deceased person. Where such a notice has been served it is up to the beneficiary to decide whether or not he or she wishes to take part in the proceedings and file an acknowledgement of service accordingly.

The position where a compromise is proposed and all beneficiaries affected are not parties to the action is dealt with on p 150.

Re Blight, Blight v Westminster Bank Ltd (1949) 96 LJ News 233 illustrates the necessity of having all interested parties before the court. The testator made provision in his will for the maintenance of his son, mentally handicapped, 42 years of age, who was living in an institution. The testator's daughter applied for maintenance under the Act of 1938, and the son was not made a party to the proceedings. Vaisey J held that he could not reach a decision which would affect the property and income of the son while the son was not present before the court. He accordingly referred the case back to chambers to join the son as defendant and to obtain further evidence (by letter from the authorities) as to what extra comforts could be obtained for the patient if funds were available, and whether the patient was able to enjoy any extra comforts if provided.

Ord 99, r 3(3) requires that there shall be lodged with the court an affidavit by the applicant in support of the summons, exhibiting an official copy of the grant of representation to the deceased's estate and of every testamentary document admitted to proof, and that a copy of the affidavit shall be served on every defendant with the summons. All affidavits must comply with Practice Direction: Chancery Division 8(A). Attention is drawn in *Practice Note (Inheritance: Family Provision)* [1976] 1 WLR 418 to the importance of setting out in the applicant's affidavit particulars of any known previous proceedings relevant to the application, and it is pointed out that such proceedings will often be material to the question whether the application ought to be transferred from the Family Division to the Chancery Division or vice versa under Ord 4, r 3. Thus reference should be made to any separation order or any maintenance order made by a court of summary jurisdiction. The affidavit should set out the main story, recite the material parts of any will and exhibit such necessary documents as birth, marriage and death certificates. The affidavit should also cover all matters concerning the financial position, health etc of the applicant (which may include health, finances etc of a spouse or other dependant of the applicant) referred to in s 3 of the Act (see further Chapter 3). It may be arguable by analogy with the position under the Matrimonial Causes Act 1973 that an applicant under the Act is under a duty of full disclosure and that failure to make full disclosure may therefore be a ground for appeal, including an application to set aside a consent order made by way of compromise. Where the plaintiff is a former spouse, a copy of the decree showing what monetary provisions have been made must be exhibited. If there is any question as to the deceased's domicile (see p 4), evidence should be adduced to show that he died domiciled in England and Wales. Any relevant memoranda left by a testator giving his reasons for his dispositions should be exhibited.

Order 99, r 5(1) provides that a defendant to an application under s 1 who is a personal representative of the deceased shall and any other defendant may, within 21 days after service of the summons on him, inclusive of the day of service, lodge with the court an affidavit in answer to the application. Rule 5(2) provides that the personal representative in his affidavit shall state to the best of his ability:

(a) full particulars of the deceased's net estate, as defined by s 25(1) of the Act;
(b) the person or classes of person beneficially interested in the estate, giving the names and (in the case of those who are not already parties) addresses of all living beneficiaries, and the value of their interests so far as ascertained;
(c) if such be the case, that any living beneficiary (naming him) is a minor or a patient within the meaning of Ord 80, r 1; and
(d) any facts known to the defendant which might affect the exercise of the court's powers under the Act.

A defendant's personal representative who is also a beneficiary is not, however, obliged to disclose particulars of his own means. It is the right of a citizen to keep private the details of his means (*Morgan v Morgan* [1977] Fam 122) and only in the rarest of cases should be a stranger to a *lis* be ordered to swear an affidavit (*Wynne v Wynne and Jeffers* [1980] 3 All ER 659). The combined effect of s 3(1)(c) of the Act (see p 26) and r 5(2)(d) is not sufficient to impose on a personal representative who is also a beneficiary a duty of disclosure from which had he not been a personal representative he would undoubtedly have been protected: *Re Clark, Clark v Clark* [1981] CLY 2884, a decision of Hollings J at Winchester Crown Court. Where a defendant who is a beneficiary chooses not to give evidence of his or her financial situation the court will assume that the beneficiary is sufficiently comfortable not to require the funds made available under the will or intestacy of the deceased.

Rule 5(3) provides that every defendant who lodges an affidavit shall at the same time serve a copy on the plaintiff and on every other defendant who is not represented by the same solicitor. In *Re Simson, Simson v National Provincial Bank Ltd* [1950] Ch 38, Vaisey J said that in a case where there were obvious complications and doubts, it was the duty of the executors to provide an informative affidavit telling the court what was known to them, and what it was necessary for the court to know in order to deal properly with the matter. In *Practice Note* (*Inheritance: Family Provision*) [1976] 1 WLR 418, however, it is pointed out that r 5(2)(d) makes it clear that it is only facts known to the deponent which have to be stated in the affidavit of a personal representative, and that he is obviously not obliged to make inquiries and investigations in order to ascertain or confirm other matters within the 21 days after service of the summons; nor is he required to set out facts (possibly distasteful) which are not necessarily relevant at that stage: if they become relevant later he may lodge a further affidavit. Bearing in mind ss 8–13 of the Act, however, the burden placed upon personal representatives is a heavy one.

Where all beneficiaries whose interest in the estate may be affected by the application have been joined or have been notified of the application and indicated that they do not wish to be joined, any personal representative who is not beneficially interested should adopt a neutral stance while giving such assistance to the court as he or she is able. If at any stage a beneficiary who may be affected has not been joined or notified of the application it will be proper for the personal representatives to bring that to the court's attention and in the meantime to act so as to protect that beneficiary's interest. Where all beneficiaries who may be affected have been joined or notified and the estate is relatively small consideration should be given to applying for leave to the personal representatives not to be represented at the hearing but simply to put in a supplementary affidavit as to the assets and liabilities of the estate immediately prior to the date of the hearing. If the applicant does not object and there is no other conflict of interest the personal representatives and the beneficiaries may in some cases be represented by the same solicitors and counsel.

Although the evidence in the High Court is given on affidavit the court has power to order the cross-examination of any deponent under RSC Ord 38, r 2 and if such an order is made and the deponent does not attend for cross-examination his affidavit cannot be used in the proceedings without leave of the court. It is usual for an order for cross-examination to be made on the first hearing of the originating summons and it is particularly important for such an order to be made where there is a conflict of evidence, eg as to the applicant's means or relationship with the deceased. Where there is such a conflict judges hearing applications under the Act have been known to comment unfavourably where no order for cross-examination has been made and no cross-examination takes place.

If the plaintiff seeks the exercise of the court's discretion under s 4 of the Act when the application is out of time, this should be asked for as a separate head of relief in the originating summons and the grounds on which the court's leave to entertain the application is sought should be included in the supporting affidavit (*Practice Note* (*Inheritance: Family Provision*) [1976] 1 WLR 418). If the failure to issue within time is the result of an oversight by the applicant's solicitor he or she should swear an affidavit as to the circumstances. If the summons is issued before the plaintiff realises that it is out of time, he should apply to amend the summons so as to ask for the court's permission to bring the application out of time as the first item of the summons: *Re Greaves, Greaves v Greaves* [1954] 1 WLR 760. The application for such permission is made after the service of the summons and filing of acknowledgement of services.

A plaintiff who desires interim relief under s 5 (see Chapter 6) need not ask for it specifically in the originating summons. He should, however, set out his case for such relief in his supporting affidavit, if it is known that an application will be made. Otherwise the summons for interim relief should be supported by a separate affidavit setting out the relief sought and the grounds.

Under Ord 99, r 8 any proceedings under the Act may, if the court so directs, be disposed of in chambers, and it is provided that Ord 32, r 14(1) (which is concerned with the jurisdiction of masters of the Chancery Division) shall apply in relation to proceedings in the Family Division as if for the reference to the masters of the Chancery Division there were substituted a reference to a district judge of the Family Division. In *Re F* ((1985) *The Times*, 11 February) however, Balcombe J having referred to the fact that in the Chancery Division the practice was to list cases under the Act for hearing in open court, whereas in the Family Division they tended to be heard in chambers, went on to say that in that Division, too, cases should, unless the court (including a district judge at the intermediate stage) had so directed, be listed for hearing in open court. Thereafter an application could always be made to the judge, when the case began, for the hearing to be in chambers. Masters, district judges of the Principal Registry of the Family Division and district judges may hear applications and make final orders disposing of proceedings under the Act, subject to the directions of the judges. No formal directions under Ord 32, r 14(1) have been made and masters and district judges may therefore deal with either contested or uncontested applications. It is envisaged that they will exercise their discretion so as to refer to a judge any case which is likely to involve a long or complex issue of fact or law or a question of jurisdiction, unless the amount of the estate in the case is small.

Since 1982 there is no longer any right to have a matter referred to the judge either before or after it has been heard by a master or district judge of the Family Division. Any party appearing before a master or district judge who considers that a matter should be referred to a judge under Ord 32, r 12 (as applied in the case of the Chancery Division by Ord 32, r 14(3)) rather than be heard by the master or district judge should mention it before any hearing takes place and seek directions.

It is open to a master, with the consent of the parties, to try the case in open court under Ord 36, r 11; and if he does so an appeal lies to the Court of Appeal under Ord 58, r 3. If, however, there is a hearing in chambers (under Ord 32, r 14), an appeal lies to the judge under Ord 58, r 1. Though the judge or the parties may require any cross-examination on affidavits or other oral evidence to be heard again in full, in most cases this should not be necessary if a full note or transcript of evidence before the master has been made. A master hearing a case in chambers should therefore ensure, if possible, that proceedings before him are recorded by a shorthand writer or a recording instrument. If he is unable to arrange this he should take as full a note as practicable of the oral evidence before him. On any adjournment or appeal to the judge there should be sent to the judge, with the affidavits, a transcript or copy of the master's note of the oral evidence and a transcript or note of the master's judgment. No provision should be made for the attendance of witnesses at the rehearing before a judge unless a judge so directs.

Where an order has been made on an application under s 1 of the Act, any subsequent application, whether made by a party to the proceedings in which such order was made, or by any other person, must be made by an ordinary summons to be taken out in the existing proceedings (r 9), so anyone who is not already a party will have to inquire whether there are any existing proceedings and, if there are, apply to be joined in them. Any of the persons referred to in s 6(5) of the Act (see p 87–90) may make such a subsequent application as is referred to in this rule. A person desiring to apply under the rule will first have to inquire whether any proceedings are or have been in progress and, if so, apply to be joined in them.

Subsection (3) of s 19, as originally enacted, provides that a copy of every order made under the Act shall be sent to the Principal Registry of the Family Division for entry and filing, and a memorandum of the order shall be endorsed on, or permanently annexed to, the probate or letters of administration under which the estate is being administered: but the subsection has been amended by the Administration of Justice Act 1982, s 52, so as to except from it with effect from 28 October 1982 (*ibid*, s 76(9), (10)) an order made under s 15(1) of the Act. The personal representatives must produce in court at the hearing of the application the probate or letters of administration, which are to remain in the custody of the court until action has been taken as required by s 19(3) (r 7). An office copy of any order made under the Act must be sent to the Principal Registry of the Family Division to be filed and entered, whether the order is for provision under the Act, or whether the application fails and is dismissed (*Practice Note* [1941] WN 185). Every final order embodying terms of compromise made in proceedings under the Act must contain a direction that a memorandum thereof be endorsed on or permanently annexed to the probate or letters of administration; and a copy of the order must be sent to the Principal Registry of the Family Division with the relevant grant of probate or letters of administration for endorsement, notwithstanding that any particular order may not, strictly speaking, be an order under the Act (*Practice Direction*: Chancery Division 16(B)(i)). The provisions of the Family Proceedings Rules 1991 (SI 1991 No 1247) as amended relating to the drawing-up and service of orders (rr 2.43, 10.16 and 10.17) apply to proceedings in the Family Division under Ord 99 as if they were proceedings under those rules (Ord 99, r 10).

Subject to the provisions of Ord 99, the procedure on an application will be in accordance with the usual Rules of the Supreme Court governing procedure on an originating summons. The Family Proceedings Rules 1991 do not apply to applications under the Act other than as provided by Ord 99, r 10 as such applications are not proceedings which are for the time being assigned to the Family Division and no other division by or under the Supreme Court Act 1981. However, where an application has been made in the Family Division directions as to discovery etc may sometimes be given by reference to the practice under those Rules.

3 Applications in county court

Applications in the county court are largely regulated by CCR Ord 48. That Order is now set out in full in Appendix III.

Care should be taken to ensure that the application is made in the right county court (CCR Ord 48, r 3). Unlike the position in the High Court the application must be begun in a specific county court, normally the court for the area in which the deceased resided at the date of his death unless the deceased did not then reside in

England and Wales in which case it should be the court for the area in which the respondent or one of the respondents resides or carries on business or the estate or part of the estate is situated. Only if none of the foregoing apply is it permissible to begin the proceedings in the court for the area in which the applicant resides or carries on business.

The application is begun by originating application in Practice Form N423. CCR Ord 48, r 2 prescribes the information to be contained in that originating application, which is largely the same information as would be included in an affidavit on an application in the High Court (see p 141). Under r 3(2) the applicant must also file an office copy of the grant of representation and a copy of all testamentary documents admitted to proof.

Without prejudice to its powers under CCR Ords 5 and 15 (which deal respectively with parties and amendment), the court may, at any stage of the proceedings, direct that any person be added as a party to the proceedings or that notice of the proceedings be served on any person: r 4(1). Rule 4(2) applies CCR Ord 5, r 6, which empowers the court to appoint one or more persons to represent any person (including an unborn person) or class of person where that person or members of that class cannot be ascertained or found, etc.

Every respondent must, within 21 days after the service of the originating application on him, inclusive of the day of service, file in the court office an answer together with a copy thereof for every other party to the proceedings. The answer must contain a statement of the respondent's case, and where the respondent is a personal representative, must state to the best of his ability:

(a) full particulars of the value of the deceased's net estate, as defined by s 25(1) of the Act;
(b) the persons or classes of persons beneficially interested in the estate, giving the names and (in the case of those who are not already parties) the addresses of all living beneficiaries, and the value of their interests so far as ascertained;
(c) if such be the case, that any living beneficiary (naming him) is a minor or a mental patient; and
(d) any facts known to the personal representative which might effect the exercise of the court's powers under the Act: r 5.

For the role to be played by the personal representatives see p 143. The proper officer must send a copy of the answer to every other party to the proceedings: CCR Ord 9, r 18(4).

An application for an interim order under s 5 may be made by an interlocutory application served on the respondent and filed in the court not less than two clear days before the hearing in accordance with CCR Ord 13, r 1.

Rule 6 provides that where an order has been made on an application under s 1, any subsequent application, whether made by a party to the proceedings or by any other person, is to be made in those proceedings in accordance with CCR Ord 13, r 1; that is to say, it must be served on the respondent and filed in the court not less than two clear days before the hearing.

Rule 7 provides that any application may be heard and determined by the registrar and may, if the court thinks fit, be dealt with in chambers.

The personal representatives of the deceased must produce at the hearing of any application the grant of administration to the deceased's estate and, if an order is made under the Act the proper officer must send to the Principal Registry of the Family Division a sealed copy thereof, together with the grant of representation and a memorandum of the order to be endorsed on, or permanently annexed to the grant in accordance with s 19(3) (as amended, see pp 145–146) of the Act (r 8).

An application for the exercise of the court's discretion when the application is out of time is dealt with by the court before the rest of the application is considered.

The general rule in the county court is that any fact required to be proved at the hearing of an action or matter by the evidence of witnesses shall be proved by the examination of the witnesses orally and in open court (CCR Ord 20, r 4). This will therefore be the position on an application under the Act in the county court unless either the application is ordered to be dealt with in chambers under CCR Ord 48, r 7, when evidence may be given by affidavit under CCR Ord 20, r 5 (and an order for cross-examination on affidavit may be made under the same rule), or an order is made either at the trial or at an earlier hearing that the evidence may be given on affidavit under CCR Ord 20, r 6. If the matter is not to be tried wholly on affidavit evidence with cross-examination, directions as to the exchange of witness statements should be given at the pre-trial review and may be given at any other time, CCR Ord 20, r 12A. The court has a wide discretion as to the form and content and time of service of such statements. Generally witness statements should cover all matters on which it is intended the witness will give evidence in chief.

4 Appeals

The same rules apply on an appeal under the Act as in any other type of case, including the usual rules as to the admission of fresh evidence (see *Leeder v Ellis* [1952] AC 52 (a decision of the Privy Council on appeal from the High Court of Australia considering an application under the Testator's Family Maintenance and Guardianship of Infants Act 1916 (New South Wales)). On the same basis the Court of Appeal will not interfere with the exercise of discretion by the trial judge or conduct a new inquiry unless it is shown that the judge misdirected himself on law or failed to take into account relevant matters (see *Re Besterman, Besterman v Grusin* [1984] Ch 458 and *Davis v Davis* [1993] 1 FLR 54). On a number of occasions the Court of Appeal has expressed strong views as to the propriety of making appeals in cases concerning small estates (see also p 26).

5 Compromise

Applications under the Act are often compromised, either before proceedings are commenced or prior to the final hearing, and the court is often asked to embody the terms of the compromise in an order. An application involving infant or unborn beneficiaries or patients can only be compromised with the approval of the court, even where agreement is reached prior to the proceedings being commenced. Where the applicant is a minor or patient, reference should be made to Ord 80, rr 11 and 12 and CCR Ord 10, rr 10 and 11. Masters of the Chancery Division (see Practice Direction: Chancery Division (13)B(A)(i)(b)) and district judges of the Family Division have an unlimited jurisdiction to sanction a compromise under the Act on behalf of minors or patients and absent, unborn and ascertained persons.

The court only has power to make an order under s 2 of the Act if it is satisfied that the disposition of the deceased's estate under the will or intestacy failed to make reasonable financial provision for the applicant. If therefore the court is asked on a compromise to make an order under that section, as opposed to an order in the Tomlin form, sufficient evidence must be available to satisfy the court that that is the case.

Although on a compromise the parties are not confined to making provision in a form which the court could have awarded under s 2 there are occasions when the terms of the order ought to be such as could have been made by the court. This is especially the case where there may be an inheritance tax advantage of coming within s 146(8) of the Inheritance Tax Act 1984 (see pp 130–132) or where one or more of the parties is legally aided and it is desired to rely on regs 94(d)(ii), 96 or 97 of the Civil Legal Aid (General) Regulations 1989 (SI 1989 No 339) (as to which see pp 129–130).

All persons whose interest in the estate is affected by the proposed compromise must be parties to it. In this respect it is important to note that beneficiaries who are neither parties to the action nor represented under Ord 15, r 13 or CCR Ord 5, r 6 will not be bound by a consent order, even if they have been notified of the action under Ord 15, r 15A or CCR Ord 48, r 4, unless they have otherwise given their consent. A claim under the Act is primarily a claim against the individual rights of the beneficiaries and not against the estate as a whole and therefore it is not thought that the personal representatives as such have power to compromise such a claim under s 15 of the Trustee Act 1925 without reference to the beneficiaries, although they could do so with the consent of all the beneficiaries providing they are of full age and mental capacity. It is important that those representing the personal representatives satisfy themselves that in complying with the agreement the personal representatives will not be committing a breach of duty.

It is sometimes suggested that beneficiaries which are charities cannot compromise proceedings under the Act without an order of the Charity Commissioners under s 27 of the Charities Act 1993 (ex gratia payments). However, charitable trustees do have power to compromise claims properly brought against them under s 15 of the Trustee Act 1925 and this would include claims made under the Act. A claim under the Act is not a claim to an ex gratia payment.

There is as yet no authority as to appealing or setting aside a consent order in respect of an application under the Act. The normal rule is that a consent order obtains its validity from the underlying contract and will only be set aside on grounds which would invalidate that contract, eg misrepresentation. However, it has been suggested that an application under the Act has more in common with an application for ancillary relief in matrimonial proceedings and that therefore such an order can be set aside where the order was made on a fundamental assumption which proves to be incorrect, for example where the compromise is based on the assumption that the applicant will require accommodation for a substantial period and the applicant dies a short time after the making of the order (see *Barder v Caluori* sub nom *Barder v Barder* (*Caluori intervening*) [1988] AC 20).

If a compromise is effected which relies for its validity on an order of the court and the applicant dies before that order is made it is thought that the compromise will be unenforceable, following the reasoning of *Whyte v Ticehurst* [1986] Fam 64 (see p 24). The position may be different where the compromise is not dependent on an order being made.

6 Associated claims

An application under the Act may be associated with a number of other claims, eg as to the validity of a will and as to the beneficial ownership of property. It is therefore appropriate to deal shortly with the practice to be adopted in such cases.

A claim under the Act presupposes the validity of any will affecting the distribution of the deceased's estate and evidence as to the validity of the will will usually be irrelevant on an application under the Act (see *Re Blanch, Blanch v Honhold* [1967] 1 WLR 987). Where probate has been obtained but a claim for revocation is being made it is sensible to issue and, if necessary, serve proceedings under the Act within the six month time limit and apply for the application to be stayed until the probate proceedings have been determined so as to avoid the necessity of making an application under s 4 of the Act at a later stage.

In the county court a claim to a beneficial interest in property forming part of the estate can be made in the same originating application as the claim under the Act. In the High Court such claims must be commenced by separate originating process but where they are commenced in the same division and it appears that the evidence in respect of one claim will be largely the same as the evidence on the other an application may be made to hear them together or one immediately after the other. A claim to a beneficial interest in real property should be made in the Chancery Division and not in the Family Division. Where the claims are to be dealt with separately the claim under the Act should be stayed until the beneficial interest claim has been determined as until that time it will not be possible to determine the net estate for the purposes of the Act.

Any claim to payment of arrears of maintenance, as opposed to claims to vary an order for periodic payments or a maintenance agreement (as to which see Chapter 4) should be dealt with separately but must be dealt with before the application under the Act.

7 Costs

There is no invariable rule that costs of all parties to an application under the Act will be payable out of the estate. Costs in applications under the Act are in the discretion of the court which therefore has power to order the costs to be paid by any party.

A useful deterrent to the making of vexatious applications is the power of the judge to order dismissal of an application with costs (see *Re Vrint, Vrint v Swain* [1940] Ch 920; *Mastaka v Midland Bank Executor and Trustee Co Ltd* [1941] Ch 192; *Re Joslin, Joslin v Murch* [1941] Ch 200; and see *Re Catmull, Catmull v Watts* [1943] WN 71; [1943] Ch 262; *Re Watkins, Hayward v Chatterton* [1949] 1 All ER 695; *Re E, E v E* [1966] 1 WLR 709; *Re Clayton, Clayton v Howell* [1966] 1 WLR 969; *Re Fullard, Fullard v King* [1982] Fam 42; *Brill v Proud* (1984) 14 Fam Law 59). The applicant may, however, be a man of straw, and in that case the personal representative's costs will have to come out of the deceased's estate. In the High Court, personal representatives will normally be awarded costs on the indemnity basis, while other parties will, if awarded costs, be awarded them on the standard basis (Ord 62).

It has become usual practice for parties to applications under the Act to make offers to compromise the proceedings 'without prejudice save as to costs', usually referred to as offers in the *Calderbank* form after *Calderbank v Calderbank* [1976] Fam 93. Such offers are now expressly regulated by Ord 22, r 14 and CCR Ord 11, r 10. The effect of such an offer is that the court will take it into account when considering the order as to costs. However, it should be noted that in the county court the offer must first have been filed in a sealed envelope and that in both the High Court (Ord 62, r 9(1)(d)) and the county court (CCR Ord 11, proviso to r 10(2)) the offer cannot be taken into account if at the time it was made the party making the offer could have protected his position by means of a payment into court. While the estate is in the course of administration it will not be possible for any one beneficiary to make a payment in out of the estate and clearly there will be no room for a payment if the claim is for non-monetary provision. However, if the claim is formulated as a claim for a lump sum out of the estate or the offer is limited to such and the estate is no longer in the course of administration and cash is available, it may be that this course should be followed. Where the offer can be taken into account and the applicant has refused the offer and then been awarded less than the terms offered he or she may be refused costs from the date of the offer or may be ordered to pay the costs of the defendants from that date.

Appendix I

Precedents

A Originating Summons for issue in the Chancery Division asking for leave to apply out of time and for reasonable financial provision to be made
B Originating Summons asking for an order pursuant to s 9 of the Act and for reasonable financial provision to be made
C Originating Summons asking for an order pursuant to s 10 of the Act and for reasonable financial provision to be made
D Standard form of executor's affidavit pursuant to RSC Ord 99, r 5
E Summons to be heard before the Master asking for an order pursuant to s 5 of the Act
F Originating Application in the county court pursuant to CCR Ord 48 r 2 asking for reasonable financial provision to be made
G Standard form of executor's answer pursuant to CCR Ord 48, r 3

Precedent A

Originating Summons for issue in the Chancery Division asking for leave to apply out of time and reasonable financial provision[1]

IN THE HIGH COURT OF JUSTICE CH 199 [ ] X No

CHANCERY DIVISION[2]
[IN THE [ ] DISTRICT REGISTRY]

IN THE MATTER OF the estate of X deceased[3]
AND IN THE MATTER OF the Inheritance (Provision for Family and Dependants) Act 1975

BETWEEN:

AB Plaintiff

—and—

(1) CD
(2) EF
(3) GH Defendants

LET CD of [*address*] and EF of [*address*] [*executors/administrators*] of the estate of the above-named deceased ('the Deceased') and GH of [*address*] [*nature of interest under the Deceased's will or intestacy*] attend [before Master [ ] at Chancery Chambers, Room No [ ], Thomas More Building, Royal Courts of Justice, Strand, London WC2A 2LL on [ ]day the [ ] day of [ ] 199[ ] at [ ] o'clock in the [fore/after]noon] *or if in a District Registry* [before the District Judge in Chambers at the [ ] district registry of the High Court of Justice at [*address*] on [ ]day the [ ] day of [ ] 199[ ]] *or* [on a day to be fixed] on the hearing of an application by the Plaintiff AB of [*address*] for:

(1) an Order that the Plaintiff be granted leave pursuant to section 4 of the Inheritance (Provision for Family and Dependants) Act 1975 to make an application for provision under the said Act notwithstanding that a period of six calendar months from the date on which representation with regard to the estate of the Deceased was first taken out has expired;
(2) an Order pursuant to section 2 of the said Act that such reasonable financial provision as this Honourable Court thinks fit be made for the Plaintiff out of the net estate of the Deceased;
(3) further or other relief;
(4) costs.

LET each Defendant within 14 days after service of this Summons on them counting the day of service, return the accompanying Acknowledgement of Service to the appropriate Court Office.

DATED the [ ] day of [ ] 199[ ]

Note: This Summons may not be served later than 4 calendar months (*or, if leave is required to effect service out of the jurisdiction, 6 months*) beginning with the above date unless renewed by Order of the Court.

This Summons was taken out by [ ], Solicitors for the Plaintiff of [*address*]

Note: If a Defendant does not attend personally or by his counsel or solicitor at the time and place above-mentioned such order will be made as the Court may think just and expedient.

A Defendant who is a personal representative must, within 21 days after service of this Summons on such Defendant, inclusive of the day of service, lodge with the Court an affidavit in answer, stating the particulars required by Order 99, r 5 of the Rules of the Supreme Court.

Important
Directions for Acknowledgement of Service are given with the accompanying form.

[1] A copy of an affidavit complying with RSC Ord 99, r 3(3) must accompany the Originating Summons when served.
[2] If the application is to be made in the Family Division then:
(a) in the title, Family Division must be substituted for Chancery Division and 'CH' removed from the case reference;
(b) references to the Master must be replaced by 'District Judge [ ] in chambers at Somerset House, Strand, London WC2R 1LP'.
[3] RSC Ord 7, r 7(1)—(5).

Precedent B

Originating Summons asking for an order under section 9 of the Act and for reasonable financial provision[1]

IN THE HIGH COURT OF JUSTICE CH 199 [ ] X No

CHANCERY DIVISION[2]

[IN THE [ ] DISTRICT REGISTRY]

IN THE MATTER OF the estate of X deceased[3]

AND IN THE MATTER OF the Inheritance (Provision for Family and Dependants) Act 1975

BETWEEN:

AB Plaintiff

—and—

(1) CD
(2) EF
(3) GH
(4) IJ Defendants

LET CD of [*address*] and EF of [*address*] [*executors/administrators*] of the estate of the above-named deceased ('the Deceased') GH of [*address*] [nature of interest under the Deceased's will or intestacy] and IJ of [*address*] jointly entitled with the Deceased (immediately prior to the Deceased's death) to [*description of property*] attend [before Master [ ] at Chancery Chambers, Room No [ ], Thomas More Building, Royal Courts of Justice, Strand, London WC2A 2LL on [ ]day the [ ] day of [ ] 199[ ] at [ ] o'clock in the [fore/after]noon] *or if in a District Registry* [before the District Judge in Chambers at the district registry of the High Court of Justice of [*address*] on [ ]day the [ ] day of [ ] 199[ ]] *or* [on a day to be fixed] on the hearing of an application by the Plaintiff AB of [*address*] for:

(1) an Order that the Deceased's severable share in [description of property] at the value thereof immediately prior to the death of the Deceased be treated to such extent as appears just to this Honourable Court as part of the net estate of the Deceased pursuant to section 9 of the Inheritance (Provision for Family and Dependants) Act 1975;
(2) an Order pursuant to section 2 of the said Act that such reasonable financial provision as this Honourable Court thinks fit be made for the Plaintiff out of the net estate of the Deceased;
(3) further or other relief;
(4) costs.

LET each Defendant within 14 days after service of this Summons on them counting the day of service, return the accompanying Acknowledgement of Service to the appropriate Court Office.

DATED the [ ] day of [ ] 199[ ]

Note: This Summons may not be served later than 4 calendar months (*or, if leave is required to effect service out of the jurisdiction, 6 months*) beginning with the above date unless renewed by Order of the Court.

This Summons was taken out by [ ], Solicitors for the Plaintiff of [*address*]

Note: If a Defendant does not attend personally or by his counsel or solicitor at the time and place above-mentioned such order will be made as the Court may think just and expedient.

A Defendant who is a personal representative must, within 21 days after service of this Summons on such Defendant, inclusive of the day of service, lodge with the Court an affidavit in answer, stating the particulars required by Order 99, r 5 of the Rules of the Supreme Court

Important
Directions for Acknowledgement of Service are given with the accompanying form.

[1] A copy of an affidavit complying with RSC Ord 99, r 3(3) must accompany the Originating Summons when served.

[2] If the application is to be made in the Family Division then:
(a) in the title, Family Division must be substituted for Chancery Division and 'CH' removed from the case reference;
(b) references to the Master must be replaced by 'District Judge [ ] in chambers at Somerset House, Strand, London WC2R 1LP'.
[3] RSC Ord 7, r 7(1)—(5).

Precedent C

Originating Summons asking for an order pursuant to section 10 of the Act and for reasonable financial provision[1]

IN THE HIGH COURT OF JUSTICE CH 199 [ ] X No

CHANCERY DIVISION[2]

[IN THE [ ] DISTRICT REGISTRY]

IN THE MATTER OF the estate of X deceased[3]

AND IN THE MATTER OF the Inheritance (Provision for Family and Dependants) Act 1975

BETWEEN:

AB Plaintiff

—and—

(1) CD
(2) EF
(3) GH
(4) IJ Defendants

LET CD of [*address*] and EF of [*address*] [*executors/administrators*] of the estate of the above-named deceased ('the Deceased') GH of [*address*] [nature of interest under the Deceased's will or intestacy] and IJ of [*address*] the donee of a disposition of [*description of property or money*] made by the Deceased attend [before Master [ ] at Chancery Chambers, Room No [ ], Thomas More Building, Royal Courts of Justice, Strand, London WC2A 2LL on [ ]day the [ ] day of [ ] 199[ ] at [ ] o'clock in the [fore/after]noon] *or if in a District Registry* [before the District Judge in Chambers at the district registry of the High Court of Justice of [*address*] on [ ]day the [ ] day of [ ]

199[ ]] *or* [on a day to be fixed] on the hearing of an application by the Plaintiff AB of [*address*] for:

(1) an Order pursuant to section 10(2) of the Inheritance (Provision for Family and Dependants) Act 1975 that IJ provides, for the purpose of making financial provision for the Plaintiff, [*description of property or money the subject of the disposition made*];
(2) an Order pursuant to section 2 of the said Act that such reasonable financial provision as this Honourable Court thinks fit be made for the Plaintiff out of the net estate of the Deceased;
(3) further or other relief;
(4) costs.

LET each Defendant within 14 days after service of this Summons on them counting the day of service, return the accompanying Acknowledgement of Service to the appropriate Court Office.

DATED the [ ] day of [ ] 199[ ]

Note: This Summons may not be served later than 4 calendar months (*or, if leave is required to effect service out of the jurisdiction, 6 months*) beginning with the above date unless renewed by Order of the Court.

This Summons was taken out by [ ] Solicitors for the Plaintiff of [*address*]

Note: If a Defendant does not attend personally or by his counsel or solicitor at the time and place above-mentioned such order will be made as the Court may think just and expedient.

A Defendant who is a personal representative must, within 21 days after service of this Summons on such Defendant, inclusive of the day of service, lodge with the Court an affidavit in answer, stating the particulars required by Order 99, r 5 of the Rules of the Supreme Court.

Important
Directions for Acknowledgement of Service are given with the accompanying form.

[1] A copy of an affidavit complying with RSC Ord 99, r 3(3) must accompany the Originating Summons when served.
[2] If the application is to be made in the Family Division then:
(a) in the title, Family Division must be substituted for Chancery Division and 'CH' removed from the case reference;
(b) references to the Master must be replaced by 'District Judge [ ] in chambers at Somerset House, Strand, London WC2R 1LP'.
[3] RSC Ord 7, r 7(1)—(5).

Precedent D

Standard form of executor's affidavit pursuant to RSC Ord 99, r 5[1]

Name of deponent : CD
Date affidavit sworn :
On behalf of : [Plaintiff/Defendants]
Number : [1st/2nd . . .]

IN THE HIGH COURT OF JUSTICE CH 199 [ ] X No

CHANCERY DIVISION

[IN THE [ ] DISTRICT REGISTRY]

IN THE MATTER OF the estate of X deceased

AND IN THE MATTER OF the Inheritance (Provision for Family and Dependants) Act 1975

BETWEEN:

AB Plaintiff

—and—

(1) CD
(2) EF
(3) GH Defendants

I, CD of [*address*] [*occupation*] MAKE OATH and say as follows:

1 I am the First Defendant herein and joint executor of the estate of the above-named deceased (hereinafter called 'the Deceased') who died testate on [ ]. I am authorised to make this affidavit on behalf of myself and the Second Defendant herein, my co-executor. Save where expressly appears to the contrary I make this affidavit of my own knowledge and belief and I believe it to be true.

2 Probate of the Deceased's will dated [ ] (hereinafter called 'the Will') was granted out of the [District Probate Registry] [Principal Registry of the Family Division] to myself and EF, my co-executor on [ ]. The Deceased's estate was sworn gross at £[ ] and net at £[ ]. There are now produced and shown to me and exhibited herewith marked 'CD 1' true copies of the Certificate of Death of the Deceased, the Will and the said grant of probate.

3 Full particulars of the composition of and present values attributed to the Deceased's net estate (as that term is defined by section 25(1) of the Inheritance (Provision for Family and Dependants) Act 1975) are contained in a Schedule of Assets produced and shown to me and exhibited herewith marked 'CD 2'.

4 By the Will the Deceased effected the following dispositions:
[*list the gifts made by the Will stating the value of each gift* (*approximate where necessary*) *and giving the name and address of each beneficiary and their relationship to the Deceased*]

5 To the best of my knowledge and belief none of the beneficiaries of the estate of the Deceased is a minor or a patient within the meaning of RSC Ord 80, r 1[2].

SWORN etc

[1] This affidavit is only suitable in the simplest case and where the deceased died testate. If the deceased died intestate it will need to be amended to exhibit the letters of administration and will need to refer to the effect of the statutory scheme of distribution on intestacy rather than disposition by will. In any case where complications exist the affidavit will need to be amended to take account of them and it must be remembered that the deponent of this affidavit must tell the court any facts known to them which might affect the exercise of the court's powers under the Act: RSC Ord 99, r 5(2)(d). (See Chapter 9).

[2] If any of the living beneficiaries is a minor or a patient this must be expressly stated in the executor's affidavit.

Precedent E

Summons to be heard by the Master asking for interim provision pursuant to section 5 of the Act

IN THE HIGH COURT OF JUSTICE CH 199 [ ] X No

CHANCERY DIVISION

IN THE MATTER OF the estate of X deceased

AND IN THE MATTER OF the Inheritance (Provision for Family and Dependants) Act 1975

BETWEEN:

	AB	Plaintiff
	—and—	
	(1) CD (2) EF (3) GH	Defendants

LET all parties concerned attend the Master in Chambers at the Central Office, Royal Courts of Justice, Strand London on [ ]day the [ ] day of [ ] 199[ ] at [ ] o'clock in the [fore/after]noon on the hearing of an application on the part of the Plaintiff:

(1) for an Order pursuant to section 5 of the Inheritance (Provision for Family and Dependants) Act 1975 for payment of such sum or sums and

(if more than one) at such intervals as this Honourable Court thinks reasonable to the Plaintiff;
(2) that provision be made for the costs of this application.

Dated the [ ] day of [ ] 199[ ]

This Summons was taken out by [ ], Solicitors for the Plaintiff of [*address*]

TO : [*a copy must be sent to each Defendant*]

Precedent F

Originating Application in the county court pursuant to Ord 48, r 2 of the County Court Rules[1]

IN THE [ ] COUNTY COURT Case No: 199[ ]/[ ]

IN THE MATTER OF the estate of X deceased

AND IN THE MATTER OF the Inheritance (Provision for Family and Dependants) Act 1975

BETWEEN:

AB Applicant

—and—

(1) CD
(2) EF
(3) GH Respondents[2]

I, AB of [*address*] apply to the Court for an Order in the following terms:

(1) an Order pursuant to section 2 of the Inheritance (Provision for Family and Dependants) Act 1975 that such reasonable financial provision as this Honourable Court thinks fit be made for me out of the net estate (as that term is defined in section 25(1) of the said Act) of the above named deceased ("the Deceased");
(2) further or other relief within the jurisdiction of this Honourable Court;
(3) costs.

The grounds on which I claim to be entitled to apply for and obtain such an order are:

1 [*CCR Ord 48, r 2 sets out the information that must be contained in the Originating Application: if a certificate of marriage, birth, adoption or other*

form of identification assists the Applicant then copies of such documents ought to be filed with the Originating Application and reference made in the body of that Application to them. Originating Applications are not affidavits and documents ought not to be exhibited to them].

The names and addresses of the persons upon whom it is intended to serve this Application are:

Messrs [ ]
Solicitors for the First and Second Respondents of [*address*]

GH
Third Respondent of [*address*]

My address for service is:

Messrs [ ] of [*address*]

Dated the [ ] day of [ ] 199[ ]

[1] The applicant must file with (*not exhibit to*) their originating application, the grant of representation in the deceased's estate and the testamentary documents that have been admitted to proof: CCR Ord 48, r 3(2).

[2] Note the use of 'Applicant' and 'Respondent' as opposed to 'Plaintiff' and 'Defendant' in the High Court regardless of the Division.

Precedent G

Standard form of executor's answer in the county court pursuant to Ord 48, r 3 of the County Court Rules[1]

IN THE [ ] COUNTY COURT Case No: 199[ ]/[ ]

IN THE MATTER OF the estate of X deceased

AND IN THE MATTER OF the Inheritance (Provision for Family and Dependants) Act 1975

BETWEEN:

AB — Applicant

—and—

(1) CD
(2) EF
(3) GH — Respondents

I, CD of [*address*] [*occupation*] the first Respondent herein, in answer to the application dated [ ] of the Applicant, AB say that[2];

1 I am one of the joint executors of the estate of the above-named deceased ('the Deceased') who died testate on [ ]. Probate of the Deceased's will dated [ ] ('the Will') was granted out of the [District Probate Registry] [Principal Registry of the Family Division] to myself and my co-executor, EF, the Second Respondent herein on [ ]. The Deceased's estate was sworn gross at £[ ] and net at £[ ].

2 Full particulars of the composition of and present values attributed to the Deceased's net estate (as that term is defined in section 25(1) of the Inheritance (Provision for Family and Dependants) Act 1975) are as follows:
[*list the assets comprised in and the values given to the assets comprised in the Deceased's net estate*]

3 By the Will the Deceased effected the following dispositions:
[*list the dispositions made including the value of each gift (approximate if necessary), to whom it is made and describing the relationship of each beneficiary to the Deceased*]

4 To the best of my knowledge and belief none of the beneficiaries of the estate of the Deceased is a minor or a patient.

Dated the [ ] day of [ ] 199[ ]

[1] This answer will require amendment in all but the simplest case, for example where the deceased died wholly or partially intestate. The person who makes the answer must state any facts known to them which might affect the exercise of the court's powers under the Act (see Chapter 9).
[2] Answers are not sworn.

Appendix II

Inheritance (Provision for Family and Dependants) Act 1975

(c 63)

Arrangement of sections

Powers of court to order financial provision from deceased's estate

Section

1 Application for financial provision from deceased's estate
2 Powers of court to make orders
3 Matters to which court is to have regard in exercising powers under s 2
4 Time-limit for applications
5 Interim orders
6 Variation, discharge etc of orders for periodical payments
7 Payment of lump sums by instalments

Property available for financial provision

8 Property treated as part of 'net estate'
9 Property held on a joint tenancy

Powers of court in relation to transactions intended to defeat applications for financial provision

10 Dispositions intended to defeat applications for financial provision
11 Contracts to leave property by will
12 Provisions supplementary to ss 10 and 11
13 Provisions as to trustees in relation to ss 10 and 11

Special provisions relating to cases of divorce, separation etc

14 Provision as to cases where no financial relief was granted in divorce proceedings, etc
15 Restriction imposed in divorce proceedings, etc on application under this Act
15A Restriction imposed in proceedings under Matrimonial and Family Proceedings Act 1984 on application under this Act
16 Variation and discharge of secured periodical payments orders made under Matrimonial Causes Act 1973
17 Variation and revocation of maintenance agreements

An Act to make fresh provision for empowering the court to make orders for the making out of the estate of a deceased person of provision for the spouse, former spouse, child, child of the family or dependant of that person; and for matters connected therewith

[12th November 1975]

Powers of court to order financial provision from deceased's estate

1 Application for financial provision from deceased's estate

(1) Where after the commencement of this Act a person dies domiciled in England and Wales and is survived by any of the following persons –

(a) the wife or husband of the deceased;
(b) a former wife or former husband of the deceased who has not remarried;
(c) a child of the deceased;
(d) any person (not being a child of the deceased) who, in the case of any marriage to which the deceased was at any time a party, was treated by the deceased as a child of the family in relation to that marriage;
(e) any person (not being a person included in the foregoing paragraphs of this subsection) who immediately before the death of the deceased was being maintained, either wholly or partly, by the deceased;

that person may apply to the court for an order under s 2 of this Act on the ground that the disposition of the deceased's estate effected by his will or the law relating to intestacy, or the combination of his will and that law, is not such as to make reasonable financial provision for the applicant.

(2) In this Act 'reasonable financial provision' –

(a) in the case of an application made by virtue of subs (1)(a) above by the husband or wife of the deceased (except where the marriage with the deceased was the subject of a decree of judicial separation and at the date of death the decree was in force and the separation was continuing), means such financial provision as it would be reasonable in all the circumstances of the case for a husband or wife to receive, whether or not that provision is required for his or her maintenance,

(b) in the case of any other application made by virtue of subs (1) above, means such financial provision as it would be reasonable in all the circumstances of the case for the applicant to receive for his maintenance.

(3) For the purposes of subs (1)(e) above, a person shall be treated as being maintained by the deceased, either wholly or partly, as the case may be, if the deceased, otherwise than for full valuable consideration, was making a substantial contribution in money or money's worth towards the reasonable needs of that person.

2 Powers of court to make orders

(1) Subject to the provisions of this Act, where an application is made for an order under this section, the court may, if it is satisfied that the disposition of the deceased's estate effected by his will or the law relating to intestacy, or the combination of his will and that law, is not such as to make reasonable financial provision for the applicant, make any one or more of the following orders –

(a) an order for the making to the applicant out of the net estate of the deceased of such periodical payments and for such term as may be specified in the order;

(b) an order for the payment to the applicant out of that estate of a lump sum of such amount as may be so specified;

(c) an order for the transfer to the applicant of such property comprised in that estate as may be so specified;

(d) an order for the settlement for the benefit of the applicant of such property comprised in that estate as may be so specified;

(e) an order for the acquisition out of property comprised in that estate of such property as may be so specified and for the transfer of the property so acquired to the applicant or for the settlement thereof for his benefit;

(f) an order varying any ante-nuptial or post-nuptial settlement (including such a settlement made by will) made on the parties to a marriage to which the deceased was one of the parties, the variation being for the benefit of the surviving party to that marriage, or any child of that marriage, or any person who was treated by the deceased as a child of the family in relation to that marriage.

(2) An order under subs (1)(a) above providing for the making out of the net estate of the deceased of periodical payments may provide for –

(a) payments of such amount as may be specified in the order;

(b) payments equal to the whole of the income of the net estate or of such portion thereof as may be so specified;

(c) payments equal to the whole of the income of such part of the net estate as the court may direct to be set aside or appropriated for the making out of the income thereof of payments under this section;

or may provide for the amount of the payments or any of them to be determined in any other way the court thinks fit.

(3) Where an order under subs (1)(a) above provides for the making of payments of an amount specified in the order, the order may direct that such part of the net estate as may be so specified shall be set aside or appropriated for the making out of the income thereof of those payments; but no larger part of the net estate shall be so set aside or appropriated than is sufficient, at the date of the order, to produce by the income thereof the amount required for the making of those payments.

(4) An order under this section may contain such consequential and supplemental provisions as the court thinks necessary or expedient for the purpose of giving effect to the order or for the purpose of securing that the order operates fairly as between one beneficiary of the estate of the deceased and another and may, in particular, but without prejudice to the generality of this subsection –

(a) order any person who holds any property which forms part of the net estate of the deceased to make such payment or transfer such property as may be specified in the order;

(b) vary the disposition of the deceased's estate effected by the will or the law relating to intestacy, or by both the will and the law relating to intestacy, in such manner as the court thinks fair and reasonable having regard to the provisions of the order and all the circumstances of the case;

(c) confer on the trustees of any property which is the subject of an order under this section such powers as appear to the court to be necessary or expedient.

3 Matters to which court is to have regard in exercising powers under s 2

(1) Where an application is made for an order under s 2 of this Act, the court shall, in determining whether the disposition of the deceased's estate effected by his will or the law relating to intestacy, or the combination of his will and that law, is such as to make reasonable financial provision for the applicant and, if the court considers that reasonable financial provision has not been made, in determining whether and in what manner it shall exercise its powers under that section, have regard to the following matters, that is to say –

(a) the financial resources and financial needs which the applicant has or is likely to have in the foreseeable future;

(b) the financial resources and financial needs which any other applicant for an order under s 2 of this Act has or is likely to have in the foreseeable future;

(c) the financial resources and financial needs which any beneficiary of the estate of the deceased has or is likely to have in the foreseeable future;

(d) any obligations and responsibilities which the deceased had towards any applicant for an order under the said s 2 or towards any beneficiary of the estate of the deceased;

(e) the size and nature of the net estate of the deceased;

(f) any physical or mental disability of any applicant for an order under the said s 2 or any beneficiary of the estate of the deceased;

(g) any other matter, including the conduct of the applicant or any other person, which in the circumstances of the case the court may consider relevant.

(2) Without prejudice to the generality of paragraph (g) of subs (1) above, where an application for an order under s 2 of this Act is made by virtue of s 1(1)(a) or 1(1)(b) of this Act, the court shall, in addition to the matters specifically mentioned in paragraphs (a) to (f) of that subsection, have regard to –

(a) the age of the applicant and the duration of the marriage;

(b) the contribution made by the applicant to the welfare of the family of the deceased, including any contribution made by looking after the home or caring for the family;

and, in the case of an application by the wife or husband of the deceased, the court shall also, unless at the date of death a decree of judicial separation was in force and the separation was continuing, have regard to the provision which the applicant might reasonably have expected to receive if on the day on which the deceased died the marriage, instead of being terminated by death, had been terminated by a decree of divorce.

(3) Without prejudice to the generality of paragraph (g) of subs (1) above, where an application for an order under s 2 of this Act is made by virtue of s 1(1)(c) or 1(1)(d) of this Act, the court shall, in addition to the matters specifically mentioned in paragraphs (a) to (f) of that subsection, have regard to the manner in which the applicant was being or in which he might expect to be educated or trained, and where the application is made by virtue of s 1(1)(d) the court shall also have regard –

(a) to whether the deceased had assumed any responsibility for the applicant's maintenance and, if so, to the extent to which and the basis upon which the deceased assumed that responsibility and to the length of time for which the deceased discharged that responsibility;

(b) to whether in assuming and discharging that responsibility the deceased did so knowing that the applicant was not his own child;

(c) to the liability of any other person to maintain the applicant.

(4) Without prejudice to the generality of paragraph (g) of subs (1) above, where an application for an order under s 2 of this Act is made by virtue of s 1(1)(e) of this Act, the court shall, in addition to the matters specifically mentioned in paragraphs (a) to (f) of that subsection, have regard to the extent to which and the basis upon which the deceased assumed responsibility for the maintenance of the applicant and to the length of time for which the deceased discharged that responsibility.

(5) In considering the matters to which the court is required to have regard under this section, the court shall take into account the facts as known to the court at the date of the hearing.

(6) In considering the financial resources of any person for the purposes of this section the court shall take into account his earning capacity and in considering the financial needs of any person for the purposes of this section the court shall take into account his financial obligations and responsibilities.

4 Time-limit for applications

An application for an order under s 2 of this Act shall not, except with the permission of the court, be made after the end of the period of six months from the date on which representation with respect to the estate of the deceased is first taken out.

5 Interim orders

(1) Where on an application for an order under s 2 of this Act it appears to the court

(a) that the applicant is in immediate need of financial assistance, but it is not yet possible to determine what order (if any) should be made under that section; and

(b) that property forming part of the net estate of the deceased is or can be made available to meet the need of the applicant;

the court may order that, subject to such conditions or restrictions, if any, as the court may impose and to any further order of the court, there shall be paid to the applicant out of the net estate of the deceased such sum or sums and (if more than one) at such intervals as the court thinks reasonable; and the court may order that, subject to the provisions of this Act, such payments are to be made until such date as the court may specify, not being later than the date on which the court either makes an order under the said s 2 or decides not to exercise its powers under that section.

(2) Subs (2), (3) and (4) of s 2 of this Act shall apply in relation to an order under this section as they apply in relation to an order under that section.

(3) In determining what order, if any, should be made under this section the court shall, so far as the urgency of the case admits, have regard to the same matters as those to which the court is required to have regard under s 3 of this Act.

(4) An order made under s 2 of this Act may provide that any sum paid to the applicant by virtue of this section shall be treated to such an extent and in such manner as may be provided by that order as having been paid on account of any payment provided for by that order.

6 Variation, discharge etc of orders for periodical payments

(1) Subject to the provisions of this Act, where the court has made an order under s 2(1)(a) of this Act (in this section referred to as 'the original order') for the making of periodical payments to any person (in this section referred to as 'the original recipient'), the court, on an application under this section, shall have power by order to vary or discharge the original order or to suspend any provision of it temporarily and to revive the operation of any provision so suspended.

(2) Without prejudice to the generality of subs (1) above, an order made on an application for the variation of the original order may –

(a) provide for the making out of any relevant property of such periodical payments and for such term as may be specified in the order to any person who has applied, or would but for s 4 of this Act be entitled to apply, for an order under s 2 of this Act (whether or not, in the case of any application, an order was made in favour of the applicant);

(b) provide for the payment out of any relevant property of a lump sum of such amount as may be so specified to the original recipient or to any such person as is mentioned in paragraph (a) above;

(c) provide for the transfer of the relevant property, or such part thereof as may be so specified, to the original recipient or to any such person as is so mentioned.

(3) Where the original order provides that any periodical payments payable thereunder to the original recipient are to cease on the occurrence of an event specified in the order (other than the remarriage of a former wife or former husband) or on the expiration of a period so specified, then, if, before the end of the period of six months from the date of the occurrence of that event or of the expiration of that period, an application is made for an order under this section, the court shall have power to make any order which it would have had power to make if the application had been made before that date (whether in favour of the original recipient or any such person as is mentioned in subs (2)(a) above and whether having effect from that date or from such later date as the court may specify).

(4) Any reference in this section to the original order shall include a reference to an order made under this section and any reference in this section to the original recipient shall include a reference to any person to whom periodical payments are required to be made by virtue of an order under this section.

(5) An application under this section may be made by any of the following persons, that is to say –

(a) any person who by virtue of s 1(1) of this Act has applied, or would but for s 4 of this Act be entitled to apply, for an order under s 2 of this Act,
(b) the personal representatives of the deceased,
(c) the trustees of any relevant property, and
(d) any beneficiary of the estate of the deceased.

(6) An order under this section may only affect –

(a) property the income of which is at the date of the order applicable wholly or in part for the making of periodical payments to any person who has applied for an order under this Act, or
(b) in the case of an application under subs (3) above in respect of payments which have ceased to be payable on the occurrence of an event or the expiration of a period, property the income of which was so applicable immediately before the occurrence of that event or the expiration of that period, as the case may be,

and any such property as is mentioned in paragraph (a) or (b) above is in subs (2) and (5) above referred to as 'relevant property'.

(7) In exercising the powers conferred by this section the court shall have regard to all the circumstances of the case, including any change in any of the matters to which the court was required to have regard when making the order to which the application relates.

(8) Where the court makes an order under this section, it may give such consequential directions as it thinks necessary or expedient having regard to the provisions of the order.

(9) No such order as is mentioned in s 2(1)(d), (e) or (f), 9, 10 or 11 of this Act shall be made on an application under this section.

(10) For the avoidance of doubt it is hereby declared that, in relation to an order which provides for the making of periodical payments which are to cease on the occurrence of an event specified in the order (other than the remarriage of a former wife or former husband) or on the expiration of a period so specified, the power to vary an order includes power to provide for the making of periodical payments after the expiration of that period or the occurrence of that event.

7 Payment of lump sums by instalments

(1) An order under s 2(1)(b) or 6(2)(b) of this Act for the payment of a lump sum may provide for the payment of that sum by instalments of such amount as may be specified in the order.

(2) Where an order is made by virtue of subs (1) above, the court shall have power, on an application made by the person to whom the lump sum is payable, by the personal representatives of the deceased or by the trustees of the property out of which the lump sum is payable, to vary that order by varying the number of instalments payable, the amount of any instalment and the date on which any instalment becomes payable.

Property available for financial provision

8 Property treated as part of 'net estate'

(1) Where a deceased person has in accordance with the provisions of any enactment nominated any person to receive any sum of money or other property on his death and that nomination is in force at the time of his death, that sum of money, after deducting therefrom any capital transfer tax payable in respect thereof, or that other property, to the extent of the value thereof at the date of the death of the deceased after deducting therefrom any capital transfer tax so payable, shall be treated for the purposes of this Act as part of the net estate of the deceased; but this subsection shall not render any person liable for having paid that sum or transferred that other property to the person named in the nomination in accordance with the directions given in the nomination.

(2) Where any sum of money or other property is received by any person as a donatio mortis causa made by a deceased person, that sum of money, after deducting therefrom any capital transfer tax payable thereon, or that other property, to the extent of the value thereof at the date of the death of the deceased after deducting therefrom any capital transfer tax so payable, shall be treated for the purposes of this Act as part of the net estate of the deceased; but this subsection shall not render any person liable for having paid that sum or transferred that other property in order to give effect to that donatio mortis causa.

(3) The amount of capital transfer tax to be deducted for the purposes of this section shall not exceed the amount of that tax which has been borne by the person nominated by the deceased or, as the case may be, the person who has received a sum of money or other property as a donatio mortis causa.

9 Property held on a joint tenancy

(1) Where a deceased person was immediately before his death beneficially entitled to a joint tenancy of any property, then, if before the end of the period of six months from the date on which representation with respect to the estate of the deceased was first taken out, an application is made for an order under s 2 of this Act, the court for the purpose of facilitating the making of financial provision for the applicant under this Act may order that the deceased's severable share of that property, at the value thereof immediately before his death, shall, to such extent as appears to the court to be just in all the circumstances of the case, be treated for the purposes of this Act as part of the net estate of the deceased.

(2) In determining the extent to which any severable share is to be treated as part of the net estate of the deceased by virtue of an order under subs (1) above, the court shall have regard to any capital transfer tax payable in respect of that severable share.

(3) Where an order is made under subs (1) above, the provisions of this section shall not render any person liable for anything done by him before the order was made.

(4) For the avoidance of doubt it is hereby declared that for the purposes of this section there may be a joint tenancy of a chose in action.

Powers of court in relation to transactions intended to defeat applications for financial provision

10 Dispositions intended to defeat applications for financial provision

(1) Where an application is made to the court for an order under s 2 of this Act, the applicant may, in the proceedings on that application, apply to the court for an order under subs (2) below.

(2) Where on an application under subs (1) above the court is satisfied –

(a) that, less than six years before the date of the death of the deceased, the deceased with the intention of defeating an application for financial provision under this Act made a disposition, and

(b) that full valuable consideration for that disposition was not given by the person to whom or for the benefit of whom the disposition was made (in this section referred to as 'the donee') or by any other person, and

(c) that the exercise of the powers conferred by this section would facilitate the making of financial provision for the applicant under this Act,

then, subject to the provisions of this section and of ss 12 and 13 of this Act, the court may order the donee (whether or not at the date of the order he holds any interest in the property disposed of to him or for his benefit by the deceased) to provide, for the purpose of the making of that financial provision, such sum of money or other property as may be specified in the order.

(3) Where an order is made under subs (2) above as respects any disposition made by the deceased which consisted of the payment of money to or for the benefit of the donee, the amount of any sum of money or the value of any property ordered to be provided under that subsection shall not exceed the amount of the payment made by the deceased after deducting therefrom any capital transfer tax borne by the donee in respect of that payment.

(4) Where an order is made under subs (2) above as respects any disposition made by the deceased which consisted of the transfer of property (other than a sum of money) to or for the benefit of the donee, the amount of any sum of money or the value of any property ordered to be provided under that subsection shall not exceed the value at the date of the death of the deceased of the property disposed of by him to or for the benefit of the donee (or if that property has been disposed of by the person to whom it was transferred by the deceased, the value at the date of that

disposal thereof) after deducting therefrom any capital transfer tax borne by the donee in respect of the transfer of that property by the deceased.

(5) Where an application (in this subsection referred to as 'the original application') is made for an order under subs (2) above in relation to any disposition, then, if on an application under this subsection by the donee or by any applicant for an order under s 2 of this Act the court is satisfied –

(a) that, less than six years before the date of the death of the deceased, the deceased with the intention of defeating an application for financial provision under this Act made a disposition other than the disposition which is the subject of the original application, and

(b) that full valuable consideration for that other disposition was not given by the person to whom or for the benefit of whom that other disposition was made or by any other person,

the court may exercise in relation to the person to whom or for the benefit of whom that other disposition was made the powers which the court would have had under subs (2) above if the original application had been made in respect of that other disposition and the court had been satisfied as to the matters set out in paragraphs (a), (b) and (c) of that subsection; and where any application is made under this subsection, any reference in this section (except in subs (2)(b)) to the donee shall include a reference to the person to whom or for the benefit of whom that other disposition was made.

(6) In determining whether and in what manner to exercise its powers under this section, the court shall have regard to the circumstances in which any disposition was made and any valuable consideration which was given therefor, the relationship, if any, of the donee to the deceased, the conduct and financial resources of the donee and all the other circumstances of the case.

(7) In this section 'disposition' does not include –

(a) any provision in a will, any such nomination as is mentioned in s 8(1) of this Act or any donatio mortis causa, or

(b) any appointment of property made, otherwise than by will, in the exercise of a special power of appointment,

but, subject to these exceptions, includes any payment of money (including the payment of a premium under a policy of assurance) and any conveyance, assurance, appointment or gift of property of any description, whether made by an instrument or otherwise.

(8) The provisions of this section do not apply to any disposition made before the commencement of this Act.

11 Contracts to leave property by will

(1) Where an application is made to a court for an order under s 2 of this Act, the applicant may, in the proceedings on that application, apply to the court for an order under this section.

(2) Where on an application under subs (1) above the court is satisfied –

(a) that the deceased made a contract by which he agreed to leave by his will a sum of money or other property to any person or by which he agreed that a sum of money or other property would be paid or transferred to any person out of his estate, and

(b) that the deceased made that contract with the intention of defeating an application for financial provision under this Act, and

(c) that when the contract was made full valuable consideration for that contract was not given or promised by the person with whom or for the benefit of whom the contract was made (in this section referred to as 'the donee') or by any other person, and

(d) that the exercise of the powers conferred by this section would facilitate the making of financial provision for the applicant under this Act,

then, subject to the provisions of this section and of ss 12 and 13 of this Act, the court may make any one or more of the following orders, that is to say –

(i) if any money has been paid or any other property has been transferred to or for the benefit of the donee in accordance with the contract, an order directing the donee to provide, for the purpose of the making of that financial provision, such sum of money or other property as may be specified in the order;

(ii) if the money or all the money has not been paid or the property or all the property has not been transferred in accordance with the contract, an order directing the personal representatives not to make any payment or transfer any property, or not to make any further payment or transfer any further property, as the case may be, in accordance therewith or directing the personal representatives only to make such payment or transfer such property as may be specified in the order.

(3) Notwithstanding anything in subs (2) above, the court may exercise its powers thereunder in relation to any contract made by the deceased only to the extent that the court considers that the amount of any sum of money paid or to be paid or the value of any property transferred or to be transferred in accordance with the contract exceeds the value of any valuable consideration given or to be given for that contract, and for this purpose the court shall have regard to the value of property at the date of the hearing.

(4) In determining whether and in what manner to exercise its powers under this section, the court shall have regard to the circumstances in which the contract was made, the relationship, if any, of the donee to the deceased, the conduct and financial resources of the donee and all the other circumstances of the case.

(5) Where an order has been made under subs (2) above in relation to any contract, the rights of any person to enforce that contract or to recover damages or to obtain other relief for the breach thereof shall be subject to

any adjustment made by the court under s 12(3) of this Act and shall survive to such extent only as is consistent with giving effect to the terms of that order.

(6) The provisions of this section do not apply to a contract made before the commencement of this Act.

12 Provisions supplementary to ss 10 and 11

(1) Where the exercise of any of the powers conferred by s 10 or 11 of this Act is conditional on the court being satisfied that a disposition or contract was made by a deceased person with the intention of defeating an application for financial provision under this Act, that condition shall be fulfilled if the court is of the opinion that, on a balance of probabilities, the intention of the deceased (though not necessarily his sole intention) in making the disposition or contract was to prevent an order for financial provision being made under this Act or to reduce the amount of the provision which might otherwise be granted by an order thereunder.

(2) Where an application is made under s 11 of this Act with respect to any contract made by the deceased and no valuable consideration was given or promised by any person for that contract then, notwithstanding anything in subs (1) above, it shall be presumed, unless the contrary is shown, that the deceased made that contract with the intention of defeating an application for financial provision under this Act.

(3) Where the court makes an order under s 10 or 11 of this Act it may give such consequential directions as it thinks fit (including directions requiring the making of any payment or the transfer of any property) for giving effect to the order or for securing a fair adjustment of the rights of the persons affected thereby.

(4) Any power conferred on the court by the said s 10 or 11 to order the donee, in relation to any disposition or contract, to provide any sum of money or other property shall be exercisable in like manner in relation to the personal representative of the donee, and –

(a) any reference in s 10(4) to the disposal of property by the donee shall include a reference to disposal by the personal representative of the donee, and

(b) any reference in s 10(5) to an application by the donee under that subsection shall include a reference to an application by the personal representative of the donee;

but the court shall not have power under the said s 10 or 11 to make an order in respect of any property forming part of the estate of the donee which has been distributed by the personal representative; and the personal representative shall not be liable for having distributed any such property before he has notice of the making of an application under the said s 10 or 11 on the ground that he ought to have taken into account the possibility that such an application would be made.

13 Provisions as to trustees in relation to ss 10 and 11

(1) Where an application is made for –

(a) an order under s 10 of this Act in respect of a disposition made by the deceased to any person as a trustee, or

(b) an order under s 11 of this Act in respect of any payment made or property transferred, in accordance with a contract made by the deceased, to any person as a trustee,

the powers of the court under the said s 10 or 11 to order that trustee to provide a sum of money or other property shall be subject to the following limitation (in addition, in a case of an application under s 10, to any provision regarding the deduction of capital transfer tax) namely, that the amount of any sum of money or the value of any property ordered to be provided –

(i) in the case of an application in respect of a disposition which consisted of the payment of money or an application in respect of the payment of money in accordance with a contract, shall not exceed the aggregate of so much of that money as is at the date of the order in the hands of the trustee and the value at that date of any property which represents that money or is derived therefrom and is at that date in the hands of the trustee;

(ii) in the case of an application in respect of a disposition which consisted of the transfer of property (other than a sum of money) or an application in respect of the transfer of property (other than a sum of money) in accordance with a contract, shall not exceed the aggregate of the value at the date of the order of so much of that property as is at that date in the hands of the trustee and the value at that date of any property which represents the first-mentioned property or is derived therefrom and is at that date in the hands of the trustee.

(2) Where any such application is made in respect of a disposition made to any person as a trustee or in respect of any payment made or property transferred in pursuance of a contract to any person as a trustee, the trustee shall not be liable for having distributed any money or other property on the ground that he ought to have taken into account the possibility that such an application would be made.

(3) Where any such application is made in respect of a disposition made to any person as a trustee or in respect of any payment made or property transferred in accordance with a contract to any person as a trustee, any reference in the said s 10 or 11 to the donee shall be construed as including a reference to the trustee or trustees for the time being of the trust in question and any reference in subs (1) or (2) above to a trustee shall be construed in the same way.

Special provisions relating to cases of divorce, separation etc

14 Provision as to cases where no financial relief was granted in divorce proceedings, etc

(1) Where, within twelve months from the date on which a decree of divorce or nullity of marriage has been made absolute or a decree of judicial separation has been granted, a party to the marriage dies and –

(a) an application for a financial provision order under s 23 of the Matrimonial Causes Act 1973 or a property adjustment order under s 24 of that Act has not been made by the other party to that marriage, or

(b) such an application has been made but the proceedings thereon have not been determined at the time of the death of the deceased,

then, if an application for an order under s 2 of this Act is made by that other party, the court shall, notwithstanding anything in s 1 or s 3 of this Act, have power, if it thinks it just to do so, to treat that party for the purposes of that application as if the decree of divorce or nullity of marriage had not been made absolute or the decree of judicial separation had not been granted, as the case may be.

(2) This section shall not apply in relation to a decree of judicial separation unless at the date of the death of the deceased the decree was in force and the separation was continuing.

15 Restriction imposed in divorce proceedings, etc on application under this Act

(1) On the grant of a decree of divorce, a decree of nullity of marriage or a decree of judicial separation or at any time thereafter the court, if it considers it just to do so, may, on the application of either party to the marriage, order that the other party to the marriage shall not on the death of the applicant be entitled to apply for an order under s 2 of this Act.

In this subsection 'the court' means the High Court or, where a county court has jurisdiction by virtue of Pt V of the Matrimonial and Family Proceedings Act 1984, a county court.

(2) In the case of a decree of divorce or nullity of marriage an order may be made under subs (1) above before or after the decree is made absolute, but if it is made before the decree is made absolute it shall not take effect unless the decree is made absolute.

(3) Where an order made under subs (1) above on the grant of a decree of divorce or nullity of marriage has come into force with respect to a party to a marriage, then, on the death of the other party to that marriage, the court shall not entertain any application for an order under s 2 of this Act made by the first-mentioned party.

(4) Where an order made under subs (1) above on the grant of a decree of judicial separation has come into force with respect to any party to a

marriage, then, if the other party to that marriage dies while the decree is in force and the separation is continuing, the court shall not entertain any application for an order under s 2 of this Act made by the first-mentioned party.

15A Restriction imposed in proceedings under Matrimonial and Family Proceedings Act 1984 on application under this Act

(1) On making an order under s 17 of the Matrimonial and Family Proceedings Act 1984 (orders for financial provision and property adjustment following overseas divorces, etc) the court, if it considers it just to do so, may, on the application of either party to the marriage, order that the other party to the marriage shall not on the death of the applicant be entitled to apply for an order under s 2 of this Act.

In this subsection 'the court' means the High Court or, where a county court has jurisdiction by virtue of Pt V of the Matrimonial and Family Proceedings Act 1984, a county court.

(2) Where an order under subs (1) above has been made with respect to a party to a marriage which has been dissolved or annulled, then, on the death of the other party to that marriage, the court shall not entertain an application under s 2 of this Act made by the first-mentioned party.

(3) Where an order under subs (1) above has been made with respect to a party to a marriage the parties to which have been legally separated, then, if the other party to the marriage dies while the legal separation is in force, the court shall not entertain an application under s 2 of this Act made by the first-mentioned party.

16 Variation and discharge of secured periodical payments orders made under Matrimonial Causes Act 1973

(1) Where an application for an order under s 2 of this Act is made to the court by any person who was at the time of the death of the deceased entitled to payments from the deceased under a secured periodical payments order made under the Matrimonial Causes Act 1973, then, in the proceedings on that application, the court shall have power, if an application is made under this section by that person or by the personal representative of the deceased, to vary or discharge that periodical payments order or to revive the operation of any provision thereof which has been suspended under s 31 of that Act.

(2) In exercising the powers conferred by this section the court shall have regard to all the circumstances of the case including any order which the court proposes to make under s 2 or s 5 of this Act and any change (whether resulting from the death of the deceased or otherwise) in any of the matters to which the court was required to have regard when making the secured periodical payments order.

(3) The powers exercisable by the court under this section in relation to an order shall be exercisable also in relation to any instrument executed in pursuance of the order.

17 Variation and revocation of maintenance agreements

(1) Where an application for an order under s 2 of this Act is made to the court by any person who was at the time of the death of the deceased entitled to payments from the deceased under a maintenance agreement which provided for the continuation of payments under the agreement after the death of the deceased, then, in the proceedings on that application, the court shall have power, if an application is made under this section by that person or by the personal representative of the deceased, to vary or revoke that agreement.

(2)In exercising the powers conferred by this section the court shall have regard to all the circumstances of the case, including any order which the court proposes to make under s 2 or s 5 of this Act and any change (whether resulting from the death of the deceased or otherwise) in any of the circumstances in the light of which the agreement was made.

(3) If a maintenance agreement is varied by the court under this section the like consequences shall ensue as if the variation had been made immediately before the death of the deceased by agreement between the parties and for valuable consideration.

(4) In this section 'maintenance agreement', in relation to a deceased person, means any agreement made, whether in writing or not and whether before or after the commencement of this Act, by the deceased with any person with whom he entered into a marriage, being an agreement which contained provisions governing the rights and liabilities towards one another when living separately of the parties to that marriage (whether or not the marriage has been dissolved or annulled) in respect of the making or securing of payments or the disposition or use of any property, including such rights and liabilities with respect to the maintenance or education of any child, whether or not a child of the deceased or a person who was treated by the deceased as a child of the family in relation to that marriage.

18 Availability of court's powers under this Act in applications under ss 31 and 36 of Matrimonial Causes Act 1973

(1) Where –

(a) a person against whom a secured periodical payments order was made under the Matrimonial Causes Act 1973 has died and an application is made under s 31(6) of that Act for the variation or discharge of that order or for the revival of the operation of any provision thereof which has been suspended, or

(b) a party to a maintenance agreement within the meaning of s 34 of that Act has died, the agreement being one which provides for the continuation of payments thereunder after the death of one of the parties, and an application is made under s 36(1) of that Act for the alteration of the agreement under s 35 thereof,

the court shall have power to direct that the application made under the said s 31(6) or 36(1) shall be deemed to have been accompanied by an application for an order under s 2 of this Act.

(2) Where the court gives a direction under subs (1) above it shall have power, in the proceedings on the application under the said s 31(6) or 36(1), to make any order which the court would have had power to make under the provisions of this Act if the application under the said s 31(6) or 36(1) as the case may be, had been made jointly with an application for an order under the said s 2; and the court shall have power to give such consequential directions as may be necessary for enabling the court to exercise any of the powers available to the court under this Act in the case of an application for an order under s 2.

(3) Where an order made under s 15(1) of this Act is in force with respect to a party to a marriage, the court shall not give a direction under subs (1) above with respect to any application made under the said s 31(6) or 36(1) by that party on the death of the other party.

Miscellaneous and supplementary provisions

19 Effect, duration and form of orders

(1) Where an order is made under s 2 of this Act then for all purposes, including the purposes of the enactments relating to capital transfer tax, the will or the law relating to intestacy, or both the will and the law relating to intestacy, as the case may be, shall have effect and be deemed to have had effect as from the deceased's death subject to the provisions of the order.

(2) Any order made under s 2 or 5 of this Act in favour of –

(a) an applicant who was the former husband or former wife of the deceased, or

(b) an applicant who was the husband or wife of the deceased in a case where the marriage with the deceased was the subject of a decree of judicial separation and at the date of death the decree was in force and the separation was continuing,

shall, in so far as it provides for the making of periodical payments, cease to have effect on the remarriage of the applicant, except in relation to any arrears due under the order on the date of the remarriage.

(3) A copy of every order made under this Act other than an order made under s 15(1) of this Act shall be sent to the principal registry of the Family Division for entry and filing, and a memorandum of the order shall be

endorsed on, or permanently annexed to, the probate or letters of administration under which the estate is being administered.

20 Provisions as to personal representatives

(1) The provisions of this Act shall not render the personal representative of a deceased person liable for having distributed any part of the estate of the deceased, after the end of the period of six months from the date on which representation with respect to the estate of the deceased is first taken out, on the ground that he ought to have taken into account the possibility –

(a) that the court might permit the making of an application for an order under s 2 of this Act after the end of that period, or
(b) that, where an order has been made under the said s 2, the court might exercise in relation thereto the powers conferred on it by s 6 of this Act,

but this subsection shall not prejudice any power to recover, by reason of the making of an order under this Act, any part of the estate so distributed.

(2) Where the personal representative of a deceased person pays any sum directed by an order under s 5 of this Act to be paid out of the deceased's net estate, he shall not be under any liability by reason of that estate not being sufficient to make the payment, unless at the time of making the payment he has reasonable cause to believe that the estate is not sufficient.

(3) Where a deceased person entered into a contract by which he agreed to leave by his will any sum of money or other property to any person or by which he agreed that a sum of money or other property would be paid or transferred to any person out of his estate, then, if the personal representative of the deceased has reason to believe that the deceased entered into the contract with the intention of defeating an application for financial provision under this Act, he may, notwithstanding anything in that contract, postpone the payment of that sum of money or the transfer of that property until the expiration of the period of six months from the date on which representation with respect to the estate of the deceased is first taken out or, if during that period an application is made for an order under s 2 of this Act, until the determination of the proceedings on that application.

21 Admissibility as evidence of statements made by deceased

In any proceedings under this Act a statement made by the deceased, whether orally or in a document or otherwise, shall be admissible under s 2 of the Civil Evidence Act 1968 as evidence of any fact stated therein in like manner as if the statement were a statement falling within s 2(1) of that Act; and any reference in that Act to a statement admissible, or given or proposed to be given, in evidence under s 2 thereof or to the admissibility or the giving in evidence of a statement by virtue of that section or to any statement falling within s 2(1) of that Act shall be construed accordingly.

22 Jurisdiction of county courts

Note Repealed by the Administration of Justice Act 1982, s 75(1) and Sched 9 Pt I. As to the jurisdiction of the county court under the Act, see now the County Courts Act 1984, s 25 and Chapter 9 of this Book.

23 Determination of date on which representation was first taken out

In considering for the purposes of this Act when representation with respect to the estate of a deceased person was first taken out, a grant limited to settled land or to trust property shall be left out of account, and a grant limited to real estate or to personal estate shall be left out of account unless a grant limited to the remainder of the estate has previously been made or is made at the same time.

24 Effect of this Act on s 46(1)(vi) of Administration of Estates Act 1925

Section 46(1)(vi) of the Administration of Estates Act 1925, in so far as it provides for the devolution of property on the Crown, the Duchy of Lancaster or the Duke of Cornwall as bona vacantia, shall have effect subject to the provisions of this Act.

25 Interpretation

(1) In this Act –

'beneficiary', in relation to the estate of a deceased person, means –

- (a) a person who under the will of the deceased or under the law relating to intestacy is beneficially interested in the estate or would be so interested if an order had not been made under this Act, and
- (b) a person who has received any sum of money or other property which by virtue of s 8(1) or 8(2) of this Act is treated as part of the net estate of the deceased or would have received that sum or other property if an order had not been made under this Act;

'child' includes an illegitimate child and a child en ventre sa mere at the death of the deceased;

'the court' unless the context otherwise requires means the High Court, or where a county court has jurisdiction by virtue of s 22 of this Act, a county court;

'former wife' or 'former husband' means a person whose marriage with the deceased was during the lifetime of the deceased either –

- (a) dissolved or annulled by a decree of divorce or a decree of nullity of marriage granted under the law of any part of the British Islands, or
- (b) dissolved or annulled in any country or territory outside the British Islands by a divorce or annulment which is entitled to be recognised as valid by the law of England and Wales;

'net estate', in relation to a deceased person, means –

(a) all property of which the deceased had power to dispose by his will (otherwise than by virtue of a special power of appointment) less the amount of his funeral, testamentary and administration expenses, debts and liabilities, including any capital transfer tax payable out of his estate on his death;

(b) any property in respect of which the deceased held a general power of appointment (not being a power exercisable by will) which has not been exercised;

(c) any sum of money or other property which is treated for the purposes of this Act as part of the net estate of the deceased by virtue of s 8(1) or (2) of this Act;

(d) any property which is treated for the purposes of this Act as part of the net estate of the deceased by virtue of an order made under s 9 of this Act;

(e) any sum of money or other property which is, by reason of a disposition or contract made by the deceased, ordered under s 10 or 11 of this Act to be provided for the purpose of the making of financial provision under this Act;

'property' includes any chose in action;

'reasonable financial provision' has the meaning assigned to it by s 1 of this Act;

'valuable consideration' does not include marriage or a promise of marriage;

'will' includes codicil.

(2) For the purposes of paragraph (a) of the definition of 'net estate' in subs (1) above a person who is not of full age and capacity shall be treated as having power to dispose by will of all property of which he would have had power to dispose by will if he had been of full age and capacity.

(3) Any reference in this Act to provision out of the net estate of a deceased person includes a reference to provision extending to the whole of that estate.

(4) For the purposes of this Act any reference to a wife or husband shall be treated as including a reference to a person who in good faith entered into a void marriage with the deceased unless either –

(a) the marriage of the deceased and that person was dissolved or annulled during the lifetime of the deceased and the dissolution or annulment is recognised by the law of England and Wales, or

(b) that person has during the lifetime of the deceased entered into a later marriage.

(5) Any reference in this Act to remarriage or to a person who has remarried includes a reference to a marriage which is by law void or voidable or to a person who has entered into such a marriage, as the case may be, and a marriage shall be treated for the purpose of this Act as a remarriage, in relation to any party thereto, notwithstanding that the previous marriage of that party was void or voidable.

(6) Any reference in this Act to an order or decree made under the Matrimonial Causes Act 1973 or under any section of that Act shall be construed as including a reference to an order or decree which is deemed to have been made under that Act or under that section thereof, as the case may be.

(7) Any reference in this Act to any enactment is a reference to that enactment as amended by or under any subsequent enactment.

26 Consequential amendments, repeals and transitional provisions

(1) Section 36 of the Matrimonial Causes Act 1973 (which provides for the alteration of maintenance agreements by the High Court or a county court after the death of one of the parties) shall have effect subject to the following amendments (being amendments consequential on this Act) that is to say –

(a) in subs (3) for the words 's 7 of the Family Provision Act 1966' there shall be substituted the words 's 22 of the Inheritance (Provision for Family and Dependants) Act 1975', for the words from 'the Inheritance (Family Provision) Act' to 'net estate' there shall be substituted the words 'that Act if the value of the property mentioned in that section' and for the words 's 26 of the Matrimonial Causes Act 1965 (application for maintenance out of deceased's estate by former spouse)' there shall be substituted the words 's 2 of that Act';

(b) in subs (7) for the words from 's 7' to 'subs (5)' there shall be substituted the words 's 22 of the Inheritance (Provision for Family and Dependants) Act 1975 (which enables rules of court to provide for the transfer from a county court to the High Court or from the High Court to a county court of proceedings for an order under s 2 of that Act) and paragraphs (a) and (b) of subs (4)' and for the words 'any such proceedings as are referred to in subs (1) of that section' there shall be substituted the words 'proceedings for an order under s 2 of that Act'.

(2) Subject to the provisions of this section, the enactments specified in the Schedule to this Act are hereby repealed to the extent specified in the third column of the Schedule; and in paragraph 5(2) of Sched 2 to the Matrimonial Causes Act 1973 for the words 'that Act' there shall be substituted the words 'the Matrimonial Causes Act 1965'.

(3) The repeal of the said enactments shall not affect their operation in relation to any application made thereunder (whether before or after the commencement of this Act) with reference to the death of any person who died before the commencement of this Act.

(4) Without prejudice to the provisions of s 38 of the Interpretation Act 1889 (which relates to the effect of repeals) nothing in any repeal made by this Act shall affect any order made or direction given under any enactment

repealed by this Act, and, subject to the provisions of this Act, every such order or direction (other than an order made under s 4A of the Inheritance (Family Provision) Act 1938 or s 28A of the Matrimonial Causes Act 1965) shall, if it is in force at the commencement of this Act or is made by virtue of subs (2) above, continue in force as if it had been made under s 2(1)(a) of this Act, and for the purposes of s 6(7) of this Act the court in exercising its powers under that section in relation to an order continued in force by this subsection shall be required to have regard to any change in any of the circumstances to which the court would have been required to have regard when making that order if the order had been made with reference to the death of any person who died after the commencement of this Act.

Note Section 38 of the Interpretation Act 1889 has been repealed by the Interpretation Act 1978, s 25(1) and Sched 3; see now *ibid* ss 16(1), 17(2) and Sched 2 para 3.

27 Short title, commencement and extent

(1) This Act may be cited as the Inheritance (Provision for Family and Dependants) Act 1975.

(2) This Act does not extend to Scotland or Northern Ireland.

(3) This Act shall come into force on 1st April 1976.

(The Schedule to the Act has not been printed.)

Appendix III

Supreme Court and County Court Rules

RSC Order 99

Inheritance (Provision for Family and Dependants) Act 1975

Interpretation (Ord 99, r 1)

1 In this Order 'the Act' means the Inheritance (Provision for Family and Dependants) Act 1975 and a section referred to by number means the section so numbered in that Act.

Assignment to Chancery or Family Division (Ord 99, r 2)

2 Proceedings in the High Court under the Act may be assigned to the Chancery Division or to the Family Division.

Application for financial provision (Ord 99, r 3)

3—(1) Any originating summons by which an application under s 1 is made may be issued out of Chancery Chambers, the principal registry of the Family Division or any district registry.

(2) The summons shall be in Form No 10 in Appendix A.

(3) There shall be lodged with the Court an affidavit by the applicant in support of the summons, exhibiting an official copy of the grant of representation to the deceased's estate and of every testamentary document admitted to proof, and a copy of the affidavit shall be served on every defendant with the summons.

Powers of Court as to parties (Ord 99, r 4)

4—(1) Without prejudice to its powers under Ord 15, the Court may at any stage of proceedings under the Act direct that any person be added as a party to the proceedings or that notice of the proceedings be served on any person.

(2) Order 15, r 13, shall apply to proceedings under the Act as it applies to the proceedings mentioned in paragraph (1) of that rule.

Affidavit in answer (Ord 99, r 5)

5—(1) A defendant to an application under s 1 who is a personal representative of the deceased shall and any other defendant may, within 21 days after service of the summons on him, inclusive of the day of service, lodge with the Court an affidavit in answer to the application.

(2) The affidavit lodged by a personal representative pursuant to paragraph (1) shall state to the best of the deponent's ability:

(a) full particulars of the value of the deceased's net estate, as defined by s 25(1);

(b) the person or classes of persons beneficially interested in the estate, giving the names and (in the case of those who are not already parties) the addresses of all living beneficiaries, and the value of their interests so far as ascertained;

(c) if such be the case, that any living beneficiary (naming him) is a minor or a patient within the meaning of Ord 80, r 1; and

(d) any facts known to the deponent which might affect the exercise of the Court's powers under the Act.

(3) Every defendant who lodges an affidavit shall at the same time serve a copy on the plaintiff and on every other defendant who is not represented by the same solicitor.

Separate representation (Ord 99, r 6)

6 Where an application under s 1 is made jointly by two or more applicants and the originating summons is accordingly issued by one solicitor on behalf of all of them, they may, if they have conflicting interests, appear on any hearing of the summons by separate solicitors or counsel or in person, and where at any stage of the proceedings it appears to the Court that one of the applicants is not but ought to be separately represented, the Court may adjourn the proceedings until he is.

Endorsement of memorandum on grant (Ord 99, r 7)

7 On the hearing of an application under s 1 the personal representative shall produce to the Court the grant of representation to the deceased's estate and, if an order is made under the Act, the grant shall remain in the custody of the Court until a memorandum of the order has been endorsed on or permanently annexed to the grant in accordance with s 19(3).

Disposal of proceedings in chambers (Ord 99, r 8)

8 Any proceedings under the Act may, if the Court so directs, be disposed of in chambers and Ord 32, r 14(1) shall apply in relation to proceedings in the Family Division as if for the words 'the masters of the Chancery Division shall' there were substituted the words 'A registrar [district judge] of the Family Division shall.'

Subsequent applications in proceedings under s 1 (Ord 99, r 9)

9 Where an order has been made on an application under s 1, any subsequent application under the Act, whether made by a party to the proceedings or by any other person, shall be made by summons in those proceedings.

Drawing up and service of orders (Ord 99, r 10)

10 The provisions of the Family Proceedings Rules relating to the drawing up and service of orders shall apply to proceedings in the Family Division under this Order as if they were proceedings under those Rules.

In this rule 'Family Proceedings Rules' means rules made under s 40 of the Matrimonial and Family Proceedings Act 1984.

Transfer to county court (Ord 99, r 11)

Note Revoked by RSC (Amendment) 1992 (SI 1992 No 638).

CCR Order 48

Family Provision

Interpretation

1 In this Order—

'the Act of 1975' means the Inheritance (Provision for Family and Dependants) Act 1975;

'the deceased' means, in the case of an application under section 1 of the Act of 1975, the person to whose estate the application relates.

Mode of application

2 An application to a county court under section 1 of the Act of 1975 for provision to be made out of the estate of a deceased person shall be made by originating application stating—

(a) the name of the deceased, the date of his death and his country of domicile at that date;
(b) the relationship of the applicant to the deceased or other qualification of the applicant for making the application;
(c) the date on which representation with respect to the deceased's estate was first taken out and the names and addresses of the personal representatives;
(d) [Omitted]
(e) whether the disposition of the deceased's estate effected by his will or the law relating to intestacy was such as to make any provision for the applicant and, if it was, the nature of the provision;
(f) to the best of the applicant's knowledge and belief, the persons or classes of persons interested in the deceased's estate and the nature of their interests;

(g) particulars of the applicant's present and foreseeable financial resources and financial needs and any other information which he desires to place before the court on the matters to which the court is required to have regard under section 3 of the Act of 1975;

(h) where appropriate, a request for the court's permission to make the application notwithstanding that the period of six months has expired from the date on which representation in regard to the estate of the deceased was first taken out, and the grounds of the request; and

(i) the nature of the provision applied for.

Filing of application

3—(1) An application to which rule 2 relates shall be filed—

(a) in the court for the district in which the deceased resided at the date of his death, or

(b) if the deceased did not then reside in England and Wales, in the court for the district in which the respondent or one of the respondents resides or carries on business or the estate or part of the estate is situate, or

(c) if neither of the foregoing sub-paragraphs is applicable, in the court for the district in which the applicant resides or carries on business.

(2) the applicant shall file with his originating application an official copy of the grant of representation to the deceased's estate and of every testamentary document admitted to proof.

(3) Unless the court otherwise directs, the return day of the originating application shall be a day fixed for the pre-trial review of the proceedings.

Parties

4—(1) Without prejudice to its powers under Orders 5 and 15, the court may, at any stage of the proceedings, direct that any person be added as a party to the proceedings or that notice of the proceedings be served on any person.

(2) Order 5, rule 6, shall apply to an application under section 1 of the Act of 1975 as it applies to the proceedings mentioned in that rule.

Answer

5 Every respondent shall, within 21 days after service of the originating application on him, file an answer, which, if the respondent is a personal representative, shall state to the best of his ability—

(a) full particulars of the value of the deceased's net estate, as defined by section 25 (1) of the Act of 1975;

(b) the persons or classes of persons beneficially interested in the estate, giving the names and (in the case of those who are not already parties) the addresses of all living beneficiaries, and the value of their interests so far as ascertained;

(c) if such be the case, that any living beneficiary (naming him) is a minor or a mental patient; and
(d) in the case of an application under section 1 of the Act of 1975, any facts known to the personal representative which might affect exercise of the court's powers under that Act.

Subsequent application

6 Where an order has been made on an application under section 1 of the Act of 1975, any subsequent application, whether made by a party to the proceedings or by any other person, shall be made in those proceedings in accordance with Order 13, rule 1.

Hearing

7 Any application under section 1 of the Act of 1975 may be heard and determined by the registrar [district judge] and may, if the court thinks fit, be dealt with in chambers.

Endorsement of memorandum on grant

8 On the hearing of an application under section 1 of the Act of 1975, the personal representative shall produce to the court the grant of representation to the deceased's estate and, if an order is made under the Act, the proper officer shall send a sealed copy thereof, together with the grant of representation, to the principal registry of the Family Division for a memorandum of the order to be endorsed on, or permanently annexed to, the grant in accordance with section 19(3) of the Act of 1975.

Transfer to High Court

9 An order transferring an application under section 1 of the Act of 1975 to the High Court shall state whether it is desired that the proceedings be assigned to the Chancery Division or to the Family Division of the High Court.

Appendix IV

Checklist of Cases

This Checklist is an aid to research on the major topics arising under the Act. It is not intended to be an exhaustive list of the relevant authorities but a useful method of checking the most relevant cases. We have therefore not included every case on each topic nor have we cross-referred to other relevant headings. The Checklist refers in brackets to the Chapter in the Book containing the principal treatment of each topic.

1 The deceased's domicile at the date of death (Chapter 2)

Mastaka v Midland Bank Executor and Trustee Co Ltd [1941] Ch 192
Eames v Hacon (1881) 18 Ch D 347
Re Harmsworth [1982] CLY 3388

2 The objective test under section 1 of the Act (Chapter 2)

Re Coventry [1980] Ch 461
Moody v Stevenson [1992] Ch 486

also: *Re Goodwin* [1969] 1 Ch 283
Millward v Shenton [1972] 1 WLR 711

3 Categories of applicant (Chapter 2)

(a) 'wife or husband of the deceased' *Re Sehota* [1978] 1 WLR 1506

(b) 'child of the deceased' *Re Coventry* [1980] Ch 461
Re Collins [1990] Fam 56

also: Adoption Act 1976
Human Fertilisation and Embryology Act 1990

(c) 'person treated by the deceased as a child of the family'
Re Callaghan [1985] Fam 1
Re Leach [1986] Ch 226

(d) 'person maintained by the deceased'
Re Wilkinson [1978] Fam 22
Re Beaumont [1980] Ch 444

Jelley v Iliffe [1981] Fam 128
Bishop v Plumley [1991] 1 WLR 582

4 The meaning of 'maintenance' (Chapters 2 & 3)

Re Coventry [1980] Ch 461
Re Dennis [1980] 2 All ER 140
Riggs v Lloyds Bank plc (CAT (Civil) No 1151 of 1992)
Re Jennings [1994] 5 WLR 67

also: *Re Duranceau* [1952] 3 DLR 714

5 Orders the court can make: section 2 of the Act (Chapter 4)

Re Debenham [1986] 1 FLR 404

(a) 'periodical payments'
Re Debenham [1986] 1 FLR 404
Re Collins [1990] Fam 56
Re Farrow [1987] 1 FLR 205
Askew v Askew [1961] 1 WLR 725
Re Goodwin [1969] 1 Ch 283

also: *Re Bateman* (1941) 85 SJ 454
Re Gale [1966] Ch 236
Re Dorgan [1948] Ch 366

(b) 'lump sum'
Re Crawford (1983) 4 FLR 273
Re Besterman [1984] Ch 458
Re Callaghan [1985] Fam 1

(c) 'transfer . . . of such property'
Re Christie [1979] Ch 168
Rajabally v Rajabally [1987] 2 FLR 390
Davis v Davis [1993] 1 FLR 54

(d) 'settlement'
Re Mason (1975) 5 Fam Law 124

(e) 'ante-nuptial or post-nuptial settlement'

also: *Hargreaves v Hargreaves* [1926] P 42
Brooks v Brooks [1994] 2 FLR 10

(f) consequential and supplemental provisions: section 3(4) of the Act
Re Bunning [1984] Ch 480

6 What the court must consider: section 3(1) of the Act (Chapter 3)

Re Rowlands [1984] FLR 813
Re Coventry [1980] Ch 461
Moody v Stevenson [1992] Ch 486

(a) resources and needs
Jessop v Jessop [1992] 1 FLR 591
Rajabally v Rajabally [1987] 2 FLR 390
Harrington v Gill (1983) 4 FLR 265
Re Besterman [1984] Ch 458
Re Ducksbury [1966] 1 WLR 1226
Re Bunning [1984] Ch 480
Re Jennings [1994] 3 WLR 67

(i) social security benefits
Re E [1966] 1 WLR 709
Re Collins [1990] Fam 56

(ii) evidence of resources and needs
Re Clarke [1981] CLV 2884
Re Clarke [1991] Fam Law 364

(b) obligations and responsibilities
Re Joslin [1941] Ch 200
Jessop v Jessop [1992] 1 FLR 591
Re Debenham [1986] 1 FLR 404
Re Callaghan [1985] Fam 1

(c) size and nature of the net estate
Re Farrow [1987] 1 FLR 205
Re Styler [1942] Ch 387
Re Wood [1982] LS Gaz 774
Re Bunning [1984] Ch 480
Stead v Stead [1985] FLR 16
Re Besterman [1984] Ch 458
Re Inns [1947] Ch 576

(d) physical or mental disability
Re Wood [1982] LS Gaz 774
Re Debenham [1986] 1 FLR 404

(e) conduct and other matters

(i) conduct
Williams v Johns [1988] 2 FLR 475

(ii) terms of divorce or separation
Re Fullard [1982] Fam 42

(iii) the deceased's reasons
Re Coventry [1980] Ch 461
Moody v Stevenson [1992] Ch 486

7 Time limits

Re Salmon [1981] Ch 167
Re Ruttie [1970] 1 WLR 89
Re Gonin [1977] 2 All ER 720
Re Dennis [1981] 2 All ER 140
Adams v Schofield (Cat (Civil(22 July 1981)
Re Longley [1981] CLY 2885
Smith v Loosely (CAT (Civil) 18 June 1986)
Stock v Brown [1994] 1 FLR 840

(a) date when grant of representation is first taken out
Re Johnson [1987] CLY 3882
Re Bidie [1949] Ch 121
Re Miller [1969] 1 WLR 583
Re Freeman [1984] 1 WLR 1419

(b) date when application is made under the Act and when to make an application
Re Chittenden [1970] 1 WLR 1618
Re McBroom [1992] 2 FLR 49

8 Interim orders: section 5 of the Act (Chapter 6)

Re Ferrar's Application [1966] P 126
Re Ralphs [1968] 1 WLR 1522
Barnsley v Ward (CAT (Civil) No 19 of 1980)

9 The net estate (Chapters 4 & 7)

(a) Section 8 of the Act
Re Cairnes (1983) 4 FLR 225
Sen v Headley [1991] Ch 425

(b) Section 9 of the Act
Re Crawford [1983] 4 FLR 273
Jessop v Jessop [1992] 1 FLR 591
Powell v Osbourne [1993] 1 FLR 1001

(c) Section 10 of the Act
Re Dawkins [1986] 2 FLR 360

(d) Section 11 of the Act
Re Basham [1986] 1 WLR 1498

10 The final order: section 19 of the Act (Chapter 8)

Enforcement
Re Pointer [1946] Ch 324

Re Jennery [1967] Ch 280

also: taxation and costs (Chapter 8)

11 Surviving spouses: applications under section 1(1)(a) of the Act (Chapters 2 & 3)

Re Besterman [1984] Ch 458
Re Bunning [1984] Ch 480
Re Clarke [1991] Fam Law 364
Moody v Stevenson [1992] Ch 486
Jessop v Jessop [1992] 1 FLR 591
Davis v Davis [1993] 1 FLR 54

also: *Wachtel v Wachtel* [1973] Fam 72
Preston v Preston [1982] Fam 17

12 Former spouses: applications under section 1(1)(b) of the Act (Chapters 2 & 3)

Re Fullard [1982] Fam 42
Brill v Proud (1984) 14 Fam Law 59
Re Crawford (1983) 4 FLR 273
Re Farrow [1987] 1 FLR 205

also: *Whiting v Whiting* [1988] 1 WLR 565

13 Children: applications under section 1(1)(c) of the Act (Chapters 2 & 3)

Re Coventry [1980] Ch 461
Re Christie [1979] Ch 168
Re Dennis [1981] 2 All ER 140
Re Debenham [1986] 1 FLR 404
Williams v Johns [1988] 2 FLR 475
Re Collins [1990] Fam 56
Riggs v Lloyds Bank plc (CAT (Civil) No 1151 of 1992)
Re Jennings [1994] 2 WLR 67

14 Persons treated as children: applications under section 1(1)(d) of the Act (Chapters 2 & 3)

Re Callaghan [1985] Fam 1
Re Leach [1986] Ch 226

15 Persons maintained by the deceased: applications under section 1(1)(e) of the Act (Chapters 2 & 3)

Re Beaumont [1980] Ch 444
Jelley v Iliffe [1981] Fam 128

Harrington v Gill (1983) 4 FLR 265
Bishop v Plumley [1991] 1 WLR 582

16 Miscellaneous

(a) approach to competing claims: Chapter 3
Malone v Harrison [1979] 1 WLR 1353
Kusminov v Barclays Bank Trust Co Ltd [1989] Fam Law 66

(b) associated claims: Chapter 9
Re Blanch [1967] 1 WLR 987

Index